A Home Away from Home

A Home Away from Home

Mutual Aid, Political Activism, and
Caribbean American Identity

Tyesha Maddox

PENN

UNIVERSITY OF PENNSYLVANIA PRESS

PHILADELPHIA

Published by
University of Pennsylvania Press
Philadelphia, Pennsylvania 19104-4112
www.upenn.edu/pennpress

Printed in the United States of America on acid-free paper
10 9 8 7 6 5 4 3 2 1

Hardcover ISBN: 978-1-5128-2454-4
eBook ISBN: 978-1-5128-2453-7

A Cataloging-in-Publication record is
available from the Library of Congress

To my loving grandmother, Addie Olivia Maddox,

and

the Maddox and Henry families

CONTENTS

Introduction

Ivy Sinclair Simons (née Philip) first immigrated to New York City in 1941 to attend dressmaking school at the age of eighteen.[1] Born in Somerset, Bermuda, on July 15, 1923, Simons, like many young West Indian immigrant women, saw New York City as a place of opportunity.[2] Following a female-led chain of immigration, Simons joined her two aunts who had previously immigrated to New York from Bermuda and now lived together on 116th Street in Harlem. Both of the women worked as domestic servants, despite one of her aunts being a trained midwife; discriminatory hiring practices rendered her aunt unable to work in her professional field. Simons quickly found community among the Bermuda Benevolent Association (BBA), joining the mutual aid society within months of her arrival in New York. She credits her aunts and the BBA, of which they were both members, with helping her acclimate to life in the United States. The BBA served as a "home away from home" for Simons, giving her a built-in social network of other West Indian immigrants.

Organizations such as the Bermuda Benevolent Association appealed to West Indian women like Simons because these groups gave them a sense of shared community in a new, unfamiliar city and were one of the few places where they could address the specific issues they faced as Black female immigrants. As a young, single, Black immigrant woman in New York, Simons faced racial and gendered discrimination, segregation, and diminished job opportunities. Membership in immigrant mutual aid societies and benevolent associations helped to combat the isolation West Indian immigrants often faced by providing members with collective strategies for survival. They assisted their members with housing, job placement, and monetary aid, and most importantly by providing an intimate network of care and support, including sick and emergency funds and burial assistance. After several years in the association, Simons would go on to be elected its president in

1959.[3] Through organizations like the BBA, Black West Indian immigrants like Simons formed mutual aid networks that helped them survive the harsh realities and frequent injustices of Jim Crow America.

The early twentieth century saw the formation of numerous Anglophone Caribbean immigrant benevolent associations and mutual aid societies in New York City. By 1940, sixty-seven distinct mutual aid societies and benevolent associations existed in New York City. They served as forums for discussions on Caribbean American affairs, hosted cultural activities, helped members find employment, and provided charity and welfare assistance, especially in the case of newly arrived immigrants. Some organizations, such as the British Virgin Islands Benevolent Association (BVIBA), had a more international scope, with programs that benefited less fortunate West Indian immigrants not only in the United States but abroad. Immigrant mutual aid societies and benevolent associations have been and continue to be integral to the history of immigration to the United States, especially in the case of early Anglophone Caribbean immigration, as these organizations were ubiquitous and often synonymous with the Caribbean immigrant experience. If you were not part of a mutual aid society or benevolent association directly, you knew someone who was, or attended one of their functions.

A Home Away from Home demonstrates how Caribbean immigrants used these organizations to unleash political activism against racial discrimination in tumultuous Jim Crow America. Moreover, participation in these organizations empowered immigrants to form a collective "Caribbean" identity and, fighting alongside African Americans, a collective Black American identity. By the late 1920s and 1930s, associations had moved from island-specific categorizations to organizing around broader principles, as with the United Brothers and Sisters of the United Islands, whose aims centered on the well-being of the wider Caribbean immigrant population. Additionally, the objectives of these organizations shifted from concern for newly arrived immigrants to advocating for the rights of Black people in the United States and abroad. Through their involvement in mutual aid societies and benevolent associations, Caribbean immigrants demonstrated their belief that they were active participants in a Black international community. They kept abreast of news affecting people of African descent globally, participated in rallies and demonstrations for Pan-African issues, raised funds for diasporic causes such as supporting Ethiopia during the Italo-Ethiopian War of 1935, and launched various international initiatives to help people of African descent worldwide.

A Home Away from Home examines the significance of Caribbean American mutual aid societies and benevolent associations to the immigrant experience, particularly their implications in the formation of a Pan-Caribbean American identity, a Black American identity, and a diasporic Black identity. As I began to research this project, I found evidence of numerous organizations established between 1884 and 1940 that had rarely been studied in depth, despite the growing historical attention to Anglophone Caribbean immigration.[4] The proliferation of these organizations and their large membership numbers led me to interrogate their importance to Caribbean immigrants. What real and/or perceived benefits did immigrants derive from these organizations? What was their appeal? Did these organizations serve as the training ground for later Caribbean political mobilization? Or were they simply a ready-made community for subsequent Caribbean immigrant political leaders? Most significantly, what role did these organizations play in developing a Pan-Caribbean ethnic identity within the United States? *A Home Away from Home* answers these important questions.

Mutual aid served as a form of both self-preservation and political action for early twentieth-century Caribbean immigrants. Mutual aid is defined by scholars as a stratagem in which a group of people work together to implement collective strategies and pool resources to meet the needs of that select group when there is a lack of governmental assistance.[5] These resources can include food, clothing, housing, medical care, and monetary assistance. Historically, they have also included burial and sick insurance, as in the case of the BBA and other Caribbean immigrant mutual aid societies and benevolent associations.

Friendly societies in the Caribbean served as the precursors to immigrant mutual aid societies and benevolent associations in the United States. They emerged at the onset of emancipation in the British Caribbean and developed out of the need for freed people to attain social security and insurance. They provided many of the same services seen in Caribbean immigrant mutual aid societies in the United States, including burial and sick assistance, emergency funds, emotional support in times of distress, and kinship networks. They took their inspiration from West African mutual assistance associations such as the *dókpwè* societies in Dahomey. Similar to Caribbean immigrant mutual aid societies, West Indian friendly societies emerged as spaces in which members of the aspiring Black elite could cultivate leadership skills, given many of the societies' political natures. For Caribbean immigrants perpetuating traditions of home, mutual aid was always an ethic of solidarity that prioritized communal welfare and encouraged collective actions.[6] Moreover, mutual aid helped develop a sense of collective political solidarity—one that remains in evidence today in contemporary Caribbean American mutual aid organizations.

The COVID-19 pandemic had a particularly large impact on the Caribbean American community in New York City, as many Caribbean Americans held frontline positions working in hospitals, grocery stores, public transportation, daycares, schools, and as caregivers in homes. These often low-wage jobs, now deemed essential, left Caribbean Americans exposed to increased risks of contagion. It was in these dark moments that marginalized and underserved communities especially relied on mutual aid networks for survival. *A Home Away from Home* is thus not just a story about Caribbean immigrants in the early twentieth century, but an unearthing of the historical roots of strategies of survival that continue to "bring marginalized people together to support one another and to ultimately demand their rights and move towards their vision of a better world."[7] Mutual aid, then and now, is an inherently political act of solidarity, survival, and community.

A Home Away from Home builds on the seminal work of scholars of Caribbean immigration and African American history to tell the story of the transnational community of Caribbean immigrants that settled in New York at the turn of the century. Historians of early twentieth-century African American history tend to gloss over the presence and contributions of Caribbean immigrants in this period, with only a slight acknowledgment—if any—of their ethnic roots and unique experiences as Black immigrants.[8] Because the largest wave of Caribbean immigrants came to the United States after 1965, most histories of Caribbean American immigration focus on this later period. Only a few historians examine Caribbean immigration in the early twentieth century prior to World War I, and even fewer highlight the relationships formed between Caribbean immigrants and African Americans in this period.[9]

Furthermore, despite the large number of Anglophone Caribbean organizations that emerged at the beginning of the twentieth century, there are few works that examine this topic in detail.[10] In the early twentieth century, participation in voluntary associations was at an all-time high, with one in every three Americans, white or Black, participating in a secret society, sick and funeral benefit society, or life insurance society.[11] Nevertheless, historians who examine African American social organizations in the early twentieth century rarely discuss Caribbean immigrants who were members and often held leadership positions in such groups.[12]

The few historians who do focus on early Caribbean immigration to the United States often include only a cursory discussion regarding the proliferation of Caribbean social and cultural organizations in this period—and make brief reference to Marcus Garvey and the Universal Negro Improvement Association (UNIA).[13] While the UNIA was inarguably the largest and one of the most successful organizations of Caribbean immigrants in the United States, historians of Caribbean immigration often focus on it to the exclusion of smaller associations that also held major significance. By highlighting these lesser-known organizations, *A Home Away from Home* provides a fuller analysis of the Caribbean immigrant experience and illuminates the previously unheralded story of smaller associations that are equally integral to this history.

Examining Caribbean immigrant mutual aid societies also significantly broadens the historical understanding of mutual aid, which tends to emphasize modern definitions of mutual aid organizing coming out of anarchist theory.[14] Scientist and anarchist activist Peter Kropotkin is thought to have first coined the term "mutual aid" with his book *Mutual Aid: A Factor in Evolution* (1902), which argued that it was human cooperation and not competition that facilitated the survival of our species.[15] As such, many have erroneously attributed the philosophy of mutual aid solely to Kropotkin and anarchist theory. Scholars of American mutual aid and immigration history illustrate a longer history of mutual aid by exploring the tradition of mutual aid organizing that has been the cornerstone of immigrant and African American communities in the United States. However, this literature mostly examines Chinese, Jewish, Mexican, and African American histories of mutual aid, with very few, if any, references to the significance of Caribbean immigrant mutual aid societies during the same time period.[16] *A Home Away from Home* centers Caribbean immigrant mutual aid societies in the discourse on the long tradition of mutual aid organizing that is integral to an examination of American immigration history.

Importantly, *A Home Away from Home* expands on our understanding of this history, which at times views West Indians as a group that was cohesive immediately upon arrival in the United States, by exploring the complex process involved in the development of shared identity.[17] Caribbean immigrants did not initially perceive themselves as a group with a collective identity. Instead, many early immigrant associations were organized by specific islands, demonstrating that members of these groups primarily saw themselves as nationals from their own individual islands—not as the united West Indian entity by which Americans both Black and white categorized them.

Later, through cross-cooperation with other associations from differing islands, an important goal of many of the organizations became consciously fostering collaboration and unity among Caribbean immigrants. Consequently, it was in the context of U.S.-based social and cultural organizations that Caribbean immigrants first began to view themselves as Caribbean or West Indian as opposed to Saint Lucian, Antiguan, or Jamaican.[18] As a result, we see the founding of Pan-Caribbean associations like the Sons and Daughters of the West Indies and the United Brothers and Sisters of the United Islands in the 1920s. Building on the groundbreaking scholarship of historians Irma Watkins-Owens and Winston James, which first examined the community of Caribbean immigrants that formed in New York City in the early twentieth century, this monograph importantly shifts the way we understand the development of Caribbean immigrant communities in New York. By utilizing mutual aid societies as a lens through which to understand notions of community building and identity formation, *A Home Away from Home* interrogates the ways in which Caribbean immigrants organized themselves as a "West Indian" immigrant group and ultimately conceptualized their identities as Black people in the United States, connected to other people of African descent in the world.

Departing from traditional male-centered immigrant narratives, *A Home Away from Home* also illuminates the prominent role of Caribbean women in immigrant mutual aid societies and benevolent associations.[19] This project explores the seemingly quotidian activities of Caribbean women in immigrant associations to explore how Caribbean immigrants blended culture and politics, and created an ethnic and transnational identity for themselves in the United States. By centering immigrant women as indispensable agents in diasporic identity and community formation, this book challenges the tendency to make the male experience of immigration normative. Caribbean immigrant women played a previously unacknowledged yet imperative role as founders and participants in many social organizations in the early twentieth century.[20] Women made up a large percentage of the general membership of these groups and often served in leadership positions. In heavily male-dominated associations, women frequently organized their own auxiliary groups; they took on important executive positions and ran their own programs, ensuring that their views and interests were addressed. In this capacity, women were able to wield full control of their own organizations and take on positions they might not have otherwise. When their needs were not being met in organizations with both male and female members,

Caribbean women formed women's associations that catered to their specific needs as immigrant women.

Finally, *A Home Away from Home* demonstrates a strong link between social organizations and larger political movements.[21] As benevolent associations became more invested in their newly adopted homes, their aims became progressively more political. Caribbean-specific at the outset, by the 1920s mutual aid societies and benevolent associations began to champion issues that affected the Black community as a whole. For example, in response to the 1931 Scottsboro case in which several Black teenagers were wrongly accused of raping two white women, Caribbean social groups such as American West Indian Ladies Aid Society (AWILAS) and the Virgin Islands Civic and Industrial Association joined together with African American organizations like the Brotherhood of Sleeping Car Porters (BSCP) and the National Association for the Advancement of Colored People (NAACP) to fight this miscarriage of justice.[22] Leading the defense of the teenagers in their trials was the Communist Party of the United States of America (CPUSA), which recruited both Caribbean immigrants and African Americans en masse in the 1920s and 1930s. Many Caribbean mutual aid society members also became involved with the CPUSA, including Grace Campbell, Claudia Jones, Bonita Williams, Hubert Harrison, and Elizabeth Hendrickson.[23] In addition to the CPUSA, many held membership in two or more mutual aid societies or labor unions. For instance, Ivy Simons was a member of both the BBA and the United Benevolent Association, as well as her local seamstress union.[24] The desire of Caribbean immigrants to expand their social networks and attend to their particular interests often resulted in their holding multiple organizational memberships.

Once merely social organizations, these Caribbean immigrant groups evolved to work together with African Americans to fight social inequality within the United States. Their political agendas become even more clear when we examine their growing transnational concerns, emphasized in the international initiatives that many associations undertook to help people of African descent within the Caribbean and throughout the world. The range of their concerns was considerable. Many of the associations gave scholarships to students in the Caribbean, provided relief for islands hit with natural disasters, and actively supported Ethiopia during the Italo-Ethiopian War of 1935 by raising funds for Ethiopian troops. Hosting social events such as dances and church services, saving and sharing money to compensate for the lack of services for immigrants, helping members find jobs and housing, and hosting forums for conversation formed strong social networks and notions of collectivity among West Indian immigrants that would eventually be used for political mobilization. *A Home Away from Home* expands on the seminal work of Winston James by illustrating the particular importance of Caribbean women to Caribbean radicalism and political organizing in the twentieth century through their involvement in mutual aid societies and benevolent associations.[25]

A Home Away from Home centers on immigrants from the Anglophone Caribbean—comprising, but not limited to, islands such as the Danish Virgin Islands (now the U.S. Virgin Islands), Antigua, Jamaica, Saint Lucia, and Trinidad. Though not located geographically in the Caribbean, immigrants from the British Crown Colony of Bermuda are also included in this examination, as they similarly came to identify as West Indians. This book focuses primarily on Anglophone Caribbean immigrants because they were one of the largest groups of Caribbean immigrants to arrive in the United States.

In addition, they were simultaneously and paradoxically the most invisible, an invisibility that at times carries over into the historiography of American immigration. Bearing no observable physical differences from African Americans and speaking English, Anglophone Caribbean immigrants were frequently seen by outsiders as part of the native African American community, an assumption that both helped and hurt Anglophone Caribbean immigrants, as it ignored their special needs as an immigrant group and granted them seemingly immediate access to an existing native community and the rights to citizenship. This work posits that entrée to Black American society was not always a seamless transition for Caribbean immigrants and explores moments of both connection and conflict that came with collaboration. The formation of Caribbean social and cultural organizations served as a way to combat invisibility and address the specific needs of Caribbean immigrants. *A Home Away from Home* in a similar way highlights the role in American history of individual Caribbean agents, who are too often seen solely as African American, ignoring their rich ethnic identity and experience as immigrants.

Because of the significant size of Caribbean immigrant populations in central Harlem and the Brooklyn neighborhood of Bedford-Stuyvesant in the early twentieth century, this book focuses on New York City. By 1950, more than 62,000 immigrants from the British West Indies were citizens of the United States, with more than 79 percent of those immigrants living in the Northeast and 70 percent in the state of New York.[26] To be sure, Caribbean immigrants lived in other regions of the United States, such as the South and the West, but there was no other location akin to the Northeast, and New York in particular, that served as the destination of choice for most Caribbean immigrants. One 1938 estimate suggested that in Harlem alone the Caribbean population (including noncitizens) was between 75,000 and 85,000.[27] Caribbean women outnumbered Caribbean men in this migratory stream, and between 1918 and 1940 New York became by far the main destination for female Caribbean immigrants.[28]

A Home Away from Home investigates Caribbean immigrant mutual aid societies and benevolent associations between the 1890s and 1940, as this was the period in which many of the first associations were formed. Beginning this examination of Caribbean immigrant social organizations in 1890 is also significant because it demonstrates Caribbean immigrants' presence in the United States prior to the twentieth century, contrary to popular belief. The year 1940 serves as an endcap for this study because it is through the decade of the 1930s that much of the politicization of Caribbean mutual aid societies and benevolent associations occurs. Several significant events take place in the decade of the 1930s, including the Scottsboro trial (1931), the Italo Ethiopian War (1935–1936), and a plethora of labor strikes throughout the Caribbean, that are integral to the politicization of these immigrant groups and require a thorough examination.

Within the Caribbean immigrant communities of New York City during this time, in addition to the mutual aid societies, there was a large and diverse grouping of organizations with different goals, memberships, funding sources, and political alliances, including labor unions, freemasons, and the Order of Free Gardeners. Even under the umbrella term "mutual aid society" there were a variety of organizations, including not just mutual aid societies but also benevolent associations and progressive societies. These latter three groups are the most commonly examined in this monograph. While they often had varying names, such as BBA, Montserrat Progressive Society (MPS), or Virgin Gorda Mutual Society, these organizations all functioned as mutual aid societies, pooling their resources to ensure the collective well-being of their members. Additionally, a common function among these groups was death and funeral assistance set up to provide proper burials for their immigrant members, a tradition carried over from Caribbean friendly societies.

To illuminate the significance of immigrant mutual aid organizations to the Caribbean immigrant experience, I use manuscripts, periodicals, consular dispatches, passenger arrival records, naturalization records, passport applications, historical photographs, oral history interviews, and the organizational records of numerous mutual aid societies and benevolent associations.

The Manuscripts, Archives, and Rare Books Division at Schomburg Center for Research in Black Culture served as an especially rich source for primary research. Within this archive are the records of numerous mutual aid societies and benevolent associations established between 1884 and 1940, such as the Antigua Progressive Society (APS), the BBA, the BVIBA, and the AWILAS. These collections house a vast amount of correspondence between different Caribbean immigrant mutual aid societies and benevolent associations in New York, as well as organization minutes, financial reports, and programs. Additionally, I have conducted interviews with several current and former members of Caribbean mutual aid societies and benevolent associations, in order to obtain firsthand accounts of the significance these groups had in the lives of their members.

To provide a rich history of the formation of these organizations and their impact within the international Black community, this book moves beyond sources based in the United States and draws on a number of archival sites within the Caribbean, including in Jamaica, Barbados, Trinidad and Tobago, Saint Lucia, and Saint Vincent and the Grenadines. I believe it is important to frame this story as a transnational one, as ideas, money, and people often flowed beyond national borders. I complement these collections with British archives that cover the colonial administration of the islands, as well as the transatlantic linkages immigrants formed with their counterparts in London evidenced in the Black Cultural Archives there.

A Home Away from Home is organized into five chapters that analyze the migratory movements of Caribbean people from emancipation in 1834 to their settlement in the United States in the twentieth century. The first two chapters take place in the Caribbean in order to highlight the origins of U.S. mutual aid societies and benevolent associations, as well as to provide a more comprehensive understanding of the Caribbean immigrants who would eventually form American social organizations. The final three chapters take place in the United States, but maintain a bilateral gaze on both the United States and the Caribbean in order to highlight the transnational nature of this immigrant group. Gender, race, and class are important themes that permeate the manuscript, with specific attention paid in every chapter to the importance of female immigrants.

Chapter 1, "Friendly Societies in the Caribbean and Their African Traditions," examines the history of friendly societies in the Caribbean, which were the forerunners of immigrant mutual aid societies and benevolent associations in the United States. Influenced by West African mutual assistance associations such as the *dókpwè* societies in Dahomey, these Caribbean friendly societies emerged at the onset of emancipation and developed out of the need for freed people to attain social security and insurance. Their objectives were to promote the moral and religious welfare of members as well as provide burial assistance and relief when members fell ill. This chapter emphasizes the significance these societies had in the lives of the formerly enslaved.

Friendly societies provided indispensable services to their members. Further, West Indian friendly societies served an ideological purpose by providing agency to newly emancipated Black people in the Caribbean. Participation in these societies functioned as a claim-making mechanism by which the formerly enslaved demonstrated both their status as free people and their self-sufficiency. They utilized friendly societies to illustrate that they were not only willing but also able to take care of themselves and, most importantly, wield control over their own lives. Finally, West Indian friendly societies emerged as spaces in which members of the aspiring Black elite could cultivate leadership skills, given the political nature of many of the societies.

Moreover, this chapter confirms the influence of West African mutual assistance associations such as the *dókpwè* societies in Dahomey on Caribbean-friendly societies, by illuminating their very similar functions. This connection is important because it demonstrates that these societies were not merely an imitation of other immigrant groups in the United States, such as the Jewish and Chinese mutual aid societies that also emerged at this time. Instead, they were a deeply rooted West Indian institution.

Chapter 2, "Whence They Came: Immigration and Mobility in the Caribbean," explores mobility within the Caribbean and migration to the United States. The abolition of slavery in the British West Indies set into motion thousands of freed people seeking to distance themselves from the plantations they had labored on and exercise their newly gained autonomy to choose when and where they worked. This chapter argues that newly freed Black people utilized migration as a tool of autonomy, demonstrating their agency in the years following emancipation. It illustrates that this mobility begins within the Caribbean and before freed people's more extensive early twentieth century migration to the United States. This chapter also focuses on the significance of female-led chains of migration to the United States and of Caribbean immigrant labor roles in understanding this history.

Beginning with an examination of Caribbean immigrants after the abolition of slavery in the British West Indies and following their migration, for both seasonal and long-term work projects, throughout the Caribbean basin, this chapter analyzes the connection between freedom and mobility. The chapter's examination of intra-Caribbean migration illustrates that migration was not unidirectional and in many cases functioned as a testing ground for later West Indian migration to the United States and the United Kingdom. Analyzing connections between nineteenth and early twentieth-century migration movements illuminates the motivations that propelled Caribbean immigrants to leave their home countries and migrate to the United States. Further, this chapter examines the identity of individuals who migrated to the United States at the turn of the twentieth century, paying specific attention to gender, class, and levels of education for observable commonalities. The push-and-pull factors that led to their initial migration are analyzed, as are the types of jobs, social standing, and U.S. cities to which they gravitated. This chapter recognizes settlement and employment patterns of Caribbean immigrants as twofold: immigrants from various West Indian countries establishing their early connection with the African American community at the same time that they form their own Caribbean community in the United States.

While men were initially more active participants in nineteenth-century West Indian migration, in the early twentieth century women took the lead in migrating to the United States. This fact troubles the historiographical trend that places men at the forefront of migration histories and has gendered ramifications for the overall Caribbean immigrant experience to the United States. Subsequently, this chapter posits that female migrants served as the guardians and proponents of Caribbean culture in the United States. They initiated female led chains of immigration, leaving behind their families and even children to migrate to the United States. Once established in the United States, having settled in a living space and secured employment for their relatives, they then sent money for their family members to immigrate and join them. These female-led chains laid the social and economic foundation for later Caribbean immigrants; they set up households in the United States that were crucial to sustaining a thriving Caribbean immigrant community. Without Caribbean immigrant women's established social networks, systems of child fostering, involvement in social and cultural organizations, rotating lines of credit, and practice of sending remittance (which kept them linked to their home islands and Caribbean identity), a Caribbean immigrant community in the United States could not have been sustained. Caribbean women were instrumental in creating a thriving ethnic community in the United States.

Chapter 3, "More Than Auxiliary: The Functions of Mutual Aid Societies and Benevolent Associations," helps us to understand the significance of social organizations to the immigrant experience by investigating the archival records of sixty-seven West Indian mutual aid societies and benevolent associations that were founded in New York City between 1890 and 1940. This chapter argues that these associations heightened a sense of West Indian ethnic identity among Caribbean immigrants in the United States and played a vital role in the formation of a Caribbean immigrant transnational identity. It is in the context of these U.S.-founded social organizations that Caribbean immigrants began to fully embrace a Caribbean or West Indian identity as opposed to an island-specific identity. Through the lens of immigrant mutual aid societies and benevolent associations, a more nuanced understanding emerges of the way that Caribbean immigrant groups conceptualized their identities as both "West Indian" and as Black in the United States and, ultimately, how they came to perceive of themselves as a transnational group and people connected to the African Diaspora.

This chapter analyzes the ways in which Caribbean American social and cultural organizations fulfilled Caribbean immigrants' needs for a supportive and familiar community at the time of their arrival and beyond. Particularly important to this process were Caribbean women, who were the proponents of Caribbean culture in the United States and played an important role in the formation of ethnically distinct Caribbean communities. This chapter further highlights the ways in which members of mutual aid societies and benevolent associations demonstrated a strong interest in staying connected to their communities back home by providing relief aid to Caribbean islands hit with natural disasters and founding various scholarships to sponsor students in the Caribbean.

This chapter posits that through their involvement in these social organizations Caribbean immigrants expressed their belief that they were active participants in a Black international community. Demonstrating a deep concern for Black peoples throughout the world, many of the associations kept their members abreast of news affecting people of African descent globally, participated in rallies and demonstrations for Pan-African issues, raised funds for diasporic causes, and launched various international initiatives to help people of African descent worldwide. This chapter contends that an examination of Caribbean immigrant mutual aid societies and benevolent associations provides a more nuanced understanding of the way in which Caribbean immigrant groups were able to conceptualize their evolving identity.

Chapter 4, "Gendering the Migrant Experience: Caribbean Women's Roles in Social Organizations and Transnational Community Development," examines the female members of mutual aid societies and benevolent associations in order to challenge the historiography of Caribbean immigration that tends to normalize the male experience of immigrants. Familiar frameworks of Caribbean migratory trends foreground, as Tina Campt and Deborah Thomas observe, "the mobility of masculine subjects as the primary agents of diasporic formation and perpetuate a more general masculinism in the conceptualization of diasporic community."[29] Illustrated through their participation in immigrant social organizations, Caribbean women were active and influential participants in the immigration experience, not just passive bystanders. First, social organizations served as training grounds for female Caribbean leaders such as Elizabeth Hendrickson, who served as the president of the AWILAS, giving them a platform from which to discuss issues of social and political reform, as well as gain professional experience running and organizing associations. These associations empowered immigrant women to become involved in organizing and political activism, in addition to giving them a built-in audience and political base. In heavily male-dominated associations, women frequently organized their own auxiliary groups; they took on important executive positions and ran their own programs, ensuring that their views and interests were addressed. In this capacity, women were able to wield full control of their own organizations and take on positions they normally might not have. They also formed women's associations that catered specifically to the needs of immigrant women, such as the AWILAS, whose purpose was to establish camaraderie among Caribbean immigrant women.

Second, mutual aid societies and benevolent associations helped immigrant women create a system of formal and informal networks through their activities and social events. For example, the BBA annually held Bermuda Week, a week of event programming celebrating the history and culture of Bermuda. Such occasions gave Caribbean immigrants living in New York an opportunity to meet and become acquainted with other Caribbean immigrants. These organizations connected more established Caribbean immigrants with newly arrived immigrants, allowing them the opportunity to exchange their experiences and advice for navigating their new city. This type of social networking effectively created a sense of community for Caribbean immigrants in New York while maintaining their connection to their home islands in the Caribbean. Through relief efforts, charity work, and a constant stream of collaboration with groups in the Caribbean, female members of immigrant social organizations in New York created diasporic networks that helped keep them abreast of events occurring in the Caribbean, ultimately engendering their West Indian identity. By placing women in the center of diasporic formation, this chapter demonstrates that Caribbean women's involvement in social organizations is essential in shaping complex and diverse immigrant narratives, as they were indispensable agents in forging diasporic connections.

Chapter 5, "Community Building and Political Mobilization: Forging a Caribbean and Black Identity," examines poignant junctures in the politicization of Caribbean immigrant mutual aid societies and benevolent associations. Specifically, this chapter explores the transition period between 1920 and 1940 in which the objectives of Caribbean immigrant mutual aid societies and benevolent associations grew progressively more political. The turn of the twentieth century was a turbulent time for Black people in America and one that would ultimately lead to a large outpouring of political engagement among men and women in the Black community, both native and foreign-born. In response to the racial antipathy, violence, and discriminatory laws that characterized the early twentieth century, the Black community in the United States mobilized politically, lobbying for anti-lynching laws, better housing, and educational and immigration reform. New York City, in particular, became a hotbed of Black radical politics and discourse, with Caribbean immigrants leading the charge. Undoubtedly influenced by the objectives of coetaneous Black radical organizations such as the UNIA and the Liberty League and emerging ideologies such as the New Negro Movement, members of Caribbean mutual aid societies and benevolent associations also became actively involved in politics.

Motivated by the idea that the struggle against racial oppression connected all Black people in Africa and the African Diaspora, Caribbean immigrant social organizations joined with African American organizations to advocate against the oppression of Black people globally. Through their participation in these associations, Caribbean immigrants were able to build on their existing social networks and mobilize politically with African Americans, championing issues that affected the Black community as a whole. They hosted politicians at their meetings, held political rallies, and partnered with African American groups such as the BSCP in order to find a solution to the injustice they faced in the United States. The welfare of people of African descent across the globe became a clear and pressing concern for Caribbean immigrant social organizations. Because this was not always a seamless connection, this chapter also discusses the tensions that sometimes characterized these collaborations.

Caribbean immigrants in New York were simultaneously engaged with the welfare of Black people in the United States and deeply invested in events occurring in the Caribbean. This chapter argues that these social organizations helped create a transnational space for Anglophone Caribbean immigrants where they could engage with the political landscapes of their home islands and the greater Caribbean region. Association members were in many cases simultaneously developing a Pan-Caribbean identity as they developed a Black identity. Consequently, social organizations' events and activities took on a more diasporic lens that reflected their new identities as members of an African Diaspora. Through their involvement with these social organizations, which advanced clear international initiatives, Caribbean immigrants demonstrated the belief that their own fate was closely intertwined with the social, economic, and political welfare of the Black international community.

A Home Away from Home weaves together the narrative of a transnational group of Black Caribbean immigrants, many of whom were meeting in the United States for the first time. By utilizing the analytical framework of mutual aid societies and benevolent associations to question notions of gender, culture, politics, and identity formation, it tells the story of how despite, and perhaps to some extent because of, the challenges of the early twentieth century, this resilient group came together using their traditions of mutual aid and collective organizing to form community and foster new identities. Caribbean mutual aid societies and benevolent associations came to serve not only as a means to create community among fellow compatriots, but also as a base for political activism in both the United States and the wider African Diaspora.

Note on Terminology

Within this work, there are some terms that should be explained before proceeding further. The phrase *West Indian* refers to people from the Anglophone or Commonwealth Caribbean. Many researchers and historians of the region include Haitian immigrants in this group. This monograph does not, though there is evidence of contemporary Haitian and Haitian American mutual aid organizing.[30] When the term *Caribbean American* is used, it is referring to Caribbean immigrants and their known descendants who settled in the United States. *African American* is used for Black individuals whose ancestors were brought to the United States through the trans-Atlantic slave trade. It is important to note that historically, until the early nineteenth century, the trans-Atlantic slave trade used a process of what was called "seasoning," in which many enslaved Africans were first brought to Caribbean plantations to be "broken" or conditioned to the grueling daily life of slavery.[31] Many of these enslaved people were later sold to plantations in the United States. The use of the terms *Caribbean American* and *African American* attempts to take this fact into account, but because it is very difficult to determine which enslaved Americans went through the process of Caribbean "seasoning," this book therefore refers to *Caribbean Americans* as those persons from the Caribbean who immigrated to the United States after 1834, when the British first abolished slavery within the Commonwealth Caribbean. *Black* is used as an all-encompassing term that refers both to Caribbean Americans and African Americans.

CHAPTER 1

_____

Friendly Societies in the Caribbean
and Their African Traditions

Beginning in the twentieth century, New York City exploded with the establishment of Caribbean mutual aid societies and benevolent associations. Caribbean immigrants, eager to find their place in a bustling new world, clung to each other and the traditions of home. Groups such as the West Indian Benevolent Association of New York City (WIBANYC), founded in 1884, provided new immigrants with various forms of support, including job and housing assistance, rotating lines of credit, help in the naturalization process, and—its most popular function—burial assistance. However, the idea of mutual aid and cooperative finance was not novel to the Caribbean immigrant experience in the United States. Similar institutions existed in the Caribbean long before these immigrants ever set foot in the United States, and the tradition of mutual assistance and care is one that has long been present in African descendant communities.

West Indian friendly societies were the forerunners of the mutual aid societies and benevolent associations Caribbean immigrants would establish in the United States. These friendly societies emerged at the onset of emancipation in the Caribbean basin, developing from the need of freed people to attain social security and insurance. The main purpose of these friendly societies was "to promote the moral and religious welfare of members and to provide relief during their illness and help at their burial."[1] Because the well-being of newly freed people was no longer the responsibility of former slaveholders, friendly societies stepped in to fill this need.

The first known friendly society in the Caribbean was the St. George's Church Mutual Relief Society of Kingston, Jamaica, organized in November 1828. The society's objectives were the mutual relief of its members in sickness and providing for the burial of its members and aid to their dependents, at the time of their death.[2] St. John's Friendly Society, founded in Antigua in 1829, was the second friendly society established in the Caribbean and had similar aims of providing mutual assistance for sick and deceased members.[3] For the most part, these West Indian friendly societies were established in cities, although some societies existed in the countryside, such as those founded by the Established Church in 1832 in rural areas of Antigua. Memberships in cities were often large and consisted of at least a hundred members per society. For instance, in Saint Vincent in 1854, there were 21 friendly societies with a total membership of 3,375. That equals to an average of 61 members per friendly society in Saint Vincent. Large memberships in friendly societies were seen throughout the entire Caribbean basin.

West Indian friendly societies emerged as spaces where members of the aspiring Black elite could cultivate leadership skills, given the political nature of many friendly societies. In the period prior to emancipation, free people of color served in leadership positions within these groups, leading the call for British ideas of respectability and demanding full rights as equal members of British colonial society. After emancipation, the aspiring Black middle class assumed the leadership of friendly societies with the intentions of not only providing mutual assistance for the disadvantaged among them, but also serving their social agenda of respectability. The Black middle class in the British Caribbean consisted of "free persons of color" and the "free Blacks of slave society." After 1838, the middle class expanded as "ex-slaves and their descendants, liberated Africans, and coloured [sic] and Black immigrants from the Eastern Caribbean rose to middle class status." Members of the colored and Black middle class were distinguished from the rest of the post-emancipation Black population by their education, their familiarity with European literary culture, and their white-collar non–manual labor jobs.[4] Thus friendly societies became a platform for the aspiring Black middle class.

Friendly societies initially developed to provide for the economic and physical needs of freed people who were no longer the responsibility of former slaveholders and the British colonial government. As Bridget Brereton has noted, the post-emancipation period in the Caribbean "left an absence of established social or governmental resources for dealing with the unmet needs of a large marginal populace."[5] Furthermore, she argues, "the void left by the absence of established social institutions help[s] explain the high incidence of voluntary mutual aid associations among the large economically vulnerable groups."[6] Friendly societies provided indispensable services to their members in the form of burial, sick, and emergency funds, as well as emotional support in times of distress, including kinship networks.

Finally, friendly societies served an ideological purpose by providing agency to the newly emancipated in the Caribbean. Participation in these societies functioned as a claim-making mechanism by which the formerly enslaved demonstrated their status as free people as well as their self-sufficiency. The formerly enslaved believed that with "freedman status" they would gain respectability; they longed for the "satisfaction that flowed from successful self-help activity. Black free people had concluded that freedom could be a temporary state unless vigorously defended, and they should trust no other agency but themselves to maintain its existence."[7] Their involvement in friendly societies demonstrates that they were not only willing to but also capable of taking care of themselves and wielding control over their own lives.

Early in their history, friendly societies emphasized demonstrating their autonomy to colonial officials. The formerly enslaved wanted to prove they would not be a burden on the new post-emancipation society; instead, they would be productive and self-reliant members of society. Friendly societies enabled the autonomy that freed people sought by guaranteeing monetary assistance in case of injury or sickness, and the funds for a proper burial.

African Traditions: Dahomey

West African mutual assistance associations greatly influenced Caribbean friendly societies, as is demonstrated by their similar functions. The connection between these societies is significant because it shows that they were not merely an imitation of other immigrant groups in the United States, such as the Jewish and Chinese mutual aid societies that also emerged at this time. Instead, they were deeply rooted West Indian institutions with some of their origins in West African collective assistance associations such as the *dókpwè* societies in Dahomey.

Between the years of 1606 and 1842, more than two million enslaved Africans were brought to the British Caribbean from the west coast of Africa—from areas such as the Bight of Benin, Sierra Leone, the Bight of Biafra, the Gold Coast, and Senegambia.[8] The enslaved brought many of the traditions of their countries with them; these traditions helped them to survive the hostile new world they were forced into. Many scholars have asserted a strong link between African and Caribbean history, contending that the enslaved carried knowledge and information that they used in the creation of a new identity once they arrived in the New World.[9] Maureen Warner-Lewis, for example, argues that ethnic language clustering by enslaved Africans occurred within plantations, where possible, for social and political functions. In addition, she contends that the survival and/or continued use of even one African lexical item in a West Atlantic location is evidence of an integral link at some point in time between a particular ethno-linguistic group and the practice and belief to which the term refers.[10] It seems certain that enslaved Africans arriving in the West Indies employed prior knowledge of mutual assistance in order to survive in their new environments and to create new kinship networks for themselves. Consequently, friendly societies of the Caribbean shared many of the same mutual aid functions as West African institutions, particularly those of the *dókpwè* of Dahomey, showing the strong likelihood that West African mutual aid societies were the predecessors to West Indian friendly societies.

West Indian friendly societies are prime examples of the resourcefulness of enslaved Africans in the Caribbean. The existence of such organizations and the shared terminology that exists among West African societies and Caribbean friendly societies, such as the term *susu,* are further evidence that knowledge and practices persevered among the enslaved. *Susu,* which means a rotating line of credit, was something that many friendly societies provided their members. The same function, known as the *esusu,* is seen among Yoruba mutual aid societies.[11] This fact illustrates that there is some truth to Warner-Lewis's theory that the survival of even a single African lexical item is evidence of a link between the practice to which the term refers and the ethno-linguistic group.

Death and funeral rituals were an important carryover from West African traditions. The Senufo people who inhabited an area including present-day Côte d'Ivoire, Burkina Faso, and Mali—much like West Indians—believed death was a significant phase of social life. For the Senufo, as Anita J. Glaze has shown, funeral services were a "reinforcement of social values, group integration within the village, [and] the stimulation of the creative arts."[12] The funeral was designed to protect the living and ensure continual integration of social groups and the village community. Its purpose was to "mark the completion of the spiritual, intellectual, and social formation of the individual member within the group and to create the necessary conditions under which the dead one will now leave the world of the living."[13] The funeral ceremony served as

the final rite of passage and ensured a sense of continuity between the living
and the dead. Much as in the West Indian context, funerals involved elaborate
funerary art and ritual, in which the entire village was expected to participate:
"the Senufo community brings the vitality of aesthetic expression to counter-
balance the psychological weight of death and loss."[14] Elaborate funeral rites
were performed in order to close the cycle of a Senufo person's life as well as to
help those left behind cope with loss.

In addition to the Senufo, several other West African societies share similar functions with friendly societies in the Caribbean. Examples include the
title associations and secret societies of the Efik and the Igbo ethnic groups,
which had provisions for sickness and death insurance, much like West
Indian friendly societies.[15] Similar to the organizational structure of Caribbean friendly societies, the Poro and Sande of Sierra Leone were organized
into lodges and local chapters within major towns and villages. These secret
societies served various functions, but at "the social level they helped reg-
ulate acceptable standards of behavior and assisted individuals and families
in times of crisis. Culturally, they provided formal education regarding what
should be known about the world and beyond and supervised the training of males and females for the purpose of producing responsible adults."[16]
Other functions of the secret societies included general education (in the
sense of social and vocational training), supervision of political and economic affairs, and the operation of various social services, ranging from
medical treatment to forms of entertainment and recreation.[17] West African
secret societies were ubiquitous and had very large memberships. For young
men, membership in these societies was mandatory, as they were initiated at
puberty by rite of circumcision. Young women were expected to join prior
to or at the onset of puberty. Like West Indian friendly societies, these societies were instrumental in uniting female leadership among household units
and kinship groups of various villages. Another similarity is the emphasis
these groups placed on preparing each member for full participation in
community affairs.[18]

In Dahomey, there were numerous associations for mutual self-help
through all stages of life; such groups included societies for cooperative
farming and the production of tools and weapons, as well as for subsidizing
the cost of funerals, marriages, and other ceremonies. The most widespread
of these societies was the *dókpwè*. The *dókpwè* was an ancient institution said
to have existed before there were kings. Its chief was the *dokpwègá*, whose
office was hereditary. The chief had command of the entire village, but was

technically a chief only to the young men of the village. The *dókpwè* aided men in fulfilling their bride-wealth duties to the parents of their wives. A Dahomean priest argued the *dókpwè* "is for everyone; whether you are a chief or a common man, the *dókpwè* will help you. If you need a house it will build one for you; if you have a field to cultivate, it will break your ground. When you are sick, it helps you; when you die, it buries you." The purpose of the *dókpwè*, Herskovits states, is "to be regarded as an organization which insures to each member the cultivation of his fields, even though he himself may be incapacitated."[19] The *dókpwè's* purpose was very similar to that of the friendly societies established in the British Caribbean and then later the mutual aid societies and benevolent associations in the United States.

It is evident that many parallels can be drawn between West Indian friendly societies and Dahomean organizations. Similar to the Caribbean *susu*, Dahomean societies practiced rotating lines of credit called *gbe* and *so*.[20] Additionally, Dahomean societies placed great importance on the funeral custom called definitive burial. Members of Dahomean societies pooled funds for proper funeral ceremonies and festivities for deceased neighbors, which consisted of partial and definitive burials, a wake after the definitive burial, a mourning period of three months, and the feeding of the familial gods at ritually stated times. In Caribbean societies, and Jamaica specifically, mourners held a wake before the burial, a funeral, and a nine-night service—which was a forty-day mourning table at the end of one year, or every year, after a family member's death.[21] Mutual aid societies and benevolent associations also helped both West Africans and West Indians in honoring their dead and providing social and financial security to their members.

Much as this chapter has done, several scholars of the Caribbean argue for connections between Caribbean friendly societies and West African institutions. Historian Howard Johnson asserts that the prompt formation of friendly societies after the abolition of slavery in the Caribbean suggests that there were informal organizations, not too different from friendly societies, which may have existed during slavery. He goes on to state that these societies, while heavily influenced by both English and African organizations, truly reflected African cultural values.[22] Upon encountering friendly societies in the Caribbean, the Wells and Wells research team also drew parallels between these organizations and earlier West African traditions, concluding that the early friendly society prior to emancipation "would seem to have been an institution founded upon traditions brought overseas by slaves themselves."[23]

The Emergence of Friendly Societies

On August 29, 1833, the British government enacted the Slavery Abolition Act
of 1833, which took full effect on August 1, 1834. This Act, however, required
periods of forced indentured servitude and allowed only gradual emancipation of the enslaved, guaranteeing an expedient labor force to planters.[24]
Colonial officials and plantation owners rationalized the restrictive measures
of the Act, claiming the formerly enslaved needed time to prepare for the
responsibilities of complete freedom. The apprenticeship system varied: four
years for artisans and six for field laborers. Under this system, the newly liberated were to work without pay for their former slaveholders. In return for
their labor, the planters were to house, clothe, and feed the apprentices, and
pay them an additional wage if they worked more than forty-five hours a
week.[25] Not surprisingly, the newly freed were extremely dissatisfied with the
Act's definition of freedom, curtailed as it was by its apprenticeship clause.
Instead, they had expected to exercise choice in their housing and employment after emancipation. Freed people expected freedom of movement, the
consolidation of their families, just and equitable wages, more flexible labor
arrangements, and easy access to provision grounds.[26] In addition, many
had envisioned moving away from the plantations where they had labored.
As historian Woodville Marshall has noted, "Blacks, with vivid recollection
of their slavery experience, were determined to immediately decamp from
the plantations, the scene of their former degradation. In short, they wanted
independence, but the plantation symbolized slavery."[27]

As the realities of the apprenticeship system set in, discontent spread
among the newly freed people of the West Indies. In many of the Caribbean
islands, apprentice strikes were common and a general feeling of unrest was
pervasive. At the very start of the apprenticeship period in 1834, the formerly
enslaved in Essequibo, British Guiana, refused to continue working for plantation owners and did not return to work until they were threatened with
physical violence.[28] In Trinidad, as apprentices refused to return to work
on plantations, the island was placed under martial law just a few days after
the start of the apprenticeship period. British colonial troops, by order of
special magistrates, apprehended and flogged a number of apprentices as a
show of civil power in order to enforce new apprentice laws.[29] Convinced
that emancipation would mean ruin for their businesses, many planters did
not participate in the apprenticeship system for fear of retaliation by workers.
Exactly four years after the Act commenced, British administrators ended

involuntary apprenticeships and officially emancipated all slaves in the British Empire without any restrictions. Inhabitants of the Caribbean islands had seemingly gained the freedom they had long sought. For the first time, their new status as freed people officially left the formerly enslaved in complete charge of their own well-being.[30]

The establishment of friendly societies can largely be seen after the enactment of the Slavery Abolition Act of 1833. However, there are several instances of mutual aid societies in the Caribbean prior to emancipation. As early as the 1600s, when large numbers of West Africans were first brought to the Caribbean, we can see early forms of mutual assistance groups that resemble friendly societies.[31] The existence of mutual assistance activities prior to emancipation reinforces the argument that friendly societies were in many ways linked to traditions brought over by enslaved Africans. Wells and Wells also note the presence of assistance organizations prior to emancipation that closely resembled friendly societies in their objectives.[32] The function of these early assistance groups, Beverly Joy Anderson argues, was adaptive. They served as unifiers and allowed a disparate group of enslaved Africans to see themselves as a community.[33] While these early informal assistance groups were organized by Black people with no outside guidance or models, further demonstrating their strong connection to West African mutual assistance traditions, formal West Indian friendly societies took influence from several factors.

The majority of early West Indian friendly societies, according to Anderson, were organized by members of the clergy as "the years immediately following emancipation brought with them a fair amount of interest in friendly societies as a means of encouraging thrift among the new class of free persons, an interest which the missionary bodies helped to foster."[34] As a result, their general aim and details resembled English friendly societies. Historian Howard Johnson and economist Leonard P. Fletcher (the latter one of the most prolific writers on West Indian friendly societies) agree that early friendly societies were based on English antecedents that emerged in the late seventeenth century and proliferated in response to worker needs during the Industrial Revolution of the late eighteenth century.[35] While it is true that West African institutions had a very strong influence on West Indian friendly societies, their form and organizational structure can undeniably be linked to English models.

In Great Britain, friendly societies were generally small and local. The structure of many of these societies tended to take on the same characteristics:

a select group of officers managed each society with regular meetings.[36] Within British societies, functions such as sick and death benefits were also seen: "When a brother [society member] fell sick, he made application to the society and was granted monetary assistance in the amount and for the period set out in the society's rules. If he died, his wife could claim a lump sum to help provide for the funeral and the members were often expected to follow the body to the graveside. For the sick member there were Sick Visitors, partly no doubt to bring him his benefit and to cheer him up, but also to see that he was not malingering. When a member felt himself once more able to carry on his work, he would 'declare off' the society's funds."[37] West Indian friendly societies borrowed heavily from the practices of older British societies. The practices of visiting ill members in their homes and providing the families of deceased members with a lump sum of money for this sole purpose was a shared feature of friendly societies in both Great Britain and the Caribbean.

Although inspired by the structure and form of English models, early iterations of West Indian friendly societies were refashioned to suit the very specific needs of the descendants of enslaved Africans. They provided enslaved people with "important cultural continuity which helped bridge the gap between life in West Africa and in the New World." [38] These institutions transformed and developed with the needs of the Black population. As Anderson points out, given that the institution of slavery provided some of the basic economic necessities for the enslaved, these early forms of friendly societies were quite different from societies formed after emancipation. It was only after emancipation that friendly societies were seen as an extremely valuable institution and the numbers of associations throughout the West Indies increased exponentially.

The Bahamas Friendly Society in Nassau was the first friendly society established in the Bahamas. Founded on Emancipation Day in 1834, the society was comprised entirely of the formerly enslaved. Johnson argues for a direct correlation between the end of slavery and the founding of friendly societies, stating that "in the immediate post-emancipation years, ex-slaves and liberated Africans in the Bahamas established friendly societies in order to insure themselves against ill-health, unemployment, old age, and funeral expenses. This was part of the process," he continues, "of adjustment of former slaves to the new responsibilities of freedom and liberated Africans to an alien social and economic environment."[39] Post-emancipation friendly societies, he argues, sprang up from the genuine need on the part of the people for something to fulfill basic social and economic needs. The colonial government and the British clergy also wanted to delegate the responsibility of meeting those needs to private organizations in order to minimize government expenses as well as the potential for social disorganization. In the years preceding complete emancipation, the creation of mutual assistance groups by the formerly enslaved populations began to grow in number. Wells and Wells note that the earliest mention of friendly societies in Barbados appears in a Barbadian newspaper dated January 7, 1835.[40] Researchers have consistently linked emancipation with the establishment of West Indian friendly societies, illuminating the importance of these organizations in a period of time in which there was a lack of established social institutions or resources for dealing with the unmet needs of a large population of newly liberated West Indians.[41]

As observed above, friendly societies served a variety of purposes for the formerly enslaved population in the precarious years after the British abolished slavery in the West Indies. Notions of British Victorian respectability were high on the list of functions. A large number of friendly societies had affiliations with religious organizations, making them appear as safe and respectable organizations for the formerly enslaved to participate in. Colonial administrators often regarded friendly societies as institutions that "promot[ed] the virtues of sobriety, good conduct and thrift which were imperatives of Victorian Bahamas."[42] For instance, one of the earliest friendly societies, the St. George's Church Mutual Relief Society of Kingston, Jamaica, was organized by the Rev. Thomas Bryett Turner—demonstrating religious interest throughout the Caribbean in these friendly societies.[43] Many other early friendly societies also had direct connections to church organizations; the 1844 *Saint Vincent Handbook, Directory, and Almanac* reports that there were seven friendly societies affiliated with religious denominations in 1843, while twenty other societies of the time were nondenominational.[44] The Moravian and Wesleyan religious denominations, for example, were instrumental in the formation of many of the first friendly societies, recruiting members for their societies directly from their congregations of mostly enslaved people. Membership numbers totaled anywhere between 300 and 650 members for each society.[45]

The Moravian denomination has a unique history in the Caribbean. They were the only religious denomination to own and manage slave estates: "The whole spirit of the Moravian mission in the West Indies was to work within the framework of society as they found it, not to change it."[46] Moravian missionaries first arrived on the island of Saint Thomas, in the Danish West

Indies, in 1731. Their arrival was in response to Anthony Ulrich, a formerly enslaved person of Saint Thomas, who was invited by Count Nikolaus Zinzendorf, bishop of the Moravian Church in Germany, to petition for missionaries to the West Indies. Two prominent Moravians, Johann Leonhard Dober and David Nitchsmann, elected to become missionaries in the Caribbean. Dober even attempted to sell himself into slavery in order to get a better understanding of the conditions of enslavement, but Danish laws prohibited such a thing. Instead, the two men opted to work on a plantation to get a sense of enslaved life in the West Indies. Soon after, planters within the islands of the British Caribbean invited Moravian missionaries to proselytize to their enslaved populations. Moravian missionaries began traveling to Jamaica in 1754.[47]

Working within the framework of society, Moravian missionaries not only failed to denounce the system of slavery, but in fact owned enslaved people themselves. Moreover, slave labor was used to build Moravian churches in the Caribbean. Selvin Hastings, a late-twentieth century Black Jamaican bishop of the Moravian Church, argued that this was an "act of necessity" as there was no hired help in the Caribbean at the time and therefore slave labor was needed for church construction. He argued that "the major issue at the time was not the *institution of slavery* itself, which was universally practiced and accepted, but the treatment meted out to the slaves." Moravian missionaries, he continued, treated the enslaved fairly and avoided physical punishment.[48] Nevertheless, Moravian slaveholders believed they owned not only the bodies of their enslaved populations, but also their souls. Thus, they provided them with religious instruction and made attendance of church services mandatory. One missionary stated, "We have ventured, in the name of the Lord, to command our slaves to attend meetings . . . we think we have a right to command them to come in."[49] Consequently, Moravian congregations in the Caribbean were made up almost entirely of the enslaved. By 1832, half of the enslaved population of Antigua belonged to the Moravian church.[50]

Moravian influence was thus especially strong in the slave community and "like the other denominations, [Moravians] were pre-occupied in a typically 'Victorian' way (though many were not English but German) with [the] moral welfare"[51] of the enslaved. While respectability remained high on the Moravian list of priorities, there was also a strong push to educate their enslaved converts. In the mid-1820s, the missionaries opened day schools where free people of color and the enslaved were taught the three "Rs" of "reading, 'riting, and 'rithematic." Moravian missionaries were dedicated to turning the enslaved into "a fully-fledged Christian community with the typ-ical tenets and institutions of a modern Christian community anywhere."[52] What missionaries did not realize was that, in doing so, they "indirectly pre-sent[ed] a forceful argument for emancipation."[53]

One of the most famous pupils of Antigua's Moravian schools was Mary Prince. Prince was born into slavery in Brackish Pond, Bermuda, and even-tually sold to a slaveholding family in Antigua. While in Antigua, she was introduced to the Moravian Church and through the church's school learned to read.[54] In 1828, she was taken to England by her slaveholders and, shortly after arriving in England, gained her freedom. Prince would go on to write her groundbreaking autobiography, *The History of Mary Prince*. Prince's nar-rative was the first autobiography of a Black woman to be published in Great Britain. The autobiography illustrated the horrors of slavery and went on to become a symbol for the abolitionist movement in London. It propelled the fight for the abolition of slavery into the British consciousness.

Prior to the passing of the Slavery Abolition Act of 1833, the Moravian church was also involved with the British government in assessing the readiness of enslaved people for freedom. British officials believed that the Moravians had properly "trained" their enslaved congregation in the ways of European "civility," with just over half the slave population of Antigua being members of the Moravian faith. As a result, the British government concluded that Black people in Antigua would be exempt from the period of apprenticeship: "a special clause in the Antigua version of the Bill provided for this, ascribing the fitness of the slaves for full freedom to sound religious influence and instruction."[55] Thus a strong connection was made between religious salvation, respectability, and the attainment of freedom.

Newly freed people understood all too well the connection between religious salvation and the attainment of respectability in the eyes of Brit-ish colonial officials. Consequently, the charters and bylaws of many early friendly societies reflected their religious affiliations and even aimed to regu-late members' conduct. In Kingstown, Saint Vincent, the Chateaubelair Prov-ident Friendly Society had strict stipulations for the type of person admitted for membership: "No person shall be admitted a member of the Society who is quarrelsome, of unsound constitution, who bears a bad character or is guilty of habitual intoxication."[56] Other organizations revoked assistance to any members who were found "disabled by drunkenness, debauchery, or dis-orderly living."[57] Additionally, "if any member of the society shall be expelled from the church to which he or she belongs, or shall commit any offence punishable by a magistrate, that member forfeits his membership in the society."[58] The society also enforced the following rule: "A member shall not whilst receiving sick benefits become intoxicated, [sic] a member breaking this rule shall be fined on the offence being proved by the committee, or he or she may be suspended from and forfeit all benefits during that illness and compelled to return all money improperly obtained."[59]

Further guidelines regulated members' behavior, including the rule that "any member of the society who shall be guilty of disorderly or boisterous conduct on the premises of the Lodge when business of the society is being conducted shall be fined one shilling."[60] The Bahamas Friendly Society, for example, forbade the consumption of alcohol at their annual anniversary dinner and at the funeral services of its members. Additionally, fines were imposed for those who swore at the society's annual dinner.[61] In Saint Vincent, the Chateaubelair Olive Society's official handbook required all society meetings to be opened and closed with prayer. There were even guidelines addressing member attire for special occasions such as funeral ceremonies of fellow members, but also for general meetings: "Members present at meetings must be decently clad."[62]

By setting these strict rules in regard to members' behavior, societies hoped that they could establish respectability for their members that would in turn lead to Black people being viewed as full British subjects. Friendly society members believed that full citizenship could not come without the adoption of British ideas of respectability. Formerly enslaved people used the founding of friendly societies to serve as evidence of their adaptation to and assimilation of English values. In a letter dated August 28, 1838, written to George Scotland, Chief Justice of the island of Trinidad, John Harpe of the Moscos' African Society and Francs Joseph of the Creoles' Damas Society stated:

> We, the undersigned free Black Persons, most of us recently emancipated, loyal Subjects of Her Most Gracious Majesty, Queen VICTORIA, beg to manifest to you, our feelings of gratitude, for the wise, impartial, and intrepid manner you have administered justice to this colony, as regards the claim for emancipation and the classification question. We also feel assured that your presence in this island, your sentiments expressed in the Council, and the votes you gave, have very materially contributed to produce that precious boon of liberty we now, under the blessings of Divine Providence happily enjoy. We

trust that our future conduct will prove us worthy of the noble and generous gift; that you will find crime diminish, industry increase, morals improve, and religious duties more punctually performed. We know that, to your mind, this conduct will be the most grateful return we can possibly make for the benefits you have conferred upon us.[63]

Freed people wanted to be seen as autonomous, respectable, and equal members of British West Indian society. They believed this goal could be achieved by adopting and reflecting the opinions of the British. This idea is constantly promulgated by the formerly enslaved, many of whom believed that membership in friendly societies would serve as a gateway into the long-sought-after respectability that they demanded. In an 1835 petition written by members of the Grant's Town Friendly Society to the King of England, society members explicitly defined respectability as knowledge of the English language and the adoption of Christian values: "In adopting the language and the habits of the English people we have learned with these the truths of the Christian Religion ... and as Christians we have formed ourselves into a Society for the relief of our Widows and Orphans, and those who are unable to support themselves in sickness and in Old Age."[64]
In another letter from the Grant's Town Friendly Society, members thank the Lieutenant-Governor of the Bahamas for his "paternal advice, regarding our own conduct, and the manner of bringing up our children under the influence of mortality, and religion; as well as for your assurance of making known to His Majesty, the existence and objects of our institution."[65]

These letters illustrate the way that freed people used their participation in friendly societies and adoption of the Christian religion as evidence of their assimilation of English values in order to win entrance, equality, and the material benefits of the colonial system.

Whites, both in the Caribbean and abroad, often promoted and reinforced the ideas held by the emancipated on respectability. At the seventh anniversary celebration of the St. John's Friendly Society, for instance, the governor of Antigua stated that the society might aid in the emancipation of millions of slaves in bondage in other countries, arguing that "a people who are capable of forming such societies as this among themselves deserve to be free, and ought no longer to be held in bondage. You are showing to the world what the negro race are capable of doing."[66] The governor essentially stated that the St. John's Friendly Society and similar societies had the power to reverse the infantile stereotype that British colonial officials and white slaveholders had of Black people—the very stereotype that led colonial officials to believe that the enslaved would not survive for very long after they achieved full emancipation. A similar sentiment about friendly societies is expressed in a letter to the Bahamas Friendly Society from the lieutenant governor, William M. G. Colebrooke:

> It is particularly pleasing for me to observe you here assembled in the full recognition of such principles, and that united with so excellent and benevolent an object, you have sought to be respectable in your family relations. . . . [Holding] out a good example to your children, and [seeking] for them that instruction, which it is the anxious desire of His Majesty, and of so many benevolent persons to aid you in acquiring for them. Following the course in which you have thus set out, you cannot fail to attain all that is truly estimable in the character of Englishmen, who will be proud to recognize you as friends and fellow-subjects of the same Sovereign.[67]

In this passage, Colebrooke extols the ideals of friendly societies and sees membership in them as key to Black West Indians acquiring the necessary skills to become what he deems as respectable citizens. The British government believed so greatly in the idea of friendly societies as civilizing institutions that it established an act on May 23, 1844, to encourage the founding of more friendly societies.[68]

Further bolstering the idea of friendly societies as civilizing institutions was the research of Americans James A. Thome and J. Horace Kimball, who in 1838 published *Emancipation in the West Indies: A Six Months' Tour in Antigua, Barbados, and Jamaica in the Year 1837*. Funded by the American Anti-Slavery Society, the two men traveled to the Caribbean to conduct research on the consequences of emancipation in the British West Indies. Based on information from Black West Indian memberships in friendly societies, they recommended and advocated to the American Anti-Slavery Society an unrestricted and immediate freeing of enslaved populations. They deduced that owing to their involvement with friendly societies, Black people in the Caribbean were more than capable of caring for their own well-being. Thome and Kimball moreover contended that friendly societies were proof that, once freed, Black people could succeed by their own efforts; such societies, they held, dispelled the notion that the formerly enslaved would end up starving, homeless, and destitute.[69]

The establishment of friendly societies in post-emancipation years was one of the strategies employed by the newly freed to collectively deal with the new responsibilities of "their own maintenance during periods of sickness and in old age."[70] The emancipated consciously used friendly societies to demonstrate their agency in making life choices in their new social and economic state. At the same time, these societies over time effectively assisted the colonial administration in providing colonial officials with a "respectable" population of newly freed Black people. Enforcing the perception of a "respectable" population with the reality of "respectable" newly freed Black people is a major reason friendly societies were able to succeed.

The Functions of Friendly Societies

More than being just an ideological tool, friendly societies were benefit-driven organizations instrumental in addressing the needs of the newly freed in the post-emancipation Caribbean. For instance, during the apprenticeship period, some friendly societies assisted apprentices in purchasing the remaining term of their servitude.[71] One of the most important objectives of these societies was to provide their members with mutual assistance and relief in times of sickness and distress, as well as to see to funeral expenses and provide financial assistance to surviving family when a member passed. In addition, provisions were set aside to provide a weekly allowance to elderly members of long standing. Some of these organizations, like the British Order of the Ancient Free Gardeners Friendly Society, provided members with medical assistance, access to medical doctors, and even prescription medicine. One example is the Saint Lucia Mutual Benefit Association, which provided medical assistance and medicine for its sick members as well as a weekly allowance to members who because of sickness were unable to pursue their "ordinary duties."[72] Taking medical benefits a step further, many friendly societies in Barbados offered a maternity or "accouchement" benefit—the equivalent of two weeks' sick pay in lump sum—for female members upon the birth of each child. However, members were then not allowed to claim sick benefits for a period of time, usually three or four weeks. Friendly societies with similar maternity benefits also existed in Trinidad. Member dental and optical benefits were provided by many societies in Saint Lucia and Trinidad. Optical benefits usually covered the cost of an eye examination and refraction tests, in addition to a pair of new glasses.[73]

Additional functions of friendly societies included setting up funds from which society members could obtain loans for various purposes.[74] Societies like the Independent Order of Rechabites and the Grand United Order of Odd Fellows lent money for members to buy houses, purchase and clear land, and acquire agricultural implements. Later West Indian friendly societies even included scholarship funds for members' children within their guidelines. Societies raised money through entrance or initiation fees, member contributions, levies, fines, donations, investments, and interest on capital.[75] Members often paid weekly, or in some cases monthly, membership dues that ranged from a pence to a pound. For instance, members of the Chateaubelair Provident Friendly Society paid a weekly contribution "of any amount not less than one penny."[76] These forms of capital helped to fund the most ubiquitous function of many friendly societies—the death benefit.[77]

From their inception, as we have seen, one of the main objectives of many friendly societies was to offer assistance in the event of untimely sickness, debilitating accidents, or death. Societies provided financial and emotional support to the spouses and dependents of late members, ensuring each member a proper and respectful burial. One of the aims of the Saint Lucia Mutual Benefit Association was "to make provision for the decent burial of deceased members and their lawful dependents [and] to afford members a ready means of social intercourse."[78] This provision illustrates the great importance the emancipated placed on proper, respectable funeral ceremonies and burials. These groups assigned respectability not only to the behavior of members while alive, but to how they were prepared for the afterlife. The large emphasis placed on funerary rights may also be seen as a corrective to the abuses and indignity the dead and their survivors suffered during enslavement. Before emancipation, funeral ceremonies for the enslaved were very low on the list of concerns for slaveholders, who were more preoccupied with the productivity of their enslaved populations. Having little resources and fewer freedoms, the enslaved were forced to make do and carry out funeral ceremonies the best they could.

Clear parallels can be drawn between New World customs and West African traditions: both societies placed a serious emphasis on death and burial rites. Many West African groups believed death was a significant transition or phase of life and consequently held elaborate funeral rituals to honor this transition. As mentioned earlier, groups such as the Senufo, Efik, Igbo, and the Poro and Sande of Sierra Leone, had title associations and secret societies with provisions for sickness and death insurance and assisted in burial ceremonies, much like West Indian friendly societies. Both West Africans and West Indians looked to mutual assistance societies to uphold their traditions and honor their dead.

In his notable work *The Reaper's Garden: Death and Power in the World of Atlantic Slavery,* historian Vincent Brown illustrates the ways in which participation in burial customs gave enduring form and pattern to Jamaica and shaped enslaved Jamaicans in ways that likely affected many areas of the British Caribbean. According to Brown, burial customs shaped the terms of social interaction by providing frequent occasion for people to indicate group boundaries and to act out their vision of social hierarchy.[79] Death rites provided an opportunity for people to enact social values, to express their vision of what bound their community together, made its members unique, and separated them from others. Evocations of kinship and ancestry during funerals connected slave participants to their African past, even in an environment primarily organized by slaveholder expectations.[80] Brown furthermore posits that burial rights are among the most basic human obligations, with burial customs having a privileged role in determining ideals and standards of human conduct. "During funerals," he contends, "enslaved Blacks created a shared moral universe: they recovered their common humanity, they assumed and affirmed meaningful social roles, and they rendered communal values sacred by associating them with the dead." [81]

While Brown's work examines Jamaica specifically, parallels can be drawn to the wider Anglophone Caribbean, where Black populations also placed great importance on funeral rights. West Indian friendly societies recognized this need and made burial assistance a priority for its members. We see the same emphasis placed on Caribbean immigrant mutual aid societies in the United States in the twentieth century.

Membership

In various areas of the Anglophone Caribbean, membership in friendly societies was overwhelmingly composed of the formerly enslaved Black population. People often held memberships in multiple societies, and membership in most societies was inclusive of both men and women. The Chateaubelair Olive Society stated that its membership "shall consist of an unlimited number of male and female members who shall contribute to the Society for their sole benefit through life and after death."[82] The society's guidelines further stated that no candidate would be admitted into the society under the age of three years, or whose age exceeded fifty years old, unless provided an exemption by the society's Committee of Management. Membership was closed to any "person who may be known to be habitually intemperate, partially paralyzed of sound constitution or mind, blind, who bears a bad character or who may tend to cause disgrace to or in the Society."[83] Membership restrictions underline the fact that friendly societies crafted the image of the ideal member who would uphold the society's mission as a place of respectability among the formerly enslaved. Also among their concerns was finding able-bodied members who would contribute financially to the society in order to build up funeral and burial funds.

Significant to note, women made up a large proportion of the membership of West Indian friendly societies. Typically, women outnumbered men in these societies throughout the Caribbean. Thome and Kimball observed this fact on one of their trips to Antigua in 1837, during the apprenticeship period. During an event sponsored by the St. John's Friendly Society, the researchers counted 100 males and 260 females in a society procession. In this particular society, women constituted more than 72 percent of the membership.[84] On average, in Jamaica and British Guiana, women made up 60 percent of the membership of friendly societies. In Barbados, there was even an exclusively female society called the St. Michael's Female Friendly Society, which in 1834 had 75 members. Its objectives were "the mutual relief of its members in sickness, infirmity and old age, and the interment of the dead."[85] Other exclusively female societies, such as the Girls Friendly Society in Saint Lucia, existed throughout the Caribbean.[86]

Several factors explain women's participation in friendly societies in such large numbers. One is that in the years following emancipation, freed people were highly mobile. Finally having the freedom to work where they chose, emancipated men chose to migrate to other Caribbean islands in search of better working conditions and higher wages. Although many freed people chose to remain on their old plantations, migration greatly increased within the Caribbean region. Planters were well aware of these demographic shifts. In Trinidad, planters sponsored recruiting programs that enlisted laborers to work on the island, offering free passage and double the wages that other islands were offering.[87]

Many inhabitants of the Eastern Caribbean moved around the Caribbean in search of a better standard of living: "Between 1835 and 1846, 19,000 persons from the Eastern Caribbean islands entered British Guiana and Trinidad and Tobago; between 1850 and 1921 Barbados alone contributed 50,000 persons to the populations of British Guiana and Trinidad and Tobago."[88] Many migrants were young adult men, who moved and worked only seasonally. Workers arriving in June returned home for Christmas crop in order to cultivate their own lands. Some laborers chose to permanently remain on the islands to which they migrated, but most were temporary workers.

While these immigrants fulfilled the need for workers in British Guiana and Trinidad and Tobago, they in turn left a shortage of workers on their own islands. More importantly, they left behind thousands of wives, mothers, and daughters. These women reached out to friendly societies for kinship networks and social insurance that they lacked in their homes, and increasingly came to rely on the protection that friendly societies afforded members.[89]

Also contributing to the large number of female members in friendly societies is the fact that in many cases men enrolled their wives as members for their household. Instead of joining themselves, men enrolled their wives, as they would often receive the same benefits no matter which spouse was officially enrolled in the society. This practice effectively raised the number of female members.[90] On the other hand, the increase in female participation in these organizations can also be ascribed to the temperance requirements of some friendly societies. The sometimes restrictive rules concerning temperance may have dissuaded and even limited male membership.[91]

The membership of friendly societies in the West Indies was predominantly Black and working class, while the leadership and founders often came from a small group of Black middle class individuals with political ambitions.[92] Many of the early societies were "patronized" societies, meaning that "while they were organisations [sic] for mutual insurance of the poor, their founders and officers generally included 'better off' people."[93] As previously mentioned, many friendly societies were connected with religious organizations whose clergy would become leaders and founders, while the general membership consisted of the laboring class. However, in the early twentieth century, the makeup of friendly society membership and leadership changed and became predominately working class as middle class leaders moved on to politics and other organizations.

Prior to 1838, the Black middle class in the British Caribbean consisted of "free persons of color" and the "free Blacks of slave society"; this demographic changed after emancipation as the middle class expanded to include some freed people and their descendants. The pronounced urban orientation of many ambitious and mobile freed people and their children was important to the emergence of this group post-emancipation. Education was the essential factor in the development of a Black middle class, serving to distinguish them from the masses. In fact, middle-class status depended on two essential criteria: "an occupation which involved no manual labor, and command of European, or British culture, especially the ability to speak and write English."[94] These requirements were more crucial than material prosperity or lightness of skin color. Public elementary school education, which was established in Trinidad in 1851 and modified in 1870, was extremely significant to Black mobility in the two post-emancipation generations. Primary schoolteachers were the nucleus of the middle class, as this was one of the few "respectable" white-collar jobs available to young men from poor families that could not afford a university education. This group would increasingly become politicized in the nineteenth century as they progressively rejected the inferior position to which they were assigned by local and European whites. As the century progressed, they would gain in numbers and self-confidence.[95]

Prevalence

Charts 1 to 3, drawn from colonial Blue Books and Annual Colonial Reports, graph a sampling of the number of friendly societies in several islands of the Caribbean. Examining these figures, we see that Barbados had the largest number of active friendly societies, with total society numbers double and triple those in Saint Vincent and the Grenadines and Trinidad and Tobago, respectively. Saint Vincent, an island whose population was only 41,054 in 1891, had fewer friendly societies than larger islands like Barbados, whose population was 182,322 in the same year.[96] The number of friendly societies in Saint Vincent reached its apex in 1893 with close to thirty societies. We also see after 1890 a significant increase in the overall number of societies. Conversely, there are very few instances of societies before this time, largely due to the fact that friendly societies were not legally required to register with colonial officials until 1890. As a result, limited reliable data exists on the number of society members and friendly societies present in each colony before this date. Another salient fact is the lack of data for friendly societies before 1850. Also, as noted earlier, little statistical data is available for West Indian friendly societies in the period closely following emancipation. However, we know for certain these societies did exist, as they left records in

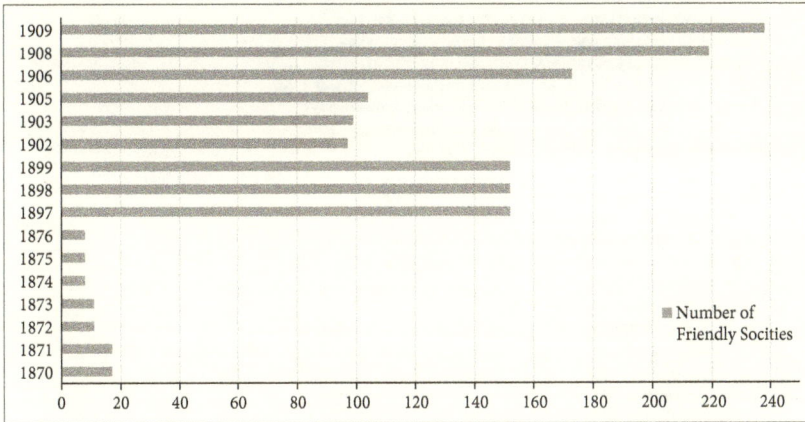

Chart 1. Friendly Societies in Barbados. *Source:* Data taken from the Barbados Blue Books, 1870–1909, and Report of the Registrar of Friendly Societies, 1897–1909. National Archives of Barbados. This chart was compiled using data taken from several sources in the National Archives of Barbados, including several Blue Books, 1870–1909, and Reports of the Registrar of Friendly Societies, 1897–1909. In the Blue Books, each year there is a category that lists the number of friendly societies in existence. Similarly, the Reports of the Registrar of Friendly Societies kept an annual tally of the number of friendly societies that were registered. Consequently, it is very possible that the total number of friendly societies could be higher for each year, as the chart does not reflect friendly societies that had not registered with the registrar.

colonial newspapers and were discussed in colonial dispatches. In addition, during this period, contemporary researchers, such as Thome and Kimball, reference them.

According to Thome and Kimball, by 1834 there were eleven Antiguan friendly societies with memberships totaling 1,602. Only two years later in 1836 this number had increased to a total of 4,560 members. They contend that the growth of friendly societies was more rapid in Antigua than in any of the other islands within the Caribbean, which was probably because Antigua received unrestricted freedom post-emancipation and was not subject to the apprentice clause.[97] An ecclesiastical return for the Diocese of Barbados and the Leeward Islands, dated July 1841, highlights the existence of five friendly societies connected with the Anglican Church in Trinidad with a membership of 656. In Barbados, there were 43 societies with 4,751 members, and nine societies with 1,128 members in Saint Vincent.[98] We can conclude therefore that although friendly societies may not be reflected in official colonial

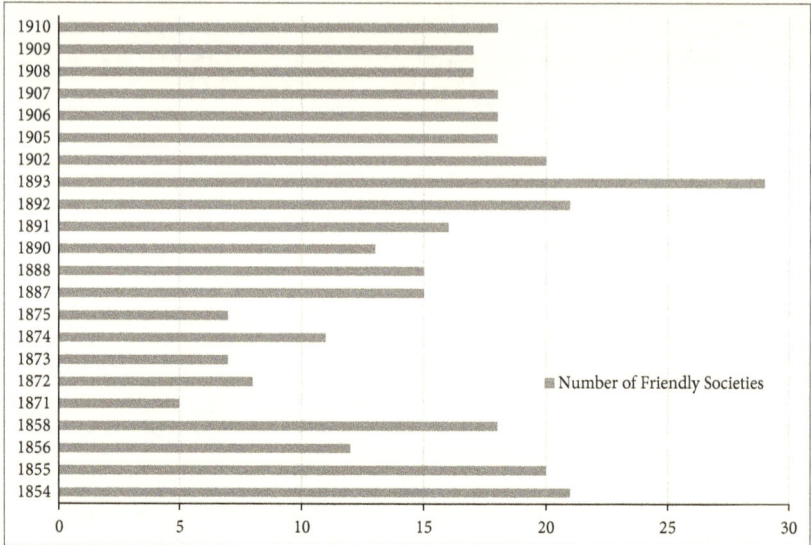

Chart 2. Friendly Societies in Saint Vincent and the Grenadines. *Source:* Data taken from the St. Vincent Blue Books, 1854–1910, and Annual Colonial Reports, 1890–1893. National Archives of St. Vincent and the Grenadines.

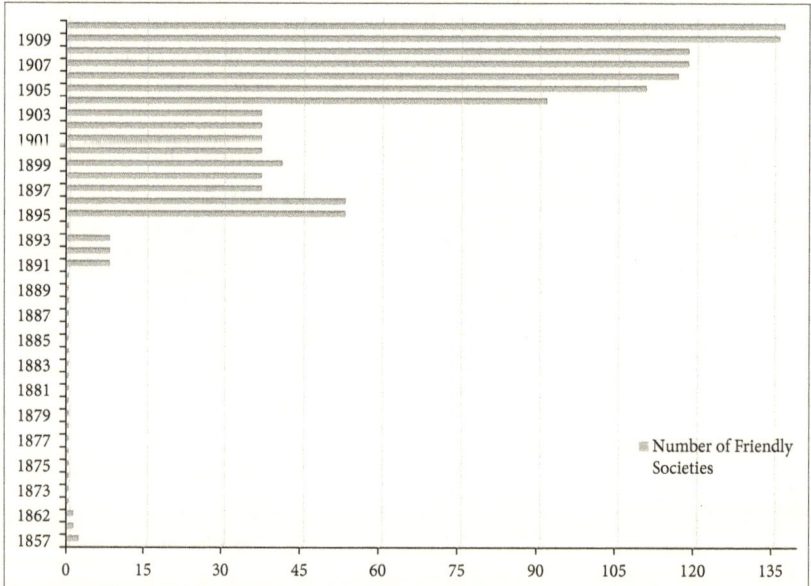

Chart 3. Friendly Societies in Trinidad and Tobago. *Source:* Data taken from the Trinidad Blue Books, 1891–1910, and Tobago Blue Books, 1857, 1859, 1862, National Archive of Trinidad.

records, supplementary sources confirm not only the existence of friendly societies but also their large memberships.

The Political Nature of Friendly Societies

Membership in a friendly society undoubtedly gave newly freed people a sense of security and kinship. However, the primary objective of many friendly societies began to shift over time, and societies came to perform a more political role for the newly emancipated in the Caribbean. The major trend among friendly societies beginning in the late 1880s was for societies to extend their activities beyond mutual aid functions to incorporate political action more fully. Subsequently, friendly societies were "increasingly used as organisational [sic] structures around which support could be mobilized for matters of vital importance to the Black community."[99] However, the political nature of many friendly societies could be observed from their very founding, as is witnessed by the numerous petitions printed in West Indian newspapers in the nineteenth century.[100] For example, the 1888 election speech of W. C. Adderley, the newly nominated president of the Bahamas Friendly Society, illustrates this point. Adderley articulates the political purpose of the society in one speech: "Gentlemen, this society has always been considered throughout this colony as being more than a common Burial society, that is, it is also a political one, and I must say that we have a right to raise our voices when we consider our rights assailed as loving subjects of Her Most Gracious Majesty Queen Victoria."[101] We can conclude that friendly societies were always somewhat political in their nature. From their genesis, many friendly societies expressed concern with the rights of their members as citizens of the British colonial empire. However, once society members had been free for a number of years, with time to settle into their new lives, their political interests became more pronounced. As a result, friendly societies became emergent political parties.

As political entities, friendly societies used various methods to lobby colonial administrations. One of the most popular and effective methods was airing their grievances in colonial newspapers in the form of letters to the editor and organized petitions that were regularly printed in these papers. Friendly society leaders also sent letters and petitions to colonial administrators and in some cases directly to the King or Queen of England. Another effective method of lobbying usually took place on major holidays or celebrations, such as the anniversary of the Slavery Abolition Act or that specific friendly society's founding date. Friendly society members used these momentous occasions, in which large groups were gathered, to address relevant political issues affecting the Black community. Members gave speeches and held large processions through the streets of the British colonies.[102] One such event occurred on March 13, 1835, the birth date of Queen Victoria, when members of the Bahamas Friendly Society and the Grant's Town Friendly Society arrived in procession to the Government House. Members of the Bahamas Friendly Society were identified by their blue ribbons. The whole event garnered public attention and is recounted in several colonial dispatches to King William IV. Having the attention of the governor of the island, members of this society then submitted a petition to the King, thanking him for granting emancipation in the British West Indies, but also asking for Black people in the West Indies to be treated as full and equal British subjects.[103] Through these various methods of lobbying, members of friendly societies received the attention of colonial administrators and demanded to be heard. Unfortunately, their requests were not often met.

One of the issues high on the political agenda for many friendly societies was a concerned interest for peoples of African descent elsewhere. Johnson notes: "Friendly societies fostered a racial consciousness and a Pan-African awareness among its [sic] membership. The link with Africa and the rest of the African diaspora was a constant theme of speeches made at the annual celebration to mark emancipation."[104] Members were not only concerned with their own islands, but also frequently expressed concern for the lives of other people of African descent. For instance, friendly societies lobbied for liberated Africans in the Caribbean to be granted the full privileges of British-born subjects.[105] Societies also expressed interest in the labor conditions of Black people in neighboring islands and countries in the Caribbean basin, where many of their friends and family members had migrated to work. By the closing decades of the nineteenth century, affiliated societies with links to organizations in Britain and the United States had also been established.[106] As members of West Indian friendly societies migrated to different countries, they brought with them the idea of friendly societies and sometimes the actual organization itself. These affiliated societies then worked closely with other friendly societies in the Caribbean, as will be discussed in a later chapter. Friendly societies, much like later American benevolent associations and mutual aid societies, served as a stellar training ground for West Indian leaders. They provided organizational experience for Black politicians and helped create a strong political base for them, demonstrating the ways in which mutual aid has historically been an inherently political act of solidarity, survival, and community for West Indians.

Conclusion

Friendly societies continued to be an important facet of Black life in the Caribbean long after the initial years post emancipation. In fact, well into the mid-twentieth century, friendly societies provided their members with kinship networks and social insurance. They also served quotidian and special functions for West Indians in the form of funeral, sick, and emergency funds; compulsory savings; emotional support in times of distress; and ritual and recreational activities. Ultimately, they helped West Indians to establish themselves in a post-emancipation society. However, friendly societies would eventually begin to lose their usefulness by the mid-twentieth century and be slowly replaced with modern institutions. Nonetheless, their legacy lived on as migrants brought the traditions of these mutual aid institutions with them as they traveled and migrated abroad.

CHAPTER 2

Whence They Came

Immigration and Mobility in the Caribbean

On June 10, 1919, Mary Layne, a forty-one-year-old native of Barbados, arrived in New York on the SS *Tivives*, operated by the United Fruit Company. Because she was illiterate, Layne was initially excluded from entering the United States; at the time literacy was one of the major requirements for the admission of immigrants. She was later granted temporary admission and placed on a $300 bond for one year because she was the domestic servant and childcare provider for Margaret and C. F. MacMurry, an American couple living in Colón, Panama. The family paid her a wage of $12.50 a month. Margaret MacMurry was the daughter of John C. Horter of Nutley, New Jersey, a sugar broker and owner of Horter & Diago S. en C. Sugars in New York. Horter had used his influence with the U.S. Secretary of Labor to allow Layne to enter the United States in 1919 with his daughter, Margaret, who would be traveling alone with her small children and would need Layne's assistance.

Prior to her employment with the MacMurrys, Layne had been living and working in Panama for a total of nine years. She was widowed in 1908, and the death of her husband may have been one of the factors that sparked her move to Panama, a country where she had no family or connections. Layne did, however, have a daughter named Ann Pounder who had been living in Harlem, New York, for three years. Pounder had invited Layne to come to the United States on numerous occasions, even offering to pay her mother's passage from Panama. In 1920, when her mother was granted a one-year stay in the United States to work for the MacMurrys, Pounder tried to have Layne's stay extended. The Board of Special Inquiry held at Ellis Island records the following exchange between officials and the mother and daughter: "Her daughter desires her to remain and is ready to care for her at any time, although it is the alien's intention to work and support herself, which she is able to do. Destined to her daughter, she may be exempted from the literacy test, which appears to be the only ground for exclusion." Ellis Island officials asked Pounder, "What would you be willing to do for your mother?" She responded, "Anything I am called upon to do, [*sic*] I am an only child." Layne was then asked how long she intended to stay and responded, "As long as my daughter is here." Layne was eventually allowed to remain in New York with her daughter; MacMurry, her employer, moved back to Panama on March 13, 1920, without her.[1] Mary Layne's narrative demonstrates the reality of immigrants' mobility within the Caribbean, female-led chains of migration to the United States, and the various labor roles available to Caribbean immigrants to the United States.

This chapter examines mobility within the Caribbean and, more extensively, early twentieth century migration to the United States. It begins with an examination of Caribbean immigrants after the abolition of slavery in the British West Indies and follows their migration, for both seasonal and long-term work projects, throughout the Caribbean basin. Analyzing the connection between freedom and mobility and investigating the labor positions Caribbean migrants held, this chapter interrogates how these initial movements led to later immigration to the United States. Further, it identifies who decided to immigrate, analyzing their gender, class, and levels of education for observable commonalities. Finally, this chapter investigates settlement and employment patterns of Caribbean immigrants as a way to understand their early connection with the African American community and the formation of their own Caribbean community through the mutual aid organizations they established.

Migration is a theme integral to the history of the Caribbean region. Nowhere was this truer than in the British West Indies, which established a long tradition of mobility both within and outside the region in the years following 1838. Seminal Caribbean historian Velma Newton asserts that freedom was the main motivation for this migration: "whatever the factors which influenced the decision to emigrate [after the abolition of slavery], British West Indians conceived of the move as a means of freeing themselves ... from plantation labour [*sic*]."[2] Taking Newton's argument a step further, this chapter demonstrates that the abolition of slavery in the British West Indies sent thousands of freed people into motion, not only to distance themselves from the plantations they had worked on, but to exercise their newly gained autonomy to choose where, when, and how they would work.

This chapter argues that newly freed Black people perceived, and ultimately utilized, migration as a tool of autonomy in the years following emancipation. Consequently, both large-scale permanent and seasonal migration commenced from smaller colonies such as Barbados and the Leeward Islands to larger and less densely populated, labor-scarce areas, such as British Guiana and Trinidad. For example, in the 1850s, large numbers of Jamaican workers flocked to Panama for the construction of the Panama Railroad. The 1860s and 1870s saw large numbers of Barbadians immigrating to South American countries for work, while Jamaicans were drawn to Costa Rica by the promise of well-paying jobs constructing a national railroad. Mass migration continued through the end of the century, with considerable movement from nearly every West Indian island to locations in Central America, South America, and other Caribbean countries in response to the labor projects financed by Europeans and Americans.

The largest intraregional movement of migrants, however, occurred between 1880 and 1914 to the Isthmus of Panama for the construction of the Panama Canal. Caribbean women, like Mary Layne, held positions in "daily social reproduction" tasks such as cooking, cleaning, providing shelter, and child-rearing, as well as providing companionship, all of which were vital to sustaining the regional workforce.[3] In total, an estimated 200,000 British West Indians traveled to Central America between 1850 and 1910.[4]

Travel to Panama had an especially transformative effect on Anglophone Caribbean societies. Caribbean immigrants were no longer migrating simply as a way to distance themselves from plantation societies or to demonstrate their autonomy. In the early twentieth century, West Indians viewed migration as a step to economic success that would help elevate them not only economically, but socially and culturally. Migration became an important social marker for upwardly mobile West Indians. Additionally, success in Panama encouraged migrants to take larger risks and seek even greater fortunes in countries outside the Caribbean basin.

"Panama silver"[5]—as money earned in this period was called—helped finance migration to the United States for canal workers, or in most cases their family members.[6] An examination of intra-Caribbean migration demonstrates that migration was far from unidirectional and often functioned as a testing ground for later West Indian migration to the United States and the United Kingdom. Analyzing connections between nineteenth and early twentieth century migration movements illuminates the larger motivations that propelled Caribbean immigrants to leave their home countries and immigrate to the United States. Moreover, this chapter interrogates in detail the identities and motives of individuals who immigrated to the United States at the turn of the twentieth century, the cities where they settled, the types of jobs they held, and their social standing.

Most significantly, while West Indian men initially made up most of the migrant population in the nineteenth century, in the early twentieth century women in larger numbers immigrated to the United States. This fact not only contradicts the historiographical assumption that places men at the forefront of many immigration histories, but has gendered ramifications in the analysis of the overall Caribbean immigrant experience to the United States.

Therefore, this work posits that female immigrants served as the guardians and proponents of Caribbean culture in the United States. In the early twentieth century, specifically between 1918 and 1940, Caribbean women were a significant immigrant group outnumbering Caribbean males in the United States. The pattern is consistent. Between 1918 and 1922, for instance, 17,504 Caribbean immigrant women arrived in the United States compared to 17,320 Caribbean men. Between 1923 and 1927, 12,283 Caribbean women arrived in the United States while 10,154 Caribbean men arrived. From 1928 to 1931, again, arriving Caribbean immigrant women outnumbered Caribbean men each year.[7] Caribbean women initiated female-led chains of immigration, leaving behind their families, including their children, to immigrate to the United States. Once established in the United States with a place to live and a job, and having secured employment for their relatives, they then sent money for their family members to join them, much as Ann Pounder tried to arrange passage for her mother Mary Layne.

These female-led chains of migration, in which families followed Caribbean women, became the social and economic foundation for later Caribbean immigrants for the simple fact that setting up households in the United States was crucial to sustaining a thriving Caribbean immigrant community. Without the social networks established by female immigrants, the Caribbean immigrant community in the United States could not have been sustained. These social networks included child fostering and the creation of social and cultural organizations that offered rotating lines of credit and their practice of remittance sending, all of which kept West Indian immigrants to the United States connected to their home islands and Caribbean identity. Caribbean women were instrumental in creating an ethnic community in the United States in which Caribbean immigrants, both women and men, could begin to find their place in a foreign country.

Circular Migration in the Caribbean

The abolition of slavery in the British Caribbean, followed by the end of involuntary apprenticeships in 1838, spurred movement in the Caribbean. This is not to say that enslaved Black people and free people of color before 1838 were stagnant and not creatively making the best of their situations; however, it was only at the end of the apprenticeship system that Black people in the British Empire for the first time had few restrictions on their movements within the region and had the right to go and come as they wished.

Freedom for these newly freed people was closely identified with freedom of movement. Equally important was land ownership. Newly freed people sought both autonomy and advancement through the purchase of land. In the years immediately following abolition, sales and registration of holdings under ten acres rose; twenty percent of the former apprentice population purchased such plots of land for residence and farming.[8] The formerly enslaved used these purchases to create customary institutions such as family land, which provided the benefits of land ownership that accrued to family groups.

Family land—understood as communal land owned by an entire family unit—was created in the generations immediately following abolition. Newly freed people pooled their money to purchase land. The undivided land was bilaterally handed down by the original property owners to their descendants, who paid property taxes and were entitled to use the land for either residential or agricultural purposes. Following generations bequeathed the land. The sale or disposal of family land was viewed as a wrong against the family and was strongly discouraged.[9] Family land was "not to be sold; not selling it. If me even dead, it can't sell. Not selling. It's fe [sic] the children: all the children."[10] Family land was especially widespread in Jamaica, but existed throughout the Anglophone Caribbean. When land was not available for purchase, many West Indians looking to provide for their families saw migration as a means for financial support.

As a result, newly freed people stretched their proverbial legs and exercised their right to move. An 1859 *Colonial Report* for Saint Vincent provides evidence of migration for these reasons, stating that "a natural withdrawal of a large number of the laboring population from estates to cultivate lands of their own, or to embark in other pursuits, has progressively gone on since emancipation."[11] There are several explanations for this movement: a simple exercise of the freedom to move, a search for better work conditions, a desire for a higher standard of living, as well as a need to separate from the plantations that had been places of degradation. Especially important to newly freed people were just and equitable wages, even if that meant leaving their islands. Newton argues that British West Indians conceived of migration as a way of removing themselves, even if only temporarily, from plantation labor and the stigma of slavery that was so deeply embedded in it.[12] Migration, she posits, was also perceived as a means of freeing themselves from a lower class status to which West Indian social structure constricted most Black individuals, and emigration became "a quest for money, freedom, and status."[13]

In places such as Trinidad and British Guiana, more land was available for settlement and wages were higher. In Trinidad, planters sponsored programs in which recruiters were sent to other islands to enlist laborers to work in Trinidad. They not only offered free passage but paid double the wages other islands offered.[14] Free passage and double wages were a huge selling point given the extremely low wages employers on other islands paid free Black people during this period. Consequently, large numbers of inhabitants of the Eastern Caribbean—many coming from Barbados—moved to Trinidad and British Guiana seeking a better standard of living: "between 1835 and 1846, 19,000 persons from the Eastern Caribbean islands entered British Guiana and Trinidad and Tobago; while between 1850 and 1921 Barbados alone contributed 50,000 persons to the populations of British Guiana and Trinidad and Tobago."[15] These migrants were often young adult men, and they migrated only seasonally for set periods of time. Workers arrived in June and returned home for Christmas crop in order to cultivate their own lands. Some laborers remained permanently on the islands to which they migrated, but much of the movement at this time was temporary.

The first substantial wave of British Caribbean emigration to foreign countries occurred during the 1850s. In Jamaica, there was a drop in sugar prices in 1846 and a bank collapse in 1847 which caused a great economic depression. As a result, a larger number of Jamaicans immigrated to Panama for the construction of the Panama Railroad until its completion in 1855. Mass migration continued throughout the end of the century. In the 1860s and 1870s, Barbadians immigrated to Saint Croix, Honduras, Suriname, Peru, Brazil, and various South American countries in search of better job opportunities. For example, thousands of Jamaicans were contracted to work on the construction of a railroad to link Puerto Limón with San José in Costa Rica.

Following the 1880s, there was considerable movement from most islands to Central America, South America, and other Caribbean countries in response to the need for labor on European- and American-financed projects and companies. For instance, in 1884, Black West Indians were contracted to construct what became known as the International Railways of Central America in Izabal, Guatemala. This railroad connected Puerto San José to several regions in Guatemala, enabling the transportation of agricultural products to export markets and harbors. It is estimated that between 15,000 and 20,000 Black West Indians migrated to the Caribbean coast of Guatemala between 1863 and 1923.[16]

The largest group of British West Indian migrant labors traveled to Panama at the turn of the twentieth century. Between 1880 and 1914, British West Indians from almost every island seeking work traveled to the Isthmus of Panama, where an estimated 150,000 Black West Indians were contracted to work on the Panama Canal, making it the largest single destination of Black migrants.[17] It is estimated that a little more than 6,000 West Indian women lived and worked in the Canal Zone between these years, with many more living in neighboring Colón and Panama City.[18]

The construction of the Panama Canal occurred in two phases. The French Compagnie Universelle du Canal Interocéanique began construction in 1880. They commissioned Ferdinand de Lesseps, who had worked on the Suez Canal in Egypt, to head the project. De Lesseps employed thousands of British West Indian laborers. In the year 1885 alone, the Panama Canal Company's labor agency sent 2,375 Black West Indians to Colón. As an incentive to recruit laborers, they paid workers' passage to Panama and set a competitive daily wage of $1.50.[19] However, the French-led project was fraught with numerous obstacles, including the challenging terrain of the Isthmus of Panama, engineering problems, and a large number of deaths due to accidents, yellow fever, malaria, and other tropical diseases. In 1889, the French went bankrupt and left the project unfinished. The United States took over the second phase of construction on the canal in 1904 and completed the project ten years later. The Panama Canal officially opened on August 15, 1914.

After the canal was completed, the United States had the responsibility of repatriating thousands of Black West Indians back to their homes. U.S. president Theodore Roosevelt assured the president of Panama that the United States would contribute financially toward the solution to the "thorny problem of alien repatriation from this country [Panama]."[20] Panamanian officials had to be guaranteed that the thousands of workers who had come to the Isthmus to work would not remain there. True to Roosevelt's promise, the United States government aided in the repatriation of many West Indian canal workers to their homes. The United States War Department proposed a grant of $150,000 for the purpose of repatriating aliens who had served three years or more working on the construction of the Panama Canal or the Panama Railroad. In total, the United States provided $150,000 in aid for resettlement costs. They also provided migrants with a lump sum of $15 to $100 each, according to their circumstances, to assist families in resettling upon return to their home islands.[21] However, even with these inducements in place, thousands of Black migrants decided to remain in Panama to establish new lives.

For most West Indians, however, Panama was a place where they could find short-term profitable employment as well as amass savings to improve their economic and social status upon their return home.[22] Additionally, British West Indian migrants acquired a certain level of prestige for having worked on the canal. Migrants returning home with "Panama money" or "Panama silver" were regarded with respect and admiration. They were thought to be worldly and, more importantly, wealthy.[23] These returnees used their "Panama silver" to advance themselves economically. Colonial administrators in Saint Lucia, as early as 1890, remarked that laborers returning from the Panama Canal "brought a considerable amount of money with them and are everywhere taking up land and building houses."[24] Many West Indians also used their Panamanian earnings to secure passage for later immigration to the United States, either for themselves or for family members. Return migrants' perceived success in Panama inspired others at home to believe that through migration they could obtain similar opportunities.[25]

During the late nineteenth century, thousands of migrants found immigration to be highly profitable economically and educationally, exposing them to different languages and customs. As a result, by 1904, foreign travel was accompanied by an aura of accomplishment. Travel was deemed a requirement in order "to become a man, to know the world, and to understand life. Thus emigration became highly desirable and sought after, even for its own sake; and as a channel to success, it became for many sectors of society a social imperative."[26]

Another factor shaping West Indian immigration was social networks. Personal ties usually guided migrants' decisions of when and where to travel. Social networks even frequently determined where migrants settled upon arrival. Within these spheres of migration in the Caribbean basin and abroad, ties of kinship and acquaintance routinely crossed national borders. Families sometimes deemed national boundaries irrelevant as they moved back and forth between them, as we have seen in the fluidity of movement between

Costa Rica and the Isthmus of Panama. However, this movement decreased when policymakers began to place border restrictions on West Indian immigrants to constrict their travel.[27] Historian Lara Putnam argues that revolving migration in the nineteenth century matched the needs of workers' ideas of "prosperity, pleasure, and obligations."[28] Many workers returned home after earning a decent amount of money and then went back to the Isthmus to work again. The completion of the Panama Canal and the ease with which British West Indian migrants traveled back and forth to Central America for work eventually led them to Cuban sugar plantations after 1914.

Once the canal project was completed, many West Indian laborers looked to Cuba for work. Between 1913 and 1920, some 6,189 West Indian migrants who had been working in Central America moved on to Cuba. They were joined by other laborers from various Caribbean islands. By the end of 1928, the British legation in Havana estimated that between 9,000 and 10,000 West Indian immigrants from countries such as Jamaica, Antigua, and Barbados were living and working in Cuba.[29] Records indicate that between 1898 and 1938, Cuba received more than 140,000 British Caribbean immigrants in total, representing every island in the British West Indies, with Jamaican migrants in the majority.[30] Immigrants were employed not only in the sugar industry and its related industries but also on coffee and fruit plantations, on railroads, and in various other occupations. However, for British West Indians, living and working in Cuba was not a smooth transition.

West Indians were not well received in Cuba. Historian Jorge Giovannetti demonstrates that the large presence of Black migrants alarmed Cubans who feared their island would become a *Black country*. This *Black fear* had haunted the Cuban psyche since the colonial era, because Cubans associated a Black outsider presence with slave uprisings and rebellions, an idea that goes back as far as the Haitian Revolution of 1804, when Cuban officials feared upheaval in their own country following the successful overthrow of the French in Saint-Domingue. Cuban officials feared that a Black presence in Cuba would "inspire with their perverse ideas those that we have in our possessions [enslaved Blacks], for the malevolent inclinations of the descendants of Ethiopia are well-known and troubling, notwithstanding the care with which we try to teach them in these dominions."[31] They did not want what they considered Black agitators inspiring or planting seeds of revolution in their own Black population.

In a similar vein, in the twentieth century, some Cubans argued that the presence of Black West Indians introduced "racism" or ideas of racial discontent, which were incompatible with Cuba's social harmony. The alleged "'racism' brought by the 'outsiders' into the Cuban social landscape thus became part of the rationale behind the way Cubans treated Black migrants."[32] In 1926, the Jamaican Secretary of State for Foreign Affairs cited the extremely unsatisfactory situation that had arisen in connection with the large number of British West Indians living, working, and seeking employment in other West Indian islands and Central American countries:

> At present, natives of the British islands are resident in such large numbers in almost all the lands washed by the Caribbean that they constitute a constant source of embarrassment to the governments within whose jurisdiction they are found. The native inhabitants, however incapable of employment themselves, resent the presence of bodies of aliens who come to undertake work. So long as labourers [sic] are in demand, this resentment is kept under a certain amount of control, but once work becomes scarce, the alien is unpopular, and incidents are always likely to arise, and have in the past arisen. As a consequence, British West Indians are gaining a bad name through-out the Caribbean, greatly to the disadvantage of British prestige.[33]

The Jamaican Secretary of State believed the large presence of British West Indians threatened the local communities. Locals resented and feared the West Indians, who they perceived were taking all the better-paying jobs.

In Central and South American countries, Black West Indian laborers working for American companies were seldom welcomed with open arms by local governments. This fact is especially true for migrants who were con-tracted to work in these countries by American companies, as they were not necessarily there at the invitation of respective local governments. Similar conditions existed in Guatemala during the late nineteenth century. U.S. State Department records recount the alarming fact that Guatemalan officials carried out violent attacks against immigrant workers. American officials expressed concern that Black migrants were often arrested without proba-ble cause and sent to jail without trial. Once imprisoned, they were forced to perform hard labor without compensation.[34] Similarly, at the turn of the twentieth century in Honduras, Black West Indian workers were met with anti-Black and anti-immigrant sentiments, reflected in the country's nation-alist rhetoric and anti-Black legislation.[35]

Giovannetti argues that there were three ways in which West Indian migrants responded both collectively and individually to Cuban hostility:

through labor activism, organization, and allegiance to British imperial traditions. In order to combat isolation, migrants developed their own communities and sociocultural infrastructure by establishing churches, associations, and social clubs. West Indian migrants also took these same actions in the Canal Zone, where they established their own churches, schools, and mutual aid societies.[36] Similar institutions could also be found among West Indian laborers in Honduras.[37] In addition, they joined labor unions and participated in strikes. In Guatemala as well, Black migrant laborers working for the railroad, on docks, and on banana plantations participated in massive strikes in 1898, 1909, 1913, 1915, 1918, and 1919, demanding higher wages and better work conditions.[38]

One of the most effective practices or tools of resistance that West Indian workers used was their allegiance to the British Empire. Migrants consistently presented complaints to the British authorities in Cuba, the Caribbean colonies, and London, demanding representatives of the British Empire to act in their favor. Migrants used the system and the language of authority of the Empire to their advantage. Whether their allegiance to the British Empire was genuine or merely a strategic tool is irrelevant as it gave them a means by which to retaliate against discriminatory practices and laws.[39] West Indian immigrants used similar tools in the United States to fight against unjust American laws and, in some cases, to separate themselves from the African American population.

Push and Pull

It is important to understand why British West Indian immigrants left their familiar homes to travel to new and unfamiliar places. High unemployment, underemployment caused by the decline of the sugar industry, few job opportunities, and low wages, as well as destructive weather phenomena and population pressure (especially in Barbados), were several of the factors that pushed mass migration of Caribbean immigrants to the United States.[40] Although the British colonial government ended involuntary apprenticeships and officially emancipated all enslaved people on August 1, 1838, conditions on many of the islands in the British Caribbean remained poor. Prior to the abolition of slavery, many of the island's planter class were in debt due to high mortgages they had taken out on their properties. After the Slavery Abolition Act of 1833, without adequate sources of free labor, planters' debt increased significantly.

In the late 1840s, the sugar industry in the Caribbean was crippled by a drastic decline in prices, which plummeted in 1840 from 49 shillings per cwt. or hundredweight (equal to 112 pounds) without duties to 23 shillings per cwt. with a duty of 5 shillings in 1848.[41] Many Caribbean economies already in danger of ruin prior to the crash of sugar prices found themselves in great despair. In 1848, the *National Era* newspaper reported that the "West India property is in a state of ruin. In these Colonies, at this moment, property cannot be sold, securities cannot be assigned, the interest upon mortgages cannot be realized, and advances are refused to enable the planter to produce a crop which cannot be relied upon to return the bare cost of production."[42] As a result of the declining sugar economy, many islands faced financial ruin and universal bankruptcy. In 1859 on the island of Saint Lucia, for example, liabilities and debt incurred prior to emancipation totaled an astronomical £1,089,865.[43] Indebted colonists received little, if any, assistance from the British colonial government, which no longer had as vested an interest in the region after the abolition of slavery. As result, the British government sent little aid to their failing colonies in the Caribbean.

Economic conditions worsened through the end of the nineteenth century on many of the islands. In the *1896 Annual Colonial Report for St. Vincent*, government officials wrote that Saint Vincent "is passing through a severe crisis, which became more acute in 1896 than in preceding years, as the causes, both local and external, to which reference has been made in this report, more fully developed their evil effects."[44] Economic and social conditions looked bleak and the new Black working class was the most affected, as the failing economy translated into even more economic hardships for them.

As was previously discussed, with the abolition of slavery, many Black West Indians sought better-paying jobs in Caribbean and Caribbean-basin countries like British Guiana and Trinidad; this exodus in turn created a shortage of workers in many of their respective islands and overpopulation in other areas.

Post emancipation, Black workers, for the first time, were in a position to demand higher wages and better conditions and were willing to relocate in order to meet these demands. This fact did not sit well with indebted planters, who were used to wielding total control over Black bodies and labor, and, most significantly, had been maximizing their profits with cheap labor. Colonial officials lamented "the steady flow of emigrants to Panama [which] increased the cost and difficulty of obtaining labour [*sic*]," and in an effort to dissuade their citizens from further migration, West Indian governments were instructed to warn Black workers of the difficulties of migration.[45] An 1878 circular dispatch to colonial officials in Saint Vincent did just this, stating that because difficulties "are constantly arising from the emigration of British subjects to the West Indian dependencies of Foreign Countries, [*sic*] you [local governments] will do all in your power to discourage such emigration." Colonial officials from overpopulated islands duly tried to discourage more immigration by issuing cautionary notices:

> Whereas numbers of the laboring classes from Barbados, St. Vincent, and other West Indian Islands are constantly arriving in Grenada under the erroneous impression that remunerative employment can at once be obtained there, and whereas they result in that after the small resources brought with them are exhausted the persons aforesaid are reduced to destitution. This is to *warn* all persons coming within the description afore intending to visit Grenada with the object of obtaining employment that there is no opening whatever for them and that if they are reduced to a state of pauperism the Government will not be responsible for their maintenance.[46]

Notices like these, as well as the lack of support from British officials for Black workers who decided to leave their home islands, were used as a tactic to deter Black migration. The British government repeatedly made it known that "Her Majesty's Government cannot undertake to be responsible for [the inhabitants of your Colony's] protection after they have entered the possessions of a Foreign Power."[47] This policy effectively abandoned West Indian immigrants to their own resources.

In an effort to cut costs, planters looked for alternative sources of labor outside of Black workers and set their sights on India, or the East Indies. From 1838 to 1917, more than half a million workers from British India were brought to the Caribbean as indentured servants in order to meet the increasing need for cheap labor. Indian immigration to Jamaica, British Guiana, and Trinidad was legalized in 1844. In 1856, immigration was legalized in Grenada and Saint Lucia in 1858.[48] It is after these years that the bulk of Indian immigration is observed.[49] In an 1859 *Colonial Report*, the Trinidadian government reported that a "stream of immigrants into this island during the last season, both from India and from West India Colonies, has been uninterrupted."[50] While indentureships existed throughout the Caribbean, they were most common in countries such as Trinidad and British Guiana, which suffered severe labor shortages. These indentureship contracts generally lasted between three and ten years before 1873, and five years after 1873.[51] Under these indentureship contracts, planters were not required to pay East Indian workers the fair wages that free Black people were now requesting, which resulted in fewer high-paying jobs for Black laborers in these areas.[52]

Thousands of British West Indian workers returned to their home countries, flooding the already oversaturated job market. This mass return of British West Indian migrants to their home islands in the twentieth century with the completion of the Panama Canal and other American- and European-financed projects in the Central American countries of Panama and Costa Rica only exacerbated the financial hardship of Black British West Indians. In a report from the British Secretary of State for the Colonies to the Parliament on labor conditions in the Caribbean, Major G. St. J. Orde Browne, O.B.E., notes the economic depression in the region that followed the return of emigrants who formerly "earned wages overseas" but now faced unemployment. As a result, immigration for work was no longer allowed, and in some cases immigrants who had already settled in foreign countries were made to repatriate. These repatriated immigrants only added to the unemployment problem in their home countries. Adverse factors thus unfortunately coincided and combined to depress the whole position of the labor market on British West Indian islands. Major G. St. J. Orde Browne, O.B.E., further states that "discontent and unrest, culminating in disorder, were the inevitable concomitants."[53]

As a result of financial hardships, labor unrest was seen in many parts of the Caribbean in the early twentieth century and culminated in a series of worker strikes and riots. Between December 1 and 3, 1919, serious rioting occurred in Port of Spain, Trinidad, as the culmination of a three-week strike of Black stevedores, who were later joined by cartermen, lightermen, and other classes of labor connected with the shipping business of the port. Workers in Trinidad were angered by unfair treatment, leading to class antagonisms between Blacks and whites:

> The disturbances which have just occurred seem to be more than merely labor troubles. They seem to afford certain ominous indications of class hatred, and especially of hostile feeling of the colored population, who are overwhelmingly in the majority, against the small minority of white people. Many comments have been heard from colored agitators, such as the following reported to me, to the effect that white people from England coming here within several years can make enough money to

buy motor cars, while we, who have lived here all our lives, cannot even make enough money to buy a decent breakfast. . . . Generally speaking, a most insolent and in some instances, dangerous temper toward white people was shown, so that the latter have felt it necessary to go about with revolvers for protection in case they were attacked.[54]

Discriminatory practices continued to keep Black laborers at the bottom of the pay ladder and infuriated Black workers who believed that they should be paid and treated equally with whites.

In addition to unemployment and low wages, in 1839 and 1843 a series of extreme hurricanes ravished the Caribbean islands, adding to West Indian misfortunes. When a hurricane hit the island of Martinique in 1839, four hundred people died and the town of St. Pierre was severely damaged, with the capital city of Fort-de-France almost totally destroyed. In 1843, another severe hurricane hit the Caribbean, causing considerable damage and the loss of nearly two thousand lives on the Leeward Islands between Saba and Dominica.[55] A series of droughts between 1840 and 1849 further depressed the economy.[56] In addition, several epidemics hit many of the islands as a result of the conditions caused by destructive weather. For instance, in 1879 a yellow fever outbreak devastated the population of Antigua.[57] In Barbados, a severe smallpox epidemic broke out on the island in 1902, and in four months, some 1,368 cases of smallpox were reported, of which 1,068 patients were released as cured, 110 died, and 190 were treated as critical. A rigorous quarantine of Barbados was imposed by neighboring islands.[58]

Further natural disasters continued to batter the Caribbean region. On May 7, 1902, after lying dormant for ninety years, the Soufrière volcano in Saint Vincent violently erupted, causing immense destruction and shock to the people of the island.[59] As the 1890–1906 Annual Colonial Report of Saint Vincent noted, the volcano "hurl[ed] death and devastation over nearly one third of the hapless Island of St. Vincent," burying alive some 1,268 people while completely covering with lava an area of sixteen square miles,[60] although a small group of survivors were able to escape the island before the volcanic eruption engulfed their homes, arriving in Castries, Saint Lucia, on May 11.[61] The Soufrière volcano erupted once again between October 15 and the early morning of October 16, 1902, causing massive destruction to the island. The volcano's eruption was so extensive that volcanic ash fell on neighboring Barbados more than one hundred miles away. As a colonial dispatch from Barbados reported, "The darkness here on that date from 9am to 1pm was so great that it was impossible to read and write without lights; the lighthouses on the coast and beacons on the pier were lighted; the street lamps in Bridgetown were lighted during that interval, and all business had to be suspended."[62] Only five months later, on March 22, the same volcano erupted for a third time.[63] With few resources to deal with such widespread destruction, many West Indians saw the United States as their best chance to rebuild their lives.

In order to understand why people migrate, it is also important to understand the attractions or "pull" factors that entice migrants to certain locations. Velma Newton argues that the conditions immigrants believe exist in the place of destination are equally important in creating an impetus for movement, yet these pull factors at the new destination are seldom discussed in detail. The pull factors, she contends, are a function of the migrant. Historically, it is through the information disseminated to migrants by recruiters and fellow migrants that potential immigrants imagine and assign a set of conditions to their country of destination, thus believing it to be superior to their home conditions, even if this is not true.[64] Newton is correct in asserting that immigrants are active participants in their own process of migration. By examining and analyzing only the push factors of immigration, scholars risk eliminating the agency migrants wield, and assigning and limiting the causes of migratory movements solely to poor conditions in countries of origin.

In the nineteenth century, freedom of movement was a major pull factor that motivated Black migrants to travel to several countries throughout the Caribbean basin. But Newton cites other reasons for immigration, contending that in addition to opportunities for self-improvement, others were motivated by a desire to broaden their experiences by traveling, learning a foreign language, and seeking adventure. Yet others, she argues, migrated simply "because it was a popular craze."[65] However, as we have seen, job opportunities continued to be one of the most important pull factors for many immigrants. British West Indians eagerly responded to the pull of job opportunities with higher-paying wages, better work conditions, and increased standards of living. In the twentieth century, similar pull factors drew Caribbean immigrants to the United States to seek more opportunities.

Moving North: Immigration to the United States

Between the years 1890 and 1940, a change occurred in Caribbean migration with just over 355,000 Caribbean immigrants coming to the United States, the majority of them, for the first time, women.[66] They flooded into cities such as New York, Boston, and Philadelphia. In the nineteenth century, Caribbean men made up much of the population of immigrants traveling within the Caribbean basin for work. However, in the twentieth century, women were often the first to immigrate to the United States, and from the years 1918 to 1940, women made up the majority of Caribbean immigrants, a fact with serious ramifications for Caribbean communities both in the United States and back home.

Caribbean women laid the foundation for subsequent family members to follow and established themselves as the preservers and proponents of Caribbean culture in the United States. This fact is most apparent between 1920 and 1924, when foreign-born Black women (mostly from the Caribbean) for the first time outnumbered male foreign-born Black immigrants to the United States, with 13,981 female migrants to 13,391 male migrants.[67]

Similar female-led lines of immigration to the United States can be seen in the lives of famous Caribbean American leaders. The Caribbean-born radical Hubert Henry Harrison, for instance, immigrated to Harlem in 1900 at the age of 17, joining his older sister, Mary, who had moved to the United States a few years earlier, securing an apartment in the San Juan Hill area of Manhattan. Harrison lived with his sister for four years until he eventually got his own apartment.[68] Cyril Briggs, W. A. Domingo, and Richard B. Moore also migrated to the United States through a chain of female networks.[69] The rise in female Caribbean immigrants to the United States may have been due to several factors, including the increased need for domestic labor and garment workers in major cities. Another possibility may be related to the fact that Caribbean women actively maintained relationships with relatives and communities back home in the Caribbean, more so than male immigrants. As a result, Caribbean women were instrumental in creating the necessary kinship networks and social contacts needed to encourage more female immigration to the United States. They provided referrals and informed female relatives and friends of job vacancies, encouraging other potential Caribbean immigrants, both female and male, to seek work opportunities in the United States.

The story of Caroline Nurse and Beatrice (Nurse) Beach seamlessly illustrates a twentieth century female-led chain of immigration. Born in Port of Spain, Trinidad, Caroline Nurse immigrated to New York City sometime in the early twentieth century, leaving her husband and two children, Beatrice and Catherine, behind. Caroline found employment in New York through the help of familial ties and existing female kinship networks and made a home for herself in Brooklyn. In 1924, Beatrice Beach (who immigrated without her husband, Edward Beach) joined her mother in the United States. Once Beatrice was established with her mother in New York, Edward and Beatrice's nephew, Eric Thomas, soon joined the two women. Edward and Eric moved into a ready-made housing arrangement organized by the two women. In 1926, with her family settled in New York, Caroline returned to Trinidad to live. Caroline's role in initiating a female-led chain illustrates the pioneering character of Caribbean women in the immigrant community in the United States during this period.[70]

In the early twentieth century, Caribbean immigrants often traveled to several cities after their initial point of entry into the United States. New York City served as a central port of entry for Caribbean immigrants, with steamships carrying both tourists and imports, such as bananas, between New York and the West Indies.[71] The United Fruit Company's steamships, which were initially designed to carry cargo, began to accommodate passengers traveling between the Caribbean and the United States. This would usher in a new age of leisure tourism to the Caribbean. New York was often viewed as a gateway for many immigrants coming from the Caribbean, who moved on to cities such as Boston, Hartford, and Philadelphia. Such was the case of James Thomas and Unilda Gooding Thomas. Natives of Barbados, the couple arrived at the port of Saint John, New Brunswick, in 1910 on the vessel SS *Ocamo*. They then took a train from Saint John to Boston, where they later caught a boat to Philadelphia.[72] Like James and Unilda Thomas, many Caribbean immigrants traveled to several cities after their initial point of entry into the United States.

By 1920, 50,000 Caribbean immigrants resided in the United States with 55,000 U.S.-born children. Ten years later, there were 72,000 Caribbean immigrants and 83,000 US-born children living in the United States.[73] Examining their rates of naturalization, 1950 U.S. census data records that more than 62,000 immigrants from the British West Indies were citizens of the United States, with more than 79 percent of those immigrants living in the Northeast and 70 percent in the state of New York.[74] Caribbean immigrants lived in other regions of the United States, such as the South and the West, but there was no other location akin to the Northeast, and New York in particular, that served as a destination of choice for most Caribbean immigrants. It is estimated that in Harlem alone the Caribbean population (including noncitizens) was between 75,000 and 85,000 in 1928.[75] The relative ease with which

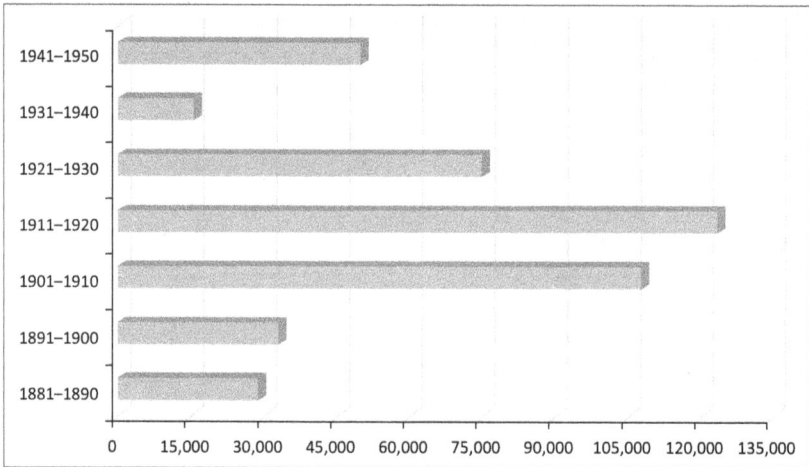

Chart 4. Caribbean Immigration to the United States. *Source:* U.S. Department of Justice, Immigration and Naturalization Service. Yearbook of Immigration Statistics, "1983 Statistical Yearbook of the Immigration and Naturalization Service," Washington, DC: U.S. Department of Homeland Security, Office of Immigration Statistics, 2002, pp. 2–5.

Caribbean immigrants could travel to New York was also a factor aiding in increased immigration to the United States. Beatrice Beach, for example, was able to travel back and forth to Trinidad several times throughout the twentieth century aboard steamships. A ticket stub from the Moore-McCormack Lines shows that Beatrice traveled from Trinidad to New York on a vessel named the SS *Brazil*. In 1928, she recorded that the journey from Trinidad to New York took about a week and a half, highlighting the relatively fast travel time between the Caribbean's southernmost island and New York City.[76]

From 1901 onward, Caribbean immigration to the United States increased exponentially from a total of 33,066 immigrants in the period from 1891 to 1900 to 107,548 between 1901 and 1910.[77] As Chart 4 indicates, the number of Caribbean immigrants continued to grow in the following decade, reaching its apex between 1911 and 1920, with a total of 123,424 immigrants. This boom in Caribbean immigration to the United States can be attributed to several factors, including lax and flexible immigration laws, less restrictive national boundaries, ease of transportation, economic opportunities, and, as previously noted, the sense of prestige associated with immigration in this period.

Chart 4 also shows the glaring decrease in Caribbean immigration in the period after 1920. This dramatic decline in Caribbean immigration can be directly linked to the restrictive immigration laws of this decade. In the years following World War I, a xenophobic United States government began to reevaluate their regulations on immigration and passed a series of laws between 1910 to 1924 that drastically limited the number of immigrants admitted into the country each year. The 1924 Immigration Act, also known as the Johnson-Reed Act, set a national quota of 2 percent of immigrants from the total of any nation's residents in the United States as reported in the 1890 census; this quota drastically limited the number of Caribbean immigrants to the United States, with the result that Caribbean immigration to the United States after 1924 all but ceased.[78] In 1924, Caribbean immigration reached an all-time high of 11,621, but the following year it fell to 554.[79] In 1925, the number of immigrants returning to the Caribbean numbered 1,094, greatly outnumbering those who immigrated to the United States that same year.[80] Thus, the Immigration Act of 1924 brought to a close the first wave of Caribbean immigration to the United States. However, as we see from Chart 4, after 1941, with the entry of the United States into World War II, Caribbean immigration again rapidly increased, largely due to the creation of the Anglo-American Caribbean Commission and the loosening of restrictive immigration laws.

It is important to note that from 1820 to 1860 there was no classification of the West Indies by individual country. Instead, all data for immigration from the Caribbean was consolidated under the heading "West Indies." As early as 1873, immigration was recorded from Antigua; in 1871 from the Bahamas; in 1869 from Barbados; in 1861 from Bermuda; in 1873 from Curaçao; in 1869 from Jamaica; in 1871 from Saint Croix; in 1872 from Saint Thomas; and in 1874 from Trinidad. In the period between 1899 and 1924 there again was no classification by country of immigration from the West Indies.[81] In 1927, Caribbean immigrants fell under the category "British Empire"—other. After the year 1953, data collected from the Caribbean began to specify individual countries, including Jamaica and Trinidad and Tobago.[82]

It should also be pointed out that the totals in Chart 4 represent the number of documented Caribbean immigrants who came to the United States each year. There was still a sizable number of Caribbean immigrants who were able to enter and remain in the United States illegally. For instance, among these in the early twentieth century were many Caribbean males who crewed ships and simply disembarked in U.S. ports upon arrival, remaining in the United States.[83] Additionally, there were cases in which Caribbean immigrants were able to enter U.S. territory unnoticed as stowaways on passenger ships. For example, on October 22, 1906, twenty-four-year-old

seaman Henry Amover from the British West Indies illegally stowed away
on the SS *Grenada*, a Trinidadian line. Found by the ship's captain, James
McGrath, upon arrival at the port of New York, Amover was handcuffed in
the officer's bathroom until he could be questioned by an inspection officer.
Somehow, however, Amover broke the lock on his handcuffs and escaped
into New York City. No trace of Amover was ever found.[84] Similar cases
occurred in the early twentieth century, such as that of Hilton L. Gooding,
a nineteen-year-old male stowaway from the British West Indies. Gooding
arrived in New York on the SS *Helen Swanzy* on September 20, 1919, without
a passport and with only fifty cents to his name, "practically destitute."[85] He
was soon employed as a boatman on the SS *Helen Swanzy*, responsible for
taking passengers from the ship to the dock. "Work was scarce and I came to
see about making a living. No one helped me on board," he stated about his
predicament. "I was discovered one day after sailing. They put me to work
painting, scrubbing and cleaning."[86]

People from the Caribbean were not the only ones entering the United
States by illegal means.[87] It was a problem that was becoming noticeable to
U.S. immigration officials; as the Assistant Secretary of Labor observed in 1917,
there were "hundreds (perhaps thousands) of cases" in which aliens entered
into the United States without inspection, conducted themselves in a "quiet
and proper manner," and were never found out.[88] This issue persisted well into
1936 when Ellis Island guards James E. Maher and Harry A. Ratzbe stated that
there was a "stowaway problem" at the port in New York City:

> Aliens are gaining entry in large numbers through our seaports as
> stowaways. This belief is strengthened by actual facts and by contacts
> we have had with stowaways who have been detained at Ellis Island.
> Each and every stowaway we have talked to, freely admits that it is no
> great feat to secrete [sic] himself on board a vessel in some foreign port
> and land in the United States without any difficulty. The alien stow-
> aways (who have been apprehended) all say that if they had money
> to pay they would not have been turned over to the authorities. The
> only reason that a few are apprehended is due to the fact that they get
> into difficulty with the local police or with their friends or relatives.
> It is very evident that at the present time a large number of aliens are
> using the stowaway route as a means of evading the Immigration Law.
> Also it would seem to appear that the majority of them are getting in,
> compared to those who are apprehended.[89]

Furthermore, Maher and Ratzbe claimed that many of the stowaways detained at Ellis Island—with few exceptions—boasted that they would try again to gain illegal entry into the United States as soon as they were deported. Officials go on to say that "it is a well-known fact that they do come back three and four times."[90] Many of the cases of British West Indian stowaways occurred after restrictive immigration laws were put into place. Prior to the Johnson Reed Act of 1924, there were not many restrictions for Caribbean immigrants and they often did not have the need to stow away. This is of course unless they were unable to afford passage or had little formal education and could not pass reading tests administered upon arrival in the United States.

Settling In

Early Caribbean immigrants established scattered communities in lower Manhattan and parts of Brooklyn. Althea Dowridge, a young Barbadian woman, was part of a female-led chain of immigration; her aunt, Constance Payne, helped her to move to Brooklyn in 1903 from St. Michael Parish, Barbados. Dowridge was able to secure housing and a job through kinship networks. Her address in Brooklyn is not recorded in her personal letters, but it is assumed she lived in the Bedford–Stuyvesant neighborhood, like many Caribbean immigrants at this time.[91]

Caribbean American women working as domestics often chose to settle near their employers' homes, including areas within Brooklyn and Manhattan.[92] For example, Susan Pounder, daughter of Mary Layne, resided at 12 West 137th Street in Harlem, just twenty blocks north of her employer on 71 Lenox Avenue.[93] The San Juan Hill section of Manhattan, which encompassed West 62nd to 66th Streets and later became known as Columbus Hill, was also a popular neighborhood for Caribbean immigrants living in Manhattan prior to 1915.[94] Notable West Indian immigrants such as Hubert Harrison lived in San Juan Hill. His first New York apartment in 1900 was located on 220 West 62nd Street.[95]

After 1915, Caribbean immigrants, along with African Americans from New York and the South, began to move into the Harlem community in upper Manhattan. Beatrice Beach, and many other Caribbean women, flooded into Harlem in the 1920s. Many rented small rooms or found housing with families that they knew. In a letter to Caroline Nurse, dated September 22, 1925, Beatrice Beach tells her mother of her move from Brooklyn to 231 West 134th

Street in Harlem in August: "I am living in the same house with Mildred [a family friend]," she says. "I got a room for $4.50 a week and 50 cents a week for gas it is very small, about the size of the bedroom you had in [*sic*] Jefferson Ave. [in Brooklyn] Sonie and Anna always come to see me and give me help."[96]

Largely responsible for this concentration of Black residents in Harlem was Philip A. Payton, an African American real estate agent, who is credited with being one of the first to convince white landlords to accept Black tenants in the then all-white area of central Harlem. Through his Afro-American Realty Company, he rented several houses on 134th Street to Caribbean tenants. By 1920, the Harlem neighborhood became a desirable location for Caribbean immigrants to settle, as it gave them the opportunity to purchase property at a more affordable rate than in other areas of Manhattan.[97]

In the late 1930s, Caribbean immigrants began moving into the Bedford–Stuyvesant area of Brooklyn as the Harlem Renaissance came to a close and left high rent rates and overcrowded housing conditions in Harlem. The Bedford–Stuyvesant neighborhood, with greater opportunities for affordable home ownership, attracted Caribbean immigrants. Second-generation Caribbean immigrant Paule Marshall, in her powerful novel *Brown Girl, Brownstones* (1959), discusses a community of Caribbean women who settled in Bedford–Stuyvesant from 1930 through the 1950s.[98] These women formed a homeowners' association that enabled other Caribbean women to purchase houses. Named the Association of Barbadian Homeowners and Businessmen, this fictionalized group served similar functions as many of the actual Caribbean American mutual aid societies and benevolent associations examined here. They not only assisted Barbadian immigrants in becoming property owners in the United States, but aided many newly arrived Barbadian immigrants in adjusting to life in the United States. While creating a place where members could celebrate their shared ethnic identities as members of a Barbadian community, they were also deeply concerned with helping members embody the ideals of American society. Additionally, education was an important principle to the group. They even sponsored scholarships for their younger members to attend college, one of which the protagonist, Selina Boyce, wins.[99]

Although it is a work of fiction, the novel closely parallels Marshall's own life growing up as the daughter of Barbadian immigrants in Brooklyn. More importantly, Marshall illustrates the social networks that Caribbean women utilized through mutual aid societies in order to establish their place in a new country.

Employment: Domestics and Elevator Operators

Many Caribbean immigrants arriving in the United States in the early twentieth century were skilled and professional workers. Between 1921 and 1925, 34 percent of arriving Caribbean immigrants were classified as industrial workers, 11.3 percent were in commerce and finance, and 4.2 percent were professionals (defined as teachers, doctors, lawyers, and so forth), while 34 percent identified as laborers and servants. In subsequent years, this trend continued; between 1931 and 1935, 40.4 percent of arriving Caribbean immigrants were classified as working in industry, 17.6 percent were in commerce and finance, and 12 percent were professionals.[100] Many are often characterized as coming from a middle-class background in the Caribbean. Historian Irma Watkins-Owens notes that Caribbean immigrants usually had a basic formal education and a skilled trade, but little money.

Trinidad-born George Padmore was one such example; he was described as so poor during his first few years in the United States that he told his sister in a 1926 letter that she had not heard from him because he could not afford a stamp to mail a letter home. He went on to say, "words are inadequate . . . to you folks what it is to live through college days without money." In an earlier letter from 1925, he writes about needing $250 to finish the school year, but having only $100. However, he describes his courage and determination to raise the money some way. Padmore would eventually go on to graduate and receive his degree from Howard University and become a successful journalist, author, and advisor on African affairs to the Ghanaian leader Kwame Nkrumah, Ghana's first prime minister and president. Many early Caribbean immigrants, similar to Padmore, were educated and traveled to the United States to attend university or receive further schooling.[101] Another such immigrant was Jamaican-born W. A. Domingo, who originally settled in Boston in 1910 to attend medical school. For two years, he attended night school in preparation for medical school, until he decided to drop out and moved to New York to pursue other opportunities.[102] Domingo would later go on to co-found the Jamaica Progressive League in 1936.

Though they were often skilled, many Caribbean immigrants in the United States were not able to secure positions in their professional fields. Ivy Simons notes that when her aunt immigrated to New York, she was trained as "a midwife but she couldn't get no other kind of work so she did the same kind of work [as a domestic]."[103] This was the fate of many skilled West Indian immigrants locked out of certain professional fields due to segregation and discrimination. Simons continues by stating that despite her uncle having a formal education, "the only job he could get was being a servant—he can't, it was—in those days, you just automatically no use doing anything else, you know, they almost told you you're wasting your time trying to better your-self."[104] Other examples include W. A. Domingo, who was a skilled tailor in Jamaica, but when he arrived in New York he took a job working at the United States Post Office—which was considered a coveted job for Black workers at the time. He eventually started a lucrative business importing Caribbean foods to New York.[105] Due to racist hiring practices that would not allow Black Caribbean immigrants to break into certain fields, many Caribbean Americans, including women, became entrepreneurs to secure better economic futures. They soon became noted for their shrewd business sense.[106] Immigrant men and women experimented with various business ventures, including tailor shops, jewelry stores, fruit and vegetable stands, candy shops, millinery stores, and grocery stores in Black neighborhoods. For example, in the AWILAS membership application file, Eliza Louise Gabriel of Saint Croix listed her occupation as hairdresser, highlighting another lucrative career field women of Caribbean descent created for themselves.[107] Beatrice Beach was also an entrepreneurial woman and sought other means of income in addition to her factory job. She owned a rental property back home in Trini-dad, which she leased out weekly, supplementing the income she made work-ing in a New York City garment factory.[108]

Real estate and insurance were other industries in which many Carib-bean immigrants worked, as they allowed them to create positions for them-selves. In 1925, Montserrat-born William H. Roach owned and operated the only Black casino and moving picture theater in Harlem—the Renaissance Theater and Casino.[109] The property was located at the northeast corner of 137th Street and Seventh Avenue; Roach bought the lot for the Renaissance complex in 1920. Together with fellow Montserratian Joseph H. Sweeney and Antiguan businessman Cleophus Charity, they built the nine-hundred-seat Renaissance Theater in 1921. The theater first featured silent films and stage performances but soon premiered "talkies," including movies by Oscar Micheaux, the first African American to produce a feature-length film. The Renaissance, nicknamed the "Renny," became a hot spot in Harlem. Musi-cians such as Duke Ellington, Cab Calloway, and Count Basie all performed there. It also hosted fights with the legendary boxer Joe Louis. The Renais-sance became home court to the Black Fives, also known as the Harlem Rens, an all-Black professional basketball team established in 1923. The Renaissance hosted the Harlem Rens at a time when Black athletes were barred from the National Basketball Association.[110]

For Caribbean men, the United States military provided additional viable employment opportunities. Employment in the U.S. military was not only a secure source of income, but in many cases allowed immigrant workers to obtain American citizenship. Barbadian John Chester Field, for instance, enlisted in the U.S. Navy in 1906 as a mess attendant with very clear goal of using this position to receive American citizenship.[111] In addition, many Caribbean men worked as elevator operators. Such was the case with Barbadian-born radical civil rights activist Richard B. Moore. Prior to immigrating, Moore had been a bright and successful student. However, due to discriminatory hiring practices in the United States, the only positions available to him were as a hotel bellhop and an elevator operator in various apartment buildings around New York City.[112]

Many Caribbean women were employed in the garment industry, taking on positions as seamstresses, dressmakers, and tailors. Upon her arrival to the United States in 1925, Beatrice Beach secured a job, which paid $12 a week, working at an embroidery factory from 8 A.M. to 7 P.M. She was also an active member of the International Ladies' Garment Workers' Union.[113] Like many West Indians emigrating from the Caribbean at this time, Beatrice was a skilled worker with a formal education. However, as with African American women at the time, one of the only viable options for employment for Caribbean immigrant women was cleaning houses and washing clothes. In the membership application files for the AWILAS, of the fourteen applications found, half of the applicants listed domestic work or housework as their occupation.[114] Domestic work was the most prevalent source of employment for Black women, foreign or native. In fact, in 1900, 36.9 percent of women in the United States, or 1,962,035 women, worked as domestics or in personal service, illustrating its prevalence among women of all races. This percentage decreased yearly as fewer white women took on these positions and mostly native and foreign-born Black women were left in the field. In 1920, 25.3 percent (2,186,682) of women in the United States worked as domestics. By 1930 the number of women working in domestic service rose to 3,180,251 (29.6 percent), as Black women from the United States and the Caribbean flooded into major cities in search of jobs.[115] Sociologist Nancy Foner has argued that there are several reasons why West Indian immigrants tended to stick to certain industries. Immigration laws, she believes, were a major factor, as they targeted specific occupations and recruited immigrants for specific jobs, such as domestic or agricultural work. Additionally, immigrant social networks were generally homogeneous, and newly arrived immigrants relied on job referrals from friends and family, who tended to work in the same industries. Finally, Foner states that discrimination and exclusion from certain industries forced immigrants into very limited positions or into entrepreneurship, as was regularly the case with Caribbean immigrants.[116]

Domestic work, particularly positions that required women to live in the homes of their employers, were very hard on immigrant and Black families. Because they worked long hours from sunup to sundown, it was difficult for single Caribbean women to form families, as much of their time was spent working. Caribbean women who were already married and/or had children were often separated from their families for long periods of time. As a result, Caribbean women relied on kinship and familial networks to aid in the rearing of their children. Many women immigrated without their children, or elected to send their children to stay with other Caribbean women in the United States or with relatives back home in the Caribbean. Grandparents were often the recipients of these returning children. In 1926, Beatrice wrote to her mother, Caroline, about sending her nephew Eric back to Trinidad to live with her. In a similar case, Althea Dowridge Chancellor left her first child, Elsie, with her mother, Harriet, in Barbados, allowing Althea to secure a job upon her arrival in New York City without having to worry about caring for her child.[117] Several cases in the Jamaican archive reveal the extent to which Caribbean women were forced to leave their children with relatives back in the Caribbean, even when they had the help of a spouse. A letter dated November 14, 1929, to the British Colonial Secretary registers a request to have fifteen-year-old Eric McKay join his parents in the United States. McKay had been left in Jamaica with a guardian family. His father was a physician in Georgia, but his parents were unable bring him with them to the United States.[118]

Child fostering became an important function of women's primary social networks.[119] Stories such as that of Laura A. Corbin, a widow who traveled to Ellis Island on the SS *Corrientes* in 1910 with her five children (eighteen-year-old Beryl, fifteen-year-old Iris, twelve-year-old Hilda, ten-year-old Doris, and five-year-old Collin) illustrate the importance of Caribbean kinship networks. When Corbin sailed to New York, she was forced to leave three of her other children (fourteen-year-old Hyathon, eight-year-old Ralph, and eight-month-old Harold) with her mother and sisters in Barbados. It was a tough choice to make, but one she believed would allow her to make the best possible living in the United States for herself and her children. The family was granted a sum of

$486.65 from the legislative branch of the Barbados government to help them immigrate to the United States. Additionally, they received aid from the Victorian Emigration Society to help pay their passage. All the children could read and write, except the youngest, Collin. The eldest, Beryl, was a seamstress and did fancy needlework. Corbin's two brothers, who lived in Philadelphia, had earlier invited her to move to the United States. Sadly, Corbin and her children were denied admission into the United States once they arrived at Ellis Island, because as "assisted aliens whose passage has been paid by a foreign government," they were "likely to become public charges."[120] Nonetheless, Corbin's story highlights the freedom of mobility child fostering granted Caribbean women. It allowed them to risk migrating to the United States for jobs they might not have otherwise pursued. Child fostering also helped to deepen kinship networks, as it required the utmost trust between both parties to raise someone else's child. Additionally, parents created close intimate connections, as they frequently sent letters, goods, and monetary remittances.

Further complicating the lack of viable labor positions for Caribbean immigrants was the large concentration of Black Southerners moving into overcrowded urban centers as a result of the Great Migration. From 1916 to 1920, half a million Black Southerners migrated to cities in the Northeast and Midwest, including New York, Chicago, Philadelphia, and Cleveland. Another one million followed in the 1920s.[121] As reported by a 1923 *New York Times* article, "Whole communities, entire streets of people, and even church congregations headed by their pastors, moved north and [re]located as units in the important industrial centres [*sic*]."[122] While racist Jim Crow policies were the major reason for the Great Migration, employment opportunities followed as a close second. With the United States entering into World War I, there were many opportunities for Black people to work in higher-paying industrial jobs. In northern cities, Black workers could make almost double what they made working in the South.[123]

Northern cities, however, faced many problems due to the mass migration, including overcrowding and health concerns. The New York Department of Health recorded a large percentage of deaths from tuberculosis in 1917.[124] Further strains on housing and competition for jobs occurred as European immigrants were added to the influx of Black Southerners who began to take unskilled positions. Tensions among Black groups in New York also emerged as Caribbean immigrants displaced African Americans in the workplace. This change in employment patterns did not sit well with some African Americans, who viewed Caribbean immigrants as threats to their

own economic opportunities. "Competition for jobs, control of Black businesses, political leadership, and status" formed the basis for frictions that
sometimes created divisions between the two groups.[125]

Despite the hostility between Caribbean immigrants and African Americans, there were in fact many similarities between the two groups. Scholar
Charles Diggs notes, "an analysis of African American residents, native born
and immigrant reveals a striking similarity in housing, occupational, and
other household characteristics during the years 1905 to 1925."[126] Native-
born African Americans and Caribbean immigrants "lived in close proxim-
ity to one another, mingling on the same block and often lodging together in
the same households. Their communities overlapped while primary social
networks formed among people from the same house in the Caribbean or
the South."[127] Sharing the same neighborhoods and similar occupations
eventually helped foster social connections and networks between the two
groups.

Changes over Time

In the fifty-year period between 1890 and 1940, there were significant changes
in the type of immigrants coming from the British West Indies. One major
transformation in the immigrant population was triggered by the United
States' purchase of the Danish Virgin Islands. Eager to expand its influence in
the Caribbean, the United States made several attempts to acquire the Danish Virgin Islands, including an 1866 treaty to procure the islands of Saint
Thomas and Saint John. [128] However, the United States was not successful
until 1917, when it purchased the islands of Saint Croix, Saint Thomas, Saint
John, and Water Island, as well as fifty smaller islets and cays, from the Danish for $25,000,000, renaming them the Virgin Islands of the United States.

Prior to Danish ownership of the islands, several nations, including Great
Britain, France, and the Netherlands, all laid claim to one or two of the islands.
However, in 1733, the Danish West India Company purchased Saint Croix
from the French and brought together all the islands to form the Danish West
Indies. Although the Danish owned the Virgin Islands for over a century and
Danish was the official language of the administration, very few Virgin Islanders actually spoke Danish. Instead, most residents spoke an English creole. As
a result of a shared language and similar cultures, Virgin Islanders often closely
aligned themselves with British West Indians both in the Caribbean and in

the United States. In the United States, they formed social organizations and kinship networks with other Black West Indian immigrants.[129] Groups such as the Virgin Islands Civic and Industrial Association, led by Virgin Island migrant Ashley L. Totten, and the AWILAS, led by Virgin Island migrant Elizabeth Hendrickson, socialized and worked together with groups such as the British Jamaican Benevolent Society and the Antillean League of New York, demonstrating their common interest as Black immigrant groups.[130]

With the U.S. acquisition of the Virgin Islands, Virgin Islanders, while culturally similar to British West Indians, held the unique status of being American nationals. Nonetheless, Virgin Islanders who migrated to the United States identified strongly with the Black immigrant community and continued to create social connections with West Indian immigrants. Those Virgin Islanders who had migrated to the United States before the acquisition, however, had a legally precarious status. Many were unclear of their legal status and not sure if they were still considered Danish citizens, as they were often labeled on their arrival documents. Records from the Immigration and Naturalization Service contain several inquiries from Virgin Islanders asking if U.S. citizenship would be extended to them. Even Virgin Islanders who came to the United States after the 1917 acquisition were unclear of their status. One example is that of Elvira Carey, born in 1883 on the island of Saint Thomas; Carey arrived at Ellis Island on the SS *Parima* in 1925. Carey was manifested as a citizen of the United States. However, two months after her arrival, she was still unclear if her status as an American citizen was correct. Proactive in making sure that she would legally be able to remain in the United States, Carey wrote the Immigration and Naturalization Service, stating that she was born in the Virgin Islands at a time when they belonged to Denmark and was a resident of those islands at the time of their transfer to the United States. She now resided in New York City and wanted her intention to become a citizen of the United States known.[131]

Much of the confusion surrounding the legal status of Virgin Islanders was a direct result of the United States' unclear colonial policy, which categorized different levels of American citizenship. With the transfer of the Virgin Islands to the United States in 1917, the islands became an unincorporated U.S. territory. As such, Virgin Islanders were initially distinguished as "nationals" or inhabitants of colonies. Under this designation they were allowed to live and work without restrictions in the U.S., but they were not granted the full rights of U.S. citizenship, such as voting rights or the ability to hold elected office.[132] However, as we see in the case of Carey, U.S. officials, especially at ports such as Ellis Island, were inconsistent in who they labeled a "national" or a "citizen."

This uncertainty persisted until 1932, when Congress ruled that full U.S. citizenship would be granted to all individuals born in the U.S. Virgin Islands. It is after this period that we see an increase in Black political activists, such as Frank Crosswaith and J. Raymond Jones, from the Virgin Islands. West Indian immigrants from the Virgin Islands were more likely to become involved in politics and political organizing because they, unlike other immigrants, were already U.S. citizens and therefore legally qualified to run for political office.

J. Raymond Jones moved to New York from Saint Thomas in 1918. He was the founder and leader of Harlem's Carver Democratic Club in 1921, which served as his political base. Through the Democratic Club, Jones organized Harlem community campaigns, collected signatures on petitions, and helped Black people register to vote. Prominent in the 1960s, he served as a city councilman, county chairman, and district leader. Known as "The Fox," Jones was influential in the appointments of state and federal judges, borough presidents, and cabinet members, and in the races of congressional representatives. Additionally, he served as a mentor to many young Black politicians who later also became prominent in New York politics, including Adam Clayton Powell, Jr., and former New York City mayor David Dinkins, who had the distinction of being the first African American to hold this office. Jones retired after a long political career and moved back to Saint Thomas with his wife.[133]

The story of J. Raymond Jones illustrates the diversity of the group of Caribbean immigrants that immigrated to the United States between 1890 and 1940. As we have seen throughout this chapter, West Indians were not a monolithic group; not only were they from different islands, they also had varying degrees of legal status in the United States—as is seen in the case of migrants from the U.S. Virgin Islands in 1917, who were for all legal purposes U.S. citizens, but continued to identify strongly with the West Indian immigrant community. Despite their differences, Virgin Islanders, along with other British West Indian immigrants, were able to form strong social and political networks with each other and with African Americans over the course of the early twentieth century.

Conclusion

The century following the British abolition of slavery in the Caribbean was one of mobility for Black British West Indians. They set out from their homes in search not only of better economic opportunities but of dignity. Weary of the plantation system that relegated them to the lowest class, they sought the autonomy needed to negotiate their own contracts and to dictate where and when they worked. In many cases, these dreams were dashed, as the reality of migrant labor often clashed with their dreams of emancipation. In countries like Panama, Costa Rica, Guatemala, and the United States, Black West Indians were treated as second-class citizens; they were segregated and asked to take the most dangerous and least desirable positions. They also frequently faced the racism of host governments and the local citizenry, who in many cases resented their presence in their countries.

However, Black West Indian immigrants persevered and continued immigrating in large numbers throughout the twentieth century. They established a place for themselves by developing their own systems of care and sociocultural infrastructure and, in the case of the United States, forged networks with the African American population. They built churches and established mutual aid societies and social clubs, making clear a determination that their dreams for a better life would not be suppressed.

African Americans and West Indians lived in the same neighborhoods and often shared similar occupations, as discriminatory Jim Crow hiring practices limited the positions available to both Caribbean immigrants and African Americans. These shared experiences allowed these two groups to form important social networks. However, this is not to take away from the unique space that Black Anglophone immigrants occupied in the United States as they joined together to navigate the terrain and make a space for themselves. They were largely ignored by the U.S. government prior to the Immigration Act of 1924, as the United States put much of its emphasis and resources in non-English-speaking, mostly European immigrants.[134] It was clear that English-speaking Black Caribbean immigrants did not fit into the United States' idea of a typical immigrant. As a result, there were very few programs set up for them, and Caribbean immigrants were left to find their own way. One way in which immigrants were able to do just that was through the support of mutual aid societies and benevolent associations.

CHAPTER 3

More Than Auxiliary

The Functions of Mutual Aid Societies
and Benevolent Associations

In the summer of 1897, two Bermudian immigrants living in New York City, Clarence William Robinson and George Lawrence Joell, rekindled their friendship. The men had both immigrated to the United States to pursue career opportunities in business. They often discussed personal as well as local matters and events in Bermuda. Robinson thought it would be useful to have a place where he and his Bermudian friends could gather, and so spoke with Joell about forming a social club that would also serve as an informal place where fellow Bermudians would be able to socialize and lend assistance to members in times of need. On January 14, 1898, the club was formed under the name Bermuda Benevolent Association (BBA) and held its first official meeting on May 6, 1898, at the home of Richard Fubler, 131 West 32nd Street. Although the organization was founded by two men, women played an integral role from the very beginning. Annie Joell-Adams was the first female member and three years later in 1901 became the association's first female president.[1] Another woman, Elmyra Gaisey, had served on the BBA's first executive board in 1898. Rosa Campbell, called the "Mother of the Association," was an active member for many years and regularly held association meetings in her home.[2]

Starting with only a handful of members, the organization grew rapidly and by 1899 had grown to include nearly one hundred members. By the 1950s, this number had tripled. In 1932, the association added a juvenile branch called the Rosebuds, geared toward younger members from six to fifteen years of age. A young adults' group was later formed for those between fifteen and twenty-five years of age. In 1932, the group purchased a building

Figure 1. Bermuda Benev-
olent Association Head-
quarters, "Home." *Source:*
Bermuda Benevolent Asso-
ciation Records, 1898–1969.
Manuscripts, Archives,
and Rare Books Division,
Schomburg Center for
Research in Black Culture.
BBA Headquarters building
was purchased in 1932 and
was located at 402 West
146th Street.

for $10,000 on 402 West 146th Street to serve as its headquarters, with some
of the funds coming from numerous building fundraising events. The association was able to pay off its mortgage in full in 1947.

The BBA served as a gathering place for biweekly meetings, educational
forums, and social affairs. Its members saw its headquarters as a home away
from home, and even nicknamed the association's building "Home." To serve
its educational aims, the group set up a borrowing library called the Library of

Negro History, which housed a collection pertaining to the African Diaspora. In 1955, the group established a five-year scholarship for the Berkeley Institute in Bermuda and donated $600 toward the establishment of the Institute's science department. That same year, reflecting more sociopolitical concerns, the association became a lifetime member of the NAACP. In 1955, it also formed an investment committee, creating a portfolio that would include real estate (and also financing mortgages), government bonds, and mutual funds. Since its establishment, the BBA had contributed to more than twenty-five charitable organizations and assisted numerous compatriots in their times of need.

The BBA would operate from these headquarters until 1989, when members sold the building and began to hold meetings at Grace Congregational Church in Harlem, where several association members were parishioners. The organization dissolved a few years later in 1998, when the last twenty remaining members liquidated the association's assets due to low membership numbers, sharing the remaining assets among themselves based on seniority in the organization and donating remaining funds as a scholarship for a local student. The BBA dissolved one hundred years after its founding.[3]

The early twentieth century witnessed the formation of a large number of Caribbean American mutual aid societies and benevolent associations. Dozens of these organizations, much like the BBA, served as forums for discussions on Caribbean American affairs, hosted cultural activities, helped their members find employment, and provided charity and welfare assistance, especially in the case of newly arrived immigrants.

This chapter surveys sixty-seven West Indian mutual aid societies and benevolent associations founded in New York City between 1884 and 1940, arguing that these prevalent social and cultural organizations played a vital role in the formation of a Caribbean American transnational identity and facilitated community building. Caribbean immigrants did not initially perceive themselves as a collective group when they arrived in the United States in the twentieth century. While some notions of a common West Indian identity existed in Central American countries like Panama, Costa Rica, and Guatemala, where Caribbean laborers had migrated in large numbers, a strong sense of island-specific identity persisted. It is important to remember that while many of the immigrants who came to the United States in the twentieth century had previously worked throughout the Caribbean basin, a large percentage of Caribbean immigrants, including many young women, were coming to the United States as first-time migrants. The issue of identity among Caribbean immigrants is complex as well as personal, and one which

Caribbean immigrants were continually working through in the nineteenth and twentieth centuries.[4] While some immigrants may have tested out bourgeoning ideas of a Pan–West Indian identity, other immigrants held strongly to their island identities.

As a result, twentieth century immigrant associations were often organized by people from specific islands, such as the Dominica Benevolent Society of New York or the British Jamaican Benevolent Society; this fact demonstrates that many Caribbean immigrants initially viewed themselves as individuals from separate islands, not as the collective "West Indian" group that outsiders categorized them as by default. In the late 1920s and 1930s, however, through cross-cooperation with other associations from differing islands, many of these organizations' members began to foster collaboration and unity among Caribbean immigrants as a whole. It is in this later period that we see the founding of more Pan-Caribbean associations like the Sons and Daughters of the West Indies and the United Brothers and Sisters of the United Islands. As a consequence, Caribbean immigrants to the United States began to fully embrace a Caribbean or West Indian identity as opposed to a Saint Lucian, Trinidadian, or Jamaican one.[5]

This chapter investigates the ways in which Caribbean American mutual aid societies and benevolent associations provided Caribbean immigrants with a supportive and familiar community at the time of their arrival and beyond. In examining the number of these organizations, their membership, and the functions they served, this chapter demonstrates that these mutual aid societies not only heightened a sense of West Indian ethnic identity among Caribbean immigrants in the United States, but also created and strengthened social and kinship networks between immigrants in the United States and those back home in the Caribbean. Particularly important to this process were Caribbean women, who I argue were the proponents of Caribbean culture in the United States, forming ethnically distinct Caribbean communities. Along the way, these societies facilitated Caribbean immigrants in identifying themselves as an American ethnic group. Activities and social events hosted by mutual aid societies and benevolent associations gave Caribbean immigrants living in New York an opportunity to meet and become acquainted with other Caribbean immigrants. This often resulted in connections being made between more established Caribbean immigrants, who had been in the United States for several years, and newly arrived immigrants.

Members of immigrant mutual aid societies in New York created diasporic networks that helped to keep them abreast of events happening in the

Caribbean and connected to their West Indian identity. They demonstrated a strong interest in staying connected to their home communities in the Caribbean by providing relief aid to Caribbean islands hit by natural disasters, founding various scholarships to sponsor students in the Caribbean, undertaking charity work, and maintaining a constant stream of collaboration with organizations in the Caribbean. Through these mutual aid societies and benevolent associations, Caribbean immigrants were not only able to stay connected to their homeland, but they also utilized these associations to celebrate their ethnic identities in the United States. For example, the BBA annually held Bermuda Week, a week of event programing celebrating the history and culture of Bermuda.[6] Other groups, like the St. Lucia United Association, held social events such as annual heritage dances that highlighted Saint Lucian culture.[7] Female association members were particularly active in this process.

Through their involvement with these mutual aid societies and benevolent associations Caribbean immigrants demonstrated their belief that their own fate was closely intertwined with the social, economic, and political welfare of the Black international community. Caribbean American mutual aid societies and benevolent associations in many ways became proto–Pan-Africanist organizations.[8] Demonstrating a deep concern for Black peoples throughout the world, association members launched various international initiatives to help people of African descent within the Caribbean and beyond. For instance, many of the associations kept their members abreast of news affecting people of African descent worldwide, participated in rallies and demonstrations for Pan-African issues, and raised funds for diasporic causes such as supporting Ethiopia during the Italo-Ethiopian War of 1935.[9] An examination of Caribbean immigrant mutual aid societies and benevolent associations provides a more nuanced understanding of the way in which Caribbean immigrant groups conceptualized their identities as both "West Indian" immigrants and as Black in the United States, and, ultimately, how they came to perceive themselves as a transnational group and people connected to the African Diaspora.

Mutual Aid Societies and Benevolent Associations

As Caribbean immigrants poured into New York City at the turn of the century, they looked for ways to provide support to each other, as the U.S. government had few programs to assist immigrants, least of all nonwhite, English-speaking immigrants. In the 1920s, the United States began setting up "Americanization" programs for female immigrants, because they believed that women were key to productive and successful immigrant groups. The programs often centered around preparing women for U.S. citizenship, however many of these programs were not for English-speaking immigrants. This fact effectively shut out Anglophone Caribbean immigrants and dismissed their needs as an immigrant group, leaving the question of where English-speaking Caribbean immigrants fit into the United States' idea of an immigrant.[10] In an unfamiliar city, in a new country, often with very few networks, Caribbean immigrants relied on the familiar structure of Caribbean friendly societies to provide networks of kinship and mutual aid: "the immediate reaction of the newly arrived immigrants was to reach out to each other for comfort and protection against a hostile environment."[11] As we saw in Chapter 1, Caribbean immigrant mutual aid societies and benevolent associations were the direct successors of Caribbean friendly societies. Caribbean immigrants took the basic principles of the Caribbean friendly society and applied them to their new realities in the United States. Ivy Simons, a prominent former member of the BBA, had been a member of a friendly society back home in Bermuda, and so it seemed natural for her to seek out a similar support network once she arrived in New York City, given the difficulties of adjusting to American life. The familiarity of mutual aid societies in New York made her feel at home. Simons stated that many of the members of American mutual aid societies had previously been involved with Caribbean-based friendly societies in some form.[12] Caribbean American mutual aid societies and benevolent associations served as gateways for Caribbean immigrants to enter and settle into their new lives in the United States by providing members with collective care and ready-made social networks, teaching them the ways of the city and "how to be good Americans," as well as helping them stay connected to their cultural identities.[13]

The first known Caribbean mutual aid society in the United States was the West Indian Benevolent Association of New York City (WIBANYC), established on April 3, 1884. Founding member A. G. Munday explained the purpose of this association: "As there are many of us West Indians in this country and among strangers, it behooves us as fellow countrymen to unite ourselves in one compact, with the help of our Heavenly Father, to assist each other in sickness or death."[14] Its members were concerned with having a place where Caribbean immigrants could fellowship and more importantly provide support for one another in times of difficulty. The WIBANYC initially had seven active members, three of whom were women. Initially, the association excluded anyone under the age of fifteen or over the age of forty-five. After members turned forty-five, they had to pay an additional fifty cents each year along with the standard initiation fee of three dollars. Monthly dues were set at forty cents. Another requirement to join the organization was that all applicants had to be West Indian natives and recommended by someone who was already a member. This requirement demonstrates the early concerns of immigrant mutual aid societies and benevolent associations to specifically support Caribbean immigrants.

Notably, this late nineteenth-century organization had no island-specific requirements for membership. Its only stipulation was that association members had to be West Indian.[15] One explanation for this may be that WIBANYC founders had already begun to develop a sense of West Indian identity due to previous experiences with migration; or perhaps their sense of Pan–West Indian identity strengthened upon arrival in New York City, where the relatively small Caribbean population at the time helped Caribbean immigrants to recognize their shared British colonial and cultural experiences. Perhaps the most practical reason for the lack of an island-specific requirement was that the Caribbean immigrant population in nineteenth-century New York was just too small, which made it hard to make island-specific demands for membership. It is in the early twentieth century that we begin to see a substantial increase in the number of Caribbean immigrants to the United States, with many new organizations admitting only members from specific islands. For instance, the Montserrat Progressive Society (MPS) of New York, founded in 1914, had a strict membership requirement based on an applicant's place of birth.

Similar patterns can be seen among Caribbean immigrant social organizations founded in Boston in the early twentieth century. Groups such as the West Indian Aid Society, founded in 1915, were formed with the aim of providing mutual assistance to all immigrants from the Caribbean, regardless of island affiliation. However, historian Violet Showers Johnson notes that "organizing along pan-West Indian lines preceded the island [specific] organizing of the 1930s."[16] Subsequently, we see the creation of island-specific groups such as the Jamaica Associates in 1934 and the Montserratian Progressive League in 1939. The formation of Caribbean communities in Boston followed a structure that was analogous to those in New York City, and as a result sociocultural structures such as immigrant mutual aid societies did as well.

Table 1 represents the sixty-seven known Caribbean mutual aid societies and benevolent associations established in New York City between the years 1884 and 1940.[17] As this table illustrates, these organizations represented the entire spectrum of the Anglophone Caribbean, from the smallest islands to the largest. We can immediately observe from Table 1 that almost half of the mutual aid societies and benevolent associations were established

Table 1. West Indian Mutual Aid Societies and Benevolent Associations in
New York, 1884–1940.

#	Organization	Founding Year	Country Affiliation	Headquarters
1	The West Indian Benevolent Association of New York City (WIBANYC)	1884	Pan-West Indian	
2	Bermuda Benevolent Association (BBA)	1897	Bermuda	
3	American West Indian Benevolent Society	Before 1899	Pan-West Indian	
4	American Virgin Islands Society	1899	Pan-West Indian	
5	Benevolent Society of the American Virgin Islands, Incorporated	1899	Pan-West Indian	
6	Danish West Indian Benevolent Society	1900	Virgin Islands	
7	Sons and Daughters of the Benevolent Society of the American Virgin Islands, Incorporated	1905	Virgin Islands	
8	Nassau Bahamas Association, Incorporated	1912	Bahamas	211 West 137th Street
9	The Nassau Bahamas Social and Beneficial Club	1912	Bahamas	
10	Sons and Daughters of St. Christopher Society in America, Incorporated	1912	British Virgin Islands	228 West 132nd Street
11	The Orange Benevolent Society	1913		
12	Beulah Wesleyan Benevolent Association	1913		
13	Windward Islands Progressive League	1914	Pan-West Indian	
14	Montserrat Progressive Society (MPS)	1914	Montserrat	Montserrat Building, 207 West 137th Street
15	American West Indian Ladies Aid Society (AWILAS)	1915	Pan-West Indian	149 West 136th Street
16	Barbuda Progressive Society	1915	Barbuda	

(continues)

Table 1. (*Continued*)

#	Organization	Founding Year	Country Affiliation	Headquarters
17	Bermuda Mutual Benevolent Association of America, Incorporated	1915	Bermuda	
18	The Ladies Aid Society of the American Virgin Islands, Incorporated	1915	Virgin Islands	
19	Antillean League of New York, Incorporated	1916	Pan-West Indian	30 West 129th Street
20	Danish-American West Indian Ladies Aid Association	Before 1917	Danish Virgin Islands	149 West 136th Street
21	The British-Jamaican Benevolent Association, Incorporated	1917	Pan-West Indian	349 West 141st Street
22	Dominica Benevolent Society of New York, Incorporated	1919	Dominica	
23	St. Lucia United Association, Incorporated	1920	Saint Lucia	125th Street
24	St. Vincent Benevolent Association, Incorporated	1920	Saint Vincent	
25	Trinidad Benevolent Association, Incorporated of New York	1920	Trinidad	
26	British Jamaican Benevolent Society	1921	Jamaica	
27	Oak Tree Benevolent Society	1921		
28	Sons and Daughters of Nevis Benevolent Society	1921?	Nevis	260 West 143rd Street
29	Virgin Islands Alliance	1923	Virgin Islands	104 West 144th Street
30	Anguilla Benevolent Society	1924	Anguilla	
31	The British Guiana Benevolent Association	1924	Guiana	127 West 120th Street
32	West Indian and American Friendly Societies Inc	1925	Pan-West Indian	
33	Sons and Daughters of the West Indies	Before 1925	Pan-West Indian	
34	The British Virgin Islands Benevolent Association of New York (BVIBA)	1926	British Virgin Islands	Montserrat Building, 207 West 137th Street

#	Organization	Founding Year	Country Affiliation	Headquarters
35	Montserrat Literary Club	Before 1927	Montserrat	
36	Third Moravian Church Benevolent Society	1928?	Pan-West Indian	
37	West Indian Society and Protective Alliance	Before 1929	Pan-West Indian	
38	American Virgin Islands Juvenile Society	Before 1933	Virgin Islands	
39	Antigua Progressive Society (APS)	1934	Antigua	Antigua and Barbuda House, 12 West 122nd Street
40	Grenada Mutual Association	Before 1936	Grenada	
41	Grenada Benevolent Association, Incorporated	Before 1936	Grenada	
42	Barbuda Benevolent Society of America, Incorporated	Before 1936	Barbuda	
43	Victoria United Benevolent Society	Before 1936	Pan-West Indian	
44	Negro Foreign Born Alliance	1938	Pan-West Indian	Harlem
45	Jamaica Unity Club, Incorporated	1938	Pan-West Indian	Harlem
46	Anegada Progressive League, Incorporated	1940	Anegada	
47	Virgin Islands Congressional Council	Unknown; seen in record prior to 1940	Virgin Islands	
48	American Virgin Islands Central Organisation	''''	Virgin Islands	
49	American Virgin Islands Mechanic Club	""	Virgin Islands	
50	Virgin Islands Civic and Industrial Association	""	Virgin Islands	207 West 140th Street
51	Negro Foreign Born Citizens League	""	Pan-West Indian	
52	The Dorcas Committee of the Virgin Islands Congressional Council	""	Virgin Islands	

(continues)

Table 1. (*Continued*)

#	Organization	Founding Year	Country Affiliation	Headquarters
53	Virgin Island Catholic Relief Committee	""	Virgin Islands	58 West 140th Street
54	Virgin Island Society	""	Virgin Islands	
55	United Brothers and Sisters of the United Islands	""	Pan-West Indian	
56	Federation of Virgin Islands Societies	""	Virgin Islands	
57	Tobago Benevolent Association	""	Tobago	10104 Park Place, Brooklyn, NY
58	St. James Mutual Aid Society	""	Pan-West Indian	
59	American Virgin Islander's Prudential Association, Incorporated	""	Virgin Islands	2 West 129th Street
60	The Guyana Benevolent Association, Inc	""	Guyana	
61	United Caribbean Youth, Inc	""	Pan-West Indian	238 East 15th Street, NY, NY
62	Antillean Benevolent Society	""	Pan-West Indian	
63	BWI War Veterans Association	""	Pan-West Indian	
64	Virgin Gorda Mutual Society	""	Virgin Gorda	
65	The Helenites Association of St Lucia Inc	""	Saint Lucia	
66	Caribbean-American Association	""	Pan-West Indian	
67	Dominican Society	""	Dominican	

Sources: "American West Indian Ladies Aid Society Records, 1915–1965," "Antigua Barbuda Progressive Society Records," "Bermuda Benevolent Association Records, 1898–1969," "British Virgin Islands Benevolent Association Records, 1926–1989," Manuscripts, Archives, and Rare Books Division, Schomburg Center for Research in Black Culture; Montserrat Progressive Society of New York, Inc., Constitution and By-Laws donated by Alan Pinado to Irma Watkins Owens; Constitution and By-laws of the West Indian Benevolent Association (1891), F128.9.W54 W47 1891, New York Historical Society; 80th Anniversary of the Jamaican Associates, Inc., 2014 Program Booklet, donated by member and former president Dr. Doreen Wilkinson.

between the years 1912 and 1924. This fact can be explained by the large influx of Caribbean immigrants to the United States between 1911 to 1920, a total of 123,424 immigrants at its peak.[18] It is during these twelve years that the largest number of Caribbean immigrants arrived in New York City prior to 1940, allowing us to draw a direct correlation between the number of arriving immigrants and the creation of immigrant mutual aid societies, and also demonstrating the extreme importance these organizations held for newly arriving Caribbean immigrants. It seemed that as new groups of immigrants arrived in the United States, they brought with them their own tradition of friendly societies and chose to create new mutual aid societies and benevolent associations instead of joining previously existing ones. As seen in Table 1, this seems to be due to the lack of island-specific organizations at the time, as new societies represented unique island nations.

After 1924, with the passing of the restrictive Johnson-Reed Act, we see a huge drop in the number of Caribbean immigrants to the United States. This Act set a national quota of 2 percent of immigrants from the total of any nation's residents in the United States as reported in the 1890 census, a requirement that drastically limited the number of Caribbean immigrants to the United States during this period. It therefore makes sense that after 1924 we see a decline in the creation of Caribbean mutual aid societies. The number of new Caribbean organizations increased again in the late 1930s when immigration laws became less restrictive and Caribbean immigrants once again came to the United States in large numbers. Caribbean mutual aid societies and benevolent associations were established and continued to operate well after this date; among these were the Virgin Gorda Mutual Society of New York, founded in 1959.

Members

The membership numbers of Caribbean mutual aid societies vary greatly; some associations, like the BBA, had as many as three hundred members in the 1940s and less than twenty in 1998. It is hard to discover the definitive membership numbers of each society, as these organizations did not leave logs recording their annual total membership. However, groups such as the AWILAS and the Antigua Progressive Society (APS) did keep annual records of new applicants. Unfortunately, nowhere in these records is a tally of either group's total membership. Even so, the pattern of new membership

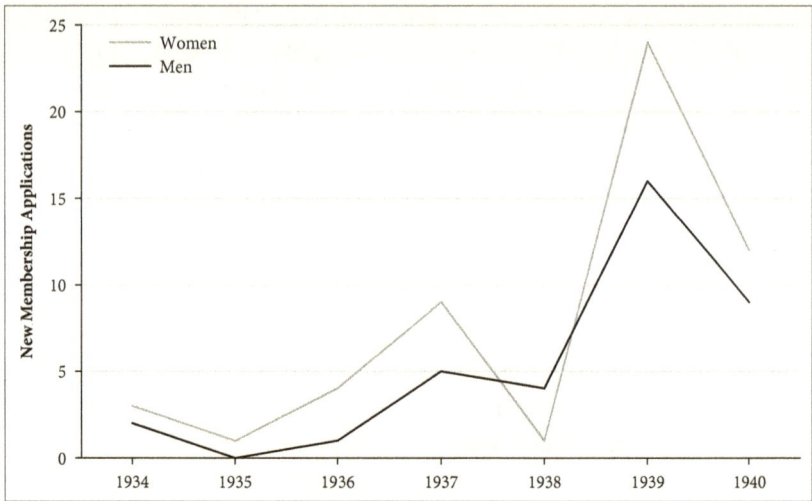

Chart 5. Antigua Progressive Society New Membership Applicants, 1934–1940.
Source: ABPS Membership Records, MARBD, SCRBC.

applications for the APS from 1934 to 1940 (Chart 5) can be taken as representative of membership applications as a whole.

Chart 5 is helpful for several reasons. First, while we do not know the total number of members in the APS at the time, we do know how many members joined the group during this period. The largest new membership intake occurs in 1939, a number that confirms that as immigration laws in the late 1930s became less restrictive, Caribbean immigrant participation in mutual aid societies and benevolent associations increased. As Table 1 demonstrates, these immigrants created several new associations, establishing a strong correlation between newly arrived Caribbean immigrants and the creation of mutual aid societies and benevolent associations. Chart 5 also highlights the fact that in many cases women joined associations at a higher rate than male immigrants. In fact, more women than men applied to join the APS every year with the exception of 1938.

The regulations and qualifications for membership outlined in Caribbean mutual aid societies and benevolent associations highlight the type of members these organizations aimed to attract and the vision each society had of itself. The mission of the APS, founded in 1934, was to "foster friendship, promote and cultivate social, economic, and intellectual intercourse among its members, and render aid in time of need, sickness, or death."[19] The APS had very strict qualifications for membership. In order to join, a potential member must have been born in Antigua or be the husband, wife, or descendant of an Antiguan. Applicants also had to be between the ages of fifteen and sixty-five and be of "good moral character" to be eligible for membership in the society.[20] Similarly, the MPS limited its membership to people born on Montserrat and their spouses and descendants.[21] The society envisioned as its purpose to be a medium through which to "unite the people from the Island of Montserrat, to assist in uplifting them socially, morally, and intellectually, to promote the general welfare of its members, to provide for the sick and those in distress, and to bury the dead."[22]

While many associations with island-specific names had very strict guidelines for their membership, this was not always the case. For instance, the objective of the Jamaica Unity Club, Inc. (founded in 1938) was to unite people of Caribbean origin and their friends for the purpose of working together to nurture the development of Caribbean people as a whole. Thus, any person, regardless of nationality, in accord with the objectives of the organization was allowed to apply for membership and was accepted.[23] Mutual aid societies and benevolent associations with more inclusive names, such as the AWILAS or the WIBANYC, were the most lenient in terms of membership qualifications and only required their members be from the West Indies or the descendants of West Indian immigrants. The AWILAS's founding principle was to establish camaraderie among Caribbean American women. As such, its only membership requirement was that its members be from the Caribbean. The same is true for the West Indian Benevolent Association, whose purpose was to unite West Indians in the United States. Their only qualification for membership was that members be West Indian natives.[24]

Examining the membership records of mutual aid societies and benevolent associations allows us a microscopic view of the types of people who participated in immigrant social organizations. For instance, the membership records of the AWILAS show that the society's applicants ranged in age from eighteen to forty-six years. However, most potential members were in their late twenties and thirties. In terms of socioeconomic standing, the members of mutual aid societies and benevolent associations came from all class levels to form social networks. An examination of fourteen AWILAS membership applications reveals that half of the potential applicants worked as domestics, two were housewives, one was a student, and one applicant was a self-employed hairdresser. More than half of the women were married and five were unmarried.[25] While the membership records of the AWILAS represent only a tiny cross-section of all potential members of Caribbean social organizations, they do provide an important sampling of the makeup of mutual aid society members and demonstrate that these groups attracted Caribbean immigrants from various socioeconomic backgrounds. These associations had neither income nor job criteria for membership. Instead, they envisioned themselves as organizations in which all Caribbean immigrants, regardless of financial or social standing, could come together and experience fellowship. Former BBA member Ivy Simons confirms this fact in speaking of the membership of the BBA during her tenure: "Most of the people were domestics and in those days, domestics would use to have Thursdays off and they decided to have their meetings on Thursdays so everything was happening on Thursdays."[26] She even confirms that the BBA scheduled meetings around the work schedules of their membership, illustrating that these groups encouraged participation from a wide range of Caribbean immigrants, regardless of socioeconomic status.

Juvenile Groups

Originally established for adult West Indian immigrants, mutual aid societies and benevolent associations expanded their functions to adapt to the growing needs of their members.

As Caribbean immigrants settled into life within the United States, they began to reunite with relatives who also immigrated to join them. Additionally, they started new families and had children born in the United States. Social organizations responded to this new population of immigrant and American-born children by creating auxiliary groups for minors.

In 1923, nine years after the founding of the original association, the MPS formed a juvenile group called the Montserrat Progressive Society Juvenile. The youth group was supervised by three members of the parent body of the MPS, with two of these members regularly attending MPS Juvenile monthly meetings and reporting back to the MPS parent body. Juvenile members were allowed to attend at least one meeting of the parent body each quarter.[27] By allowing junior members to attend these meetings, the MPS was preparing younger members to transition into the parent association when they turned eighteen. As noted above, the Bermuda Benevolent Society also formed a juvenile branch and young adults' group called the Rosebuds, as the needs of their members changed. In 1934, thirty-nine young people were inducted into the first Rosebud juvenile group. Juvenile members ranged in age from six to fifteen years. Later, a young adults' group was formed and catered to members fifteen to twenty-five years of age.[28]

In 1933, the British Virgin Islands Benevolent Association (BVIBA) proposed to found a Juvenile Society that would be known as The Juvenile Society of the British Virgin Islands Benevolent Association, with the objectives of "promot[ing] unity and friendship among the children of the people of the Islands, and members of the Parent Association. To render sick aid, and Death benefits, to assist in their Educational and Social progress, and provide a system for transferring the children into the Parent body."[29] Children between the ages of four and sixteen years old were allowed to join.

Juvenile auxiliary groups were important because they exhibited a model for younger immigrant children and provided continuity with a second generation of Caribbean immigrants, who continued the tradition of mutual aid societies and benevolent associations in the United States. Associations such as The Juvenile Society of the British Virgin Islands Benevolent Association explicitly outlined these goals in their bylaws.[30]

Additionally, juvenile auxiliary groups taught children about their West Indian heritage so that transnational identities could be fostered, even if the children had never visited the Caribbean islands of their parents' birth. Children born in the United States could connect to a West Indian identity through the different programs hosted for children. The Juvenile Society of the British Virgin Islands Benevolent Association, for instance, regularly hosted concerts, which undoubtedly highlighted traditional music and dance from the British Virgin Islands. Through mutual aid societies and benevolent associations, the children of Caribbean immigrants cultivated kinship networks that were essential to the survival of Caribbean immigrant groups in the United States.

Functions

Caribbean immigrant mutual aid societies and benevolent associations served many purposes for Caribbean immigrants living in New York City. The most common of these functions was to provide sick and death benefits. Every association (see Table 1) had some form of death benefit for its members from its inception. The BBA, for example, guaranteed a funeral fund of $100 upon the death of a member to his or her beneficiary, and $20 for juvenile members.[31] In 1932, the AWILAS raised its death benefit from $50 to $75 to stay competitive with other associations that offered their members larger sums.[32] In the MPS, when a member (in good financial standing) of one full year or more passed away, the society paid the member's beneficiary the sum of $125. In addition, the association provided a funeral wreath and every member was notified, so they could attend the funeral service.[33] These death benefits served as a form of health insurance to association members and their families. They also provided association members with a network of people who provided emotional and spiritual support. As noted in Chapter 2, many early Caribbean immigrants came to the United States alone, having left spouses and children behind. The intimate services these networks offered to Caribbean immigrants made them feel less isolated and better able to successfully navigate events like death in their new country.

The benefit, however, that members most regularly took advantage of was the sick benefit. Each association had its own rules concerning when and how much each member in good standing would receive, but most benefits followed a common pattern. Once members became ill and could no longer work, they were entitled to a weekly stipend for a set amount of time. Association members made sick visits to their members and provided them with financial assistance. The MPS, for instance, gave members $6 a week for five weeks, and then $4 a week for five additional weeks if they were still sick and unable to work. The total amount of sick benefits payable to a member for one year could not exceed fifty dollars.[34]

In addition, associations established visiting committees in order to check on the well-being of their members, bring them flowers, and keep them in good spirits. The visiting committee of the WIBANYC made hospital or home visits to check in on members who fell ill. Sick members were given $5 for eight weeks; after which they were given $2.50 for the following weeks if they still could not return to work. During this period, association members would also take up a voluntary collection at meetings soliciting extra funds for sick members. These monetary benefits, however, were all contingent on the member's standing in the association.[35] Additionally, there were stipulations regarding for which illnesses members could receive sick benefits. The MPS's constitution and bylaws explicitly stated that "sick benefits shall not be paid for incapacity due to child-birth, alcoholism, self-mutilation, and venereal diseases."[36] This clause illustrates the MPS's notion of respectability and which illnesses would be deemed proper to recognize for financial assistance.

Sick and death benefits were deeply beneficial to association members and they regularly took advantage of such financial assistance. This fact is confirmed by the large number of thank-you cards and letters in each association's records. In one letter to the AWILAS, dated September 12, 1933, member Rose Thomas writes how grateful she was to the association for having given her a sick benefit: "Through this medium, I beg to acknowledge the receipt of your kind and sympathetic letter also your generous gift of $20.00. . . . I wish therefore to express my sincere gratitude for this assistance given me during my time of distress. I appreciate your noble act of kindness and wish to thank you from the bottom of my heart, and to add with few feeble words the grateful appreciation of my entire family. Your assistance has been a source of cheer to us; it has given us courage and hope in the midst of our troubles and difficulties."[37] Thomas's letter is one of many similar letters from members thanking their organizations for making home visits, as well as for sending flowers and monetary gifts. This practice of financial assistance provided immigrants with a sense of security that they could not receive elsewhere, as worker's compensation and other disability benefits did not exist at this time, while also comforting members and helping them feel less alienated by providing a community. This type of kinship was very important and powerful for an immigrant who might have been in New York City without family members. Mutual aid societies in many ways became families to their members.

In addition, mutual aid societies offered educational workshops or forums, which provided members with information on a wide array of subjects including child rearing, job placement, the naturalization process, and even how to resolve immigration problems, obtain U.S. citizenship, and use voting machines.[38] For example, in 1934 the American Virgin Islands Society invited members of the AWILAS to their December 14 meeting, where a presentation on "child rearing and its influence on adult life" was given by a physician.[39] These workshops or forums aimed to be informative and educational, providing association members with useful information for navigating their new lives in the United States. Immigrant mutual aid societies wanted their members to be active participants in their new surroundings, and they believed hosting educational forums would help them to achieve that objective. In an effort to reach a larger number of the West Indian immigrant population, groups often invited other organizations to their educational forums.

Charitable causes were also of great importance to members of immigrant mutual aid societies and benevolent associations. The most common were scholarship funds established for members' children.[40] However, charitable efforts were not limited to members. Mutual aid societies often donated to local organizations, such as public schools, churches, hospitals, and associations for the disabled. For instance, the St. Lucia United Association, formed in 1920 in Harlem, lived up to their motto of "Friendship, Love, and Charity" by their commitment to public service; the association's bylaws contain a pledge to continue "the tradition of improvement of our brothers and sisters socially and physically, and to extend the hand of goodwill to our larger community." They furthermore stated that their "primary obligation is to provide aid in [the] time of adversity."[41] The association hosted an annual scholarship for first-year college students, and members later created the College of Preceptor Scholarship for local teachers. The St. Lucia United Association supported a children's orphanage named the Holy Family Home in Saint Lucia and donated to various nursing homes for the elderly, and members regularly sent monetary donations and gifts to the children of the orphanage. The Association also provided books, stationery, printers, and other supplies to the island's elementary schools over the years.[42]

Other groups such as the APS (founded under the direction of Antiguan-born Rev. James P. Roberts), also had many charitable missions. The APS's overarching mission—to be "a beacon of light to us all"—was boldly inscribed on an emblem on their membership badges, and the society strived to do just that.[43] APS members raised money for various causes and participated in charitable organizations both in the United States and at home in Antigua. Notable was their annual donation of clothing and toys to the St. John's Day Nursery in St. John's, Antigua. Additionally, they donated to the Halberton Hospital in Antigua toward the purchase of modern medical equipment; participated in a 1950 post-hurricane relief effort in the Caribbean; raised money for the St. John's Girls School to provide free lunches for "needy pupils"; and started a Reserve Land Fund at the Steven's Memorial Domestic Science Class of the St. John's Girls School.[44]

Education was very important to these mutual aid societies, as is witnessed by the numerous academic scholarship funds they established. The Virgin Islands Alliance held various fundraisers to raise capital for scholarships for students. One such fundraiser was the 1934 "Cocktail Musicale."[45] The Alliance also held an annual Christmas drive for students attending the historically Black college and university, Hampton University, to which other immigrant groups such as the AWILAS donated, demonstrating their growing race consciousness.[46]

Mutual aid societies' charitable efforts also extended to those in need within the Caribbean. The BVIBA was very active in donating money to charities within the British Virgin Islands. In 1936, they donated a large sum of money and an "invalid chair" to the Tortola Cottage Hospital. The same year, they also donated musical instruments to the Sunnyside Ragtimers, an orchestra based in Tortola. In 1938, they provided money and books to a local school in Tortola, an organ to the Methodist School in Virgin Gorda, and $2,500 to a hospital in Tortola, which used the donation to purchase an X-ray machine.[47] Many of these organizations were still intimately connected to Caribbean charities and could therefore donate not only money, but very specific items they needed.

A final and very significant function of mutual aid societies and benevolent associations was their potential for financial investments for their members. Separate from their monthly association dues, some groups such as the Jamaican Associates of Boston offered their members rotating lines of credit or *susus*, which worked as a collective savings plan in which a group of people could pool their money and distribute it among themselves periodically. For instance, ten people might contribute $200 each into the pool every month for a year. In the first month, one person would receive $2,000. The next month, the next person would receive $2,000, and so on. At the end of the year, each person had contributed $2,000 and received $2,000. *Susus* helped start businesses, provided down payments on new homes, and even paid the passage for a relative to the United States.

Susus were not specific to any one British West Indian island. Instead, they were utilized by numerous Anglophone Caribbean immigrants, with varying names, including *partners* or *box*. Additionally, the concept was not unique to mutual aid societies or benevolent associations. There were many separate informal savings groups or *susus* not connected to social organizations. While these groups were not organized by specific islands, most people tended to join *susus* affiliated with their home islands, as they usually had some connection to or personally knew the people running the *susu*.[48] In addition to *susus*, groups such as the BBA offered an investment bond fund, where members paid money for a bond and were promised a 4 or 5 percent return on their investment, which at the time was more than what was offered in a standard savings account. Bonds allowed both members and the groups an investment with an assured profit.[49]

Paule Marshall, in her novel *Brown Girl, Brownstones* (1959), discusses a similar phenomenon among the community of Caribbean immigrants that settled in the Bedford–Stuyvesant area of Brooklyn from 1930 through the 1950s.[50] These immigrants formed a homeowners' association with a similar bond fund that enabled Caribbean immigrants to purchase houses in New

York. While it is a fictionalized account, *Brown Girl, Brownstones* closely parallels Marshall's own life growing up as the daughter of Barbadian immigrants in Brooklyn. In the novel, the Association of Barbadian Homeowners and Businessmen is a dominant force in main character Selina Boyce's family's life. Marshall's depiction of the networks created by immigrants through mutual aid societies illustrates both the size and significance to Caribbean immigrants of Caribbean American mutual aid societies and benevolent associations throughout the twentieth century, including their potential for economic collaboration.

Kinship

Caribbean immigrant mutual aid societies and benevolent associations were essential in creating vital kinship networks among Caribbean immigrants in the United States. These groups provided many benefits to their members, including important aspects of socialization such as fellowship and the development of imperative social networks. Mutual aid societies held various social events that served as spaces in which Caribbean immigrants could socialize with people from their home islands, as well as from other islands. Dances, holiday parties, and group trips were just some of the activities offered to members. The entertainment committees of organizations like the BVIBA and the APS were responsible for planning and coordinating events. The APS entertainment committee held annual dances for Thanksgiving, as well as bus trips to national parks and tourist attractions.[51] In addition to an entertainment committee, the BVIBA had a floral committee, which handled flower arrangements for their dances and other events. This committee was also largely responsible for sending flowers to sick members or the families of deceased members.[52] In addition, the BBA had a community social and recreation club that held events, such as Bermuda Week, which celebrated the history and culture of Bermuda.[53]

These West Indian groups often coordinated events with other West Indian social organizations as well as African American organizations, such as the Eton Benevolence Society and the Associated Clubs of Harlem. Members of the American West Indian Benevolent Society, for instance, held an annual reception and dance that drew many members from several other associations, including the AWILAS.[54] The AWILAS itself held numerous receptions and dances that were open to other West Indian mutual aid societies and benevolent associations to come together for fellowship.[55] It was also quite common for associations to host their social events at local churches where association members were part of the congregation. Mutual aid societies that did not have an office or headquarters building regularly used churches as places for monthly meetings and special events since association members tended to frequent those churches.[56]

Religion, while not the main function of mutual aid societies and benevolent associations, played an important role in the lives of their members. As a result, projecting religious values became an important aspect of many associations. Religious ceremonies and services were often incorporated into an organization's social calendar. Almost every organization held an annual sermon for Thanksgiving or Christmas as part of its roster of activities. The women of the AWILAS, for example, sponsored an annual Thanksgiving sermon at the Church of the Transfiguration on 74 West 126th Street, and APS members held an annual Thanksgiving service at Advent Episcopal Mission Church.[57] Additionally, many organizations such as the MPS had a chaplain who opened and closed meetings with a prayer.[58] As with friendly societies in the Caribbean, displaying religious piety remained important to immigrant mutual aid societies and benevolent associations. Moreover, religion and religious ceremony became a way that members could further advance kinship networks.

In an effort to create broader and deeper ties to the Caribbean immigrant community in the United States and to expand their social networks, these organizations frequently collaborated with one another. Associations regularly invited one another to attend each other's meetings, workshops, and social events. The records of the AWILAS demonstrate the eagerness with which these West Indian organizations collaborated. More than fifty letters of correspondence exist between the AWILAS and various other Caribbean immigrant mutual aid societies and benevolent associations. Within the records of the BBA there are dozens of letters from various Caribbean organizations representing almost every island of the Caribbean, thanking the organization for its participation in their association's social events.[59] Associations like the BBA supported other groups with their fundraising efforts, contributing both money and materials. They frequently took out paid advertisements in each other's event and program booklets. Groups such as the Virgin Island Society, American West Indian Benevolent Society, Antillean Benevolent Society, and the United Brothers and Sisters of the United Islands attended each other's meetings and closely worked together. In 1929, members of the BVIBA even bestowed Robert Potter of the Dominican Society and James H. Van Putten of the West Indian Society and Protective Alliance with honorary memberships, illustrating the importance these associations placed on creating partnerships with one another.[60] Groups such as the BVIBA even had members of other Caribbean mutual aid societies serve as delegates and speakers at their meetings.[61] The AWILAS also collaborated with organizations such as the Virgin Islands Congressional Council, and the two groups regularly sent representatives to each other's meetings. In AWILAS records, there are dozens of letters between the groups discussing their partnership.[62] The AWILAS and the American Virgin Island Correspondence Committee also exchanged correspondence for more than a decade, attended each other's meetings and social events, and helped each other to fundraise for charities. These mutual aid societies worked together to create kinship networks and foster a sense of community among immigrant members.[63]

The AWILAS would eventually emerge as an umbrella organization for other immigrant mutual aid societies and benevolent associations. As such, the AWILAS organized many events in an effort to unite West Indian social organizations. In 1934, the AWILAS initiated a joint committee called the Federation of American Virgin Islands Societies, holding its first conference in October of that year. In attendance were several New York–based mutual aid societies, including the American West Indian Benevolent Society, the American West Indian Islands Society, the Virgin Islands Congressional Council, the American Virgin Islands Central Organisation, the American Virgin Islands Mechanic Club, and the Virgin Islands Civic and Industrial Association. While this federation was open to all West Indian groups, there was a focus on groups with members that identified with the American Virgin Islands.[64]

Relations among West Indian mutual aid societies and benevolent associations were not perfect, nor without dissent about how the groups could best achieve their goals. In the records of the AWILAS, Ashley L. Totten, president of the Virgin Islands Civic and Industrial Association and national secretary-treasurer for the BSCP New York City chapter, writes that he and members of the Virgin Islands Civic and Industrial Association had been repeatedly accused of being unwilling to work with other Virgin Islands leaders. He asserted not only that "nothing is farther from the truth than that," but also that he had repeatedly reached out to cooperate with other immigrant groups and his requests had all been turned down: "We want to be helpful to our native people and have no desire to improve the motives of any individuals. We do not feel that it is fair to be accused of blocking the cooperation or unification of the natives when we are and have always been ready and willing to cooperate. If unity of action is the solution to the masses of unorganized Virgin Islanders who it is said are in a state of bewilderment as to which leader to follow, then we are prepared to do the logical thing—a meeting of minds of all leaders."[65] Totten's letter illustrates the reality that although his organization may have had the intention of collaborating with other immigrant groups, tensions among leadership still existed. While this letter is the only record of discord that can be found in the thousands of association files examined, it illustrates that cooperation among West Indian immigrant groups was not a given, nor was it an easy process.

The emphasis that Caribbean mutual aid societies and benevolent associations placed on unity and cooperation among groups in the 1920s and 1930s is complex, and it was an objective that changed over time. As mentioned earlier in this chapter, late nineteenth-century West Indian mutual aid societies often had no island-birth requirements for their members. Their only stipulation was that association members be West Indian. The relatively small number of Caribbean immigrants in the United States in this period may have been the reason for these early Pan-Caribbean associations. As we move into the twentieth century, however, there is a substantial increase in the number of Caribbean immigrants coming to the United States, with the result that many new immigrant mutual aid societies began to cater to people from specific islands, implementing strict membership requirements. Associations often stipulated that potential members be from the island associated with the organization. For instance, the MPS of New York's stated objective was to "unite the people from the Island of Montserrat, to assist in uplifting them socially, morally, and intellectually, to promote the general welfare of its members." As a result, the society's qualifications for membership stated that members must have been born on the island of Montserrat or be the descendant or spouse of a person born in Montserrat.[66] Similarly, the Bermuda Mutual Benevolent Association, founded in 1915, restricted its membership to those who were born in Bermuda or were descendants of Bermudian immigrants. These examples of island-specific mutual aid societies with very strict membership requirements demonstrate that Caribbean immigrants did not necessarily see themselves as part of a unified Caribbean group. Instead, they were simply Montserratian or Bermudian, and as such clung to their island identities.

In the decade following 1924, there was a huge drop in the number of arriving Caribbean immigrants due to the United States' adoption of the restrictive Johnson-Reed Act. As a result, many mutual aid societies and benevolent associations began to see forming a more consolidated community with other Caribbean immigrant groups as an important objective. Island affiliation and

strict membership requirements became less important as the number of arriving immigrants drastically dwindled. Many mutual aid societies changed their
objectives to become more inclusive. Building fully transnational communities
concerned with the welfare of those in the Caribbean became another important goal. Consequently, groups like the Jamaica Unity Club, Incorporated,
which allowed any person, regardless of nationality, to apply for membership
to their association, became more prevalent. The Jamaica Unity Club's objectives were: "To unite people of Caribbean origin and their friends for the purpose of working together to foster development of Caribbean people. To seek
and acquire information on Caribbean affairs, and to spread such information
appropriately so as to foster the best interest and development of the Caribbean people. To stimulate economic, cultural and social projects, compatible
with the basic interest of people in the Caribbean. To develop adequate appreciation of the national heritage of the Caribbean area so as to encourage the
preservation of these facilities."[67] These radical objectives were a deliberate step
toward the creation of a strong connection between Caribbean communities
in the United States and within the Caribbean region.

Mutual aid societies like the MPS of Boston expanded their membership
to "anyone who [was] willing to join and help others in the community" and
worked vigilantly to foster relationships between groups of Caribbean immigrants by opening their meetings and events to all West Indian immigrants.[68]
The St. Lucia United Association started out as an association where newly
arrived Lucians could meet, but as their membership grew they became "more
conscious of those who are less fortunate in [the] homeland and in [the] com
munity in New York. With a motto of Friendship, Love, and Charity, we are
strongly committed to continue the tradition of improvement of our brothers
and sisters socially and physically, and to extend the hand of goodwill to our
larger community."[69] Other organizations such as the AWILAS focused on
developing camaraderie among Caribbean American women. The AWILAS's
only membership requirement was that its members be from the Caribbean.
As a result, their members represented various Caribbean islands.[70]

As Caribbean immigrant mutual aid societies and benevolent associations became more established in the United States, their objectives shifted
to adapt to the newer concerns of their members, which now leaned toward
creating intimate connections with other West Indians in the United States as
well as back home. Subsequently, this new objective forced many associations
to revise their membership requirements. They began to allow any person
who was aligned with their objectives, regardless of island of origin, to apply

for membership in their associations. For instance, the Negro Foreign Born Alliance, founded in Harlem in 1924, worked vigilantly to foster relationships between groups of Caribbean immigrants in New York by hosting mass meetings, educational forums, and social events. They also endeavored to keep immigrants in New York connected to the Caribbean by updating them on Caribbean news and keeping them actively involved in current social and political affairs affecting the region. Over time, many of these organizations began to embrace Pan-Caribbean aims and sentiments in order to foster larger connections with the entire New York immigrant community.

Diasporic Leanings

While the primary objective of many members of mutual aid societies and benevolent associations was to facilitate the acclimation of Caribbean immigrants to the United States and form social networks with other Caribbean immigrants, the welfare of people of African descent throughout the world became a clear and pressing concern for these organizations in the twentieth century. Often referred to as the "nadir of American history," the early twentieth century witnessed the eruption of violent and deadly race riots in cities across the United States. In the period between June and early autumn of 1919, dubbed the "Red Summer" by NAACP secretary and civil rights leader James Weldon Johnson, more than thirty race riots occurred in U.S. cities.[71] Lynchings and Jim Crow segregationist laws defined the era. Internationally, the well-being of people of African descent in various parts of the world was also under constant threat. Italy invaded Ethiopia in 1935, beginning the Second Italo-Ethiopian War; labor unrest erupted all over the British Caribbean between 1934 and 1939; and feelings of anticolonial unrest and African nationalism were expressed in strikes throughout West Africa.

As a consequence of this international unrest and threats to people of African descent, New York City became a hotbed of Black radical politics. Groups such as Jamaican-born Marcus Garvey's Universal Negro Improvement Association (UNIA; established a New York City headquarters in 1917), Hubert Harrison of Saint Croix's 1917 Liberty League, and Cyril Briggs of Nevis's African Blood Brotherhood for African Liberation and Redemption (founded in 1919) led the call for Black self-determination and political equality. These groups undoubtedly influenced the objectives of mutual aid societies and benevolent associations, whose members were often also members of these political groups. Thus, we see immigrant mutual aid societies begin to take a more diasporic approach in response to the social injustices Black people faced throughout the world. This fact is best demonstrated in the goals of organizations such as the APS, which stated, "we in America should help those in the islands to obtain and enjoy the same privileges which we have and enjoy here . . . we should fight for better conditions in the islands through the frame-work of the British Constitution."[72] The APS demonstrated such a strong commitment to Antiguan affairs, it was asked by the West Indies Royal Commission in 1938 to make recommendations for the improvement of conditions on the island of Antigua. The APS formed a special committee addressing economic, social, sanitary, and educational concerns as well as general improvements that could be made to their homeland.[73]

In 1928, the APS sent a representative to the Pan-American Nations Conference in Havana, Cuba. On the conference's agenda, APS members noted, were "plans and proposals . . . being acted upon to decide the fate of all our brothers in the West Indies, the Guianas, and British Honduras." The APS thought it vital to send representatives to the conference, because they believed that their destiny was connected to that of all Black people: "our fate is hanging in the balance, and it is most important to demonstrate our unity and strength" and to advocate the "demand for the right [to] self-determination" for Black people in the circum-Caribbean.[74] APS members drew a strong connection between themselves and other people of the African Diaspora. They believed that it was their duty to fight for the rights and freedom of all Black people throughout the world. This recurring sense of diasporic concern is evident in many of the records of Caribbean immigrant mutual aid societies and benevolent associations.

Amended to the 1926 constitution of the BVIBA is the association's overwhelmingly diasporic objective: "whereas we the people of the British Virgin Islands joined ourselves together for the purpose of having an organization to assist in giving alms to the needy among our people; not only here but to the homeland also."[75] Even before this modification, the BVIBA had been actively hosting programs that would benefit British Virgin Islanders in the Caribbean. The group had a Home Committee, which held events for and was in charge of outreach to the British Virgin Islands. The committee donated money and books to local schools in the British Virgin Islands. They even established a sister society in Anegada, British Virgin Islands. Furthermore, they hosted dinners with the consulate of the British Virgin Islands "in order to bring about co-operation among West Indians in the United States for giving relief and assistance for those of our people who may become distressed and deserving of help."[76]

The BVIBA was active in creating transnational social fields, with representatives throughout the Caribbean, including in Saint Thomas, Tortola, and Anegada, in order to keep abreast of current events on the islands. Representatives frequently wrote letters to the main organization in New York, updating them on island news. The BVIBA was so deeply invested in the development of the British Virgin Islands that in 1949 it was commissioned to work in conjunction with the Commissioner of the British Virgin Islands on an economic subcommittee. This subcommittee was created to develop an economic reconstruction plan to improve the depressed economic condition of the British Virgin Islands. In a detailed seventeen-page report, the subcommittee made recommendations regarding communications, economic development, education, medical facilities, health care, and water supplies, highlighting the close political involvement of Caribbean American mutual aid societies with the affairs of their home country and also demonstrating the diasporic direction that many associations like the BVIBA would take in the twentieth century.[77]

Members of the St. Lucia United Association also forged transnational connections with Lucians throughout the world in order to provide support to their island home. The St. Lucia United Association was a founding member of the Union of Overseas Associations, which linked Saint Lucian associations in London, Saint Croix, Barbados, the United States, Canada, and Saint Lucia in order to collectively discuss, coordinate, and combine their efforts to help those in Saint Lucia. The Union met every two years and drafted detailed plans outlining actions to be taken in Saint Lucia.[78] From its inception in 1897, the BBA also dedicated itself to the welfare of Bermudians in the New York and back home, as well as Black people around the world. In 1938, the BBA participated in a mass meeting hosted by the British Jamaican Progressive League, called in response to a massive workers' demonstration that ended in the brutal shooting of Jamaican protesters by the police. Four people were killed, while dozens were wounded and 103 were jailed. This event was the culmination of labor unrest taking place all over the Caribbean between 1934 and 1939.[79] By participating in the British-Jamaican Benevolent Association's mass meeting, members of the BBA demonstrated their solidarity with a Pan–West Indian movement calling for fair work practices throughout the Caribbean.

Members of the BBA also participated in a 1939 conference held by the United Aid for Peoples of African Descent to discuss plans of the British government to set aside ten thousand square miles of land in the highlands of British Guiana for the settlement of German refugees. While the group was optimistic that the project would bring a large flow of capital into the country and create employment opportunities, they believed the interest and future welfare of the Negro population of the colony should be made top priority. They advocated heavily to ensure that Black Guyanese people would not be negatively affected by the British government's plans.[80]

Another area of great concern in the 1930s for the BBA and many of the mutual aid societies and benevolent associations was the Italo-Ethiopian War of 1935. Seen as a bastion of African independence, Ethiopia held a symbolic place in the hearts of many in the African Diaspora. The Italian invasion was a cause of great consternation for Caribbean immigrant mutual aid societies and benevolent associations. The groups joined together to host mass meetings to discuss actions they could take in support of the Ethiopian army. Members of the BBA, for instance, organized a Peace Parade Conference to discuss how to provide aid to the Ethiopian people in their fight for independence, and even collected money, along with other immigrant mutual aid societies, to purchase surgical supplies for wounded Ethiopian soldiers. These groups also sent monetary donations directly to support the Ethiopian army, further highlighting the very real sense of diasporic connection Caribbean immigrants felt to the African Diaspora in the twentieth century.[81]

Conclusion

Understanding the purposes and activities of Caribbean immigrant mutual aid societies and benevolent associations in New York City is essential in shaping a more comprehensive and nuanced narrative of the immigrant experience. These mutual aid societies and benevolent associations provided much-needed services to incoming immigrant populations and filled a social void for the Black immigrant population that often felt overlooked. They provided socializing opportunities and fostered a sense of community in a new foreign city. They served as early insurance companies and provided members with security against illness and death, and in addition helped foster a common West Indian ethnic identity among Caribbean immigrants to the United States, providing immigrants with a way to conceptualize themselves as West Indian in addition to their specific island affiliations. Participation in these organizations allowed Caribbean immigrants frequent opportunities to collaborate and draw parallels among their experiences. Additionally, mutual aid societies strengthened kinship networks among immigrants in the United States and those back in the Caribbean, illustrating their deep concern with staying intimately connected to communities in the Caribbean.

Furthermore, through their involvement with these mutual aid societies and benevolent associations, which pushed international initiatives, Caribbean immigrants demonstrated their belief that their own fate was closely intertwined with the social, economic, and political welfare of the Black international community. As Caribbean immigrants integrated themselves into the American landscape through their participation in mutual aid societies and benevolent associations, they began to transform the goals of these organizations. No longer were they merely social or welcoming organizations for Caribbean immigrants; instead, they took on the political agendas of their members, who were deeply concerned with political issues faced by the new country in which they lived.

CHAPTER 4

Gendering the Migrant Experience

Caribbean Women's Roles in Social Organizations and Transnational Community Development

Following a female-led chain of migration typical of Caribbean immigrants in the twentieth century, Elizabeth Hendrickson, at the age of twelve, was sent by her family to New York City to live with one of her female relatives. Born on December 13, 1884, in Frederiksted, Saint Croix, in the Danish Virgin Islands (now the U.S. Virgin Islands), the youngest of three children and the only daughter, Elizabeth lived in Harlem with her aunt, Rosaline Fredricks.[1] Hendrickson attended P.S. 89 on 135th Street and Lenox Avenue. She later won a scholarship to attend the Rand School of Social Science, where she excelled at public speaking. At the age of twenty-four, she moved out of her aunt's home and into a boarding house on West 135th Street, where she lived with several other young immigrants from the Caribbean.[2] She worked as a laundress for the next several years and later went on to become a social worker.[3]

Hendrickson's life was marked by her initiatives and service in various Caribbean immigrant mutual aid societies and benevolent associations. In 1915, Hendrickson, along with several other Virgin Island women, founded the AWILAS. Its purpose was to foster connections and friendships among Caribbean American women as well as to address their concerns as both immigrant and minority women. Hendrickson served as president of the AWILAS from 1923 to 1928 and in various other executive board positions. Hendrickson's involvement with mutual aid societies in New York did not end with the AWILAS. She also served as the secretary of the Virgin Islands Congressional Council and of the Virgin Island Catholic Relief Committee, and she established the Benevolent Societies of the American Virgin Islands.

Hendrickson and Ashley L. Totten, a prominent Virgin Islander and national secretary-treasurer of the BSCP, co-founded the Virgin Islands Protective League. Hendrickson was also one of the founders of the Harlem Tenants League and served as its secretary. Established on February 12, 1928, with Captain Harry Allen Elys, Victor C. Gasper, and Grace P. Campbell, the league advocated on behalf of Harlem tenants against oppressive rent hikes and unsanitary conditions. Richard B. Moore later served as the president of the organization.[4] Additionally, Hendrickson served as the treasurer and secretary general of the Community Progressive Painter's Union, Inc., an organization of Black painters and decorators in the greater New York area. In 1928, the union broadened its scope to tackle wider labor issues affecting all Black workers in New York State. Hendrickson was also an active member of the Communist Party of the United States of the America, which was enthusiastically recruiting both Caribbean and African American women in the 1920s and 1930s. Hendrickson cited American-born A. Philip Randolph and his fight for better working conditions for laborers and the opposition of racial discrimination and oppression as a major influence on her own social and civic engagement. Similarly, Hendrickson advocated for the rights of Virgin Islanders and Caribbean people as a whole through her involvement with Caribbean immigrant mutual aid societies.

In the early twentieth century, the street corners of Harlem were filled with Black speakers expounding their political views, and Hendrickson joined their ranks as a passionate street corner speaker widely known among the Black community of New York City. Historian Irma Watkins-Owens notes: "the street corner became the most viable location for an alternative politics and the place where new social movements gained a hearing and recruited supporters."[5] As a result, Hendrickson was frequently asked to speak at events for the New York Colored Democratic Association, the National Joint Conference Committee, and many other groups.

Through her involvement with various Caribbean immigrant organizations, Hendrickson collaborated with numerous influential Caribbean leaders and mutual aid societies in New York to educate and inform their members of the wider social, economic, and political oppression faced by people in the U.S. Virgin Islands and the larger Caribbean region. In 1918, she and Ashley L. Totten were chosen as delegates to the U.S. Virgin Islands to collect firsthand information on the conditions on the islands after their incorporation as territories of the United States. And in 1920, Hendrickson was instrumental in helping fellow Virgin Islander and civil rights activist

Rothschild Francis to fundraise and secure the finances necessary to establish his seminal newspaper the *Emancipator* (published in Saint Thomas, U.S. Virgin Islands) that discussed social, economic, and political matters relevant to all peoples of the Caribbean basin.

Advocating for Caribbean and African American women's rights was another major priority for Hendrickson. Through the AWILAS and her involvement in several other social organizations, Hendrickson made it a priority to not just symbolically include women in the conversations, but to integrate their issues into the agenda. She made sure that Caribbean immigrant mutual aid societies were a place where women's voices were heard and their concerns addressed. She regularly used these groups as a platform to advocate for women's issues and encourage Black women to participate in political and social justice movements. In a 1928 *New York Age* newspaper article titled "Working Women Asked to Attend Celebration," colored women workers were urged to attend the celebration of the Painters' Union on March 29 of that same year. There is no doubt that as an executive board member of this organization, Hendrickson was involved with this call for more women's involvement in the union.[6]

At the turn of the twentieth century, there were few opportunities for women at large, and Black immigrant women in particular, to hold leadership positions in organizations in order to voice their political beliefs. Not until the passage of the Nineteenth Amendment in 1920 were American women allowed to vote or run for public office. Hendrickson's story demonstrates how Caribbean immigrant mutual aid societies and benevolent associations gave Caribbean women the opening to assume leadership roles unavailable to women overall. These mutual aid organizations opened a door for Caribbean women.

By examining the prominence of female members of Caribbean mutual aid societies, this chapter challenges the historiography of Caribbean immigration that tends to privilege the male experience. Familiar frameworks of Caribbean migratory trends foreground, as Tina Campt and Deborah Thomas observe, "the mobility of masculine subjects as the primary agents of diasporic formation and perpetuate a more general masculinism in the conceptualization of diasporic community."[7]

As their participation in mutual aid societies demonstrates, Caribbean women were active and influential participants in the immigration experience, not just passive bystanders. As we have seen, immigrant mutual aid societies served as training grounds for female Caribbean leaders such as

Elizabeth Hendrickson. In addition to Hendrickson, numerous other women took advantage of these groups, using them as platforms to discuss social issues and political reform, and in the process gained professional experience organizing and running organizations. These mutual aid societies empowered immigrant women to become involved in organizing and political activism. As the practice of mutual aid is inherently political, these groups also proved to be a built-in audience for female leaders and would eventually become a political base. In heavily male-dominated mutual aid societies, women frequently organized their own auxiliary groups; they took on important executive positions and ran their own programs, ensuring that their views and interests were addressed, even forming exclusively female mutual aid societies like the AWILAS.

Mutual aid societies and benevolent associations helped immigrant women create formal and informal networks. The activities and social events hosted by these associations provided Caribbean immigrants living in New York City an opportunity to form social relationships with other Caribbean immigrants, including women, connecting more established immigrants who may have already been in the United States for some time with newly arrived immigrants. This allowed immigrants the opportunity to exchange their experiences and advice for navigating their new city. This form of social networking created a sense of community for Caribbean immigrants in New York. Moreover, through these mutual aid societies, Caribbean women were able to stay connected to their home islands. Through their relief efforts, charity work, and collaboration with other Caribbean organizations, female members of these New York mutual aid societies and benevolent associations created larger diasporic networks that kept them abreast of events happening in the Caribbean and connected to their West Indian identity.

Through these organizations Caribbean women were able to stay connected to the homeland, but they also utilized these mutual aid societies to celebrate their ethnic identities in the United States. For example, the BBA held an annual Bermuda Week, a week of events celebrating the history and culture of Bermuda.[8] Other groups, like the St. Lucia United Association, held events such as annual heritage dances that highlighted Saint Lucian culture.[9] Caribbean women thus created new communities that celebrated their ethnic identities for themselves and their families within the larger American community.

This chapter demonstrates that it is indisputable that women served as vital proponents of Caribbean culture in the United States in the early twentieth century. A failure to take account of the activities and achievements of

Caribbean women in this period leaves us with only half the story: an inadequate analysis of the formation of diasporic and transnational identity, of Caribbean American identity and community, and the relationship between culture and politics. An examination of the role of Caribbean women in mutual aid societies and benevolent associations is essential to shaping complex and diverse immigrant narratives. Women must be placed at the center of diasporic formation as indispensable agents in forging diasporic connections.

Women in Mutual Aid Societies and Benevolent Associations

Caribbean immigrant women played a vital role as founders of and participants in mutual aid societies and benevolent associations in the early twentieth century. Additionally, numerous women took on leadership positions in these organizations. Annie Joell served as the president of the BBA in 1901.

Figure 2. Bermuda Benevolent Association House Committee. *Source:* Bermuda Benevolent Association Records, 1898–1969. Manuscripts, Archives, and Rare Books Division, Schomburg Center for Research in Black Culture. Dated November 1947. Seventeen members of the BBA's House Committee are depicted in Fig.1; twelve of them are women.

Figure 3. Bermuda Benevolent Association Ways and Means Committee. *Source:* Bermuda Benevolent Association Records, 1898–1969. Manuscripts, Archives, and Rare Books Division, Schomburg Center for Research in Black Culture. Twelve of the sixteen BBA Ways and Means Committee members pictured are women.

Edith Gilbert Hawkins (Fig. 4), a charter member of the BBA, served as the association's vice president and treasurer.[10] Gladys Innis served as vice president of the Nassau Bahamas Social and Beneficial Club in 1912.[11] Although their presence and participation overall is not always reflected in the leadership of some Caribbean mutual aid societies, women made up a large percentage of the general membership. The participation of Caribbean women in immigrant mutual aid societies and benevolent associations was equal to and oftentimes surpassed that of men. As Chart 5 in Chapter 3 shows, many groups like the APS saw higher female membership enrollments on a yearly basis. Photographs from the BBA in the 1930s and 1940s show the large number of women involved in various committees. In a photo of the BBA's House Committee (Fig. 2), seventeen members are pictured and more than half of them (12) are women. Similarly, a picture of the BBA's Ways and Means

MRS. EDITH (GILBERT) HAWKINS
CHARTER MEMBER
Has served the Association as Vice-President and Treasurer

Figure 4. Bermuda Benevolent Association Charter Member—Edith Hawkins. *Source:* Bermuda Benevolent Association Records, 1898–1969. Manuscripts, Archives, and Rare Books Division, Schomburg Center for Research in Black Culture.

Committee (Fig. 3) shows that 75 percent (12 of the 16) committee members pictured are women. "Women were always there, especially unmarried women," according to former Jamaican Associates president Dr. Doreen Wilkinson, who also noted that women "were always more active in these groups."[12] Women were the backbone of many Caribbean immigrant mutual aid societies and benevolent associations. They served on a disproportionate number of planning and organizing committees, responsible for the daily operations of the mutual aid societies, including planning and executing meetings and activities.

Elizabeth Hendrickson was an extraordinarily politically active immigrant by any standard for men or women, but her involvement with multiple organizations was not uncommon. At the start of the twentieth century, many Caribbean immigrant women held membership in two or more mutual aid societies and benevolent associations. For instance, Virgin Islander Isabelle George was a member of the AWILAS, the Federation of American Virgin Islands Society, the United Benevolent & Social League, and the Virgin Island Civic and Industrial Association. Ivy Simons was a member of both the BBA and the United Benevolent Association. The desire of Caribbean women to expand their social networks and attend to their particular interests often resulted in their holding multiple memberships in female-only, coeducational, or auxiliary organizations.

Women were also integral to the founding of many Caribbean mutual aid societies and benevolent associations in this period. For instance, Ernestine McNeil-Rogers was one of the two original founders of the Jamaican Associates, Inc. of Boston, established in 1934.[13] In 1934, when the APS was founded, half of the society's original members were women.[14] One of these founders was Salome Drysdale, an immigrant from the Antigua who came to New York in 1917 at the age of fourteen.[15] Drysdale was so committed to the mission of the APS that she mortgaged her own home to help purchase the society's headquarters building, the Antigua House located at 12 West 122nd Street in Harlem.[16] Years later, members of the APS continue to commemorate Drysdale's legacy and leadership. The main meeting space at the now renamed Antigua and Barbuda House is named Salome Drysdale Hall in honor of Drysdale. Additionally, an award was established in her name—the Salome Drysdale Award of Excellence for Women. Drysdale would also serve as president of the APS.[17]

In mutual aid societies not established by women, male founders often included women in the language of their society's constitution. For instance, the authors of the constitution of the BVIBA made it clear that although the language of the association's bylaws used male pronouns, the mutual aid society openly welcomed women as members, illustrating the group's strong desire to incorporate and encourage female participation.[18] The MPS's constitution and bylaws also explicitly stated that one of their goals as a society was to unite "our brothers and sisters," language that highlights the desire of these immigrant mutual aid societies to include female membership.[19] Most importantly, the substantive policies enacted by mutual aid societies and benevolent associations reflected their inclusion of women. For example, when the APS formed a special committee at the request of the Antiguan government for the improvement of conditions on the island of Antigua, the APS committee advocated for Antiguan women's rights. The APS recommended that women working in agriculture and other manual labor or in government or public service receive a minimum wage,[20] demonstrating the society's commitment not only to the inclusion of women, but to providing equity and real opportunities for women.

There are several explanations for the large rate of female participation in Caribbean immigrant mutual aid societies and benevolent associations.

Statistically, in the early twentieth century there were simply more female Caribbean immigrants in the United States than male immigrants.[21] An official report by American Vice Consul William T. Hunt Jr., Director of the U.S. census of 1921, confirms that "the great majority of the immigrants are women."[22] The sheer number of female Caribbean immigrants present in the United States during this period certainly accounts for their high participation in mutual aid societies. However, another factor was at play. In the twentieth century, Caribbean women were largely responsible for creating chains of migration that brought groups of new Caribbean immigrants, especially other women, to the United States. These immigrant women often set up housing arrangements for or boarded other immigrants, and introduced them in turn to their social networks, mutual aid societies and benevolent associations.

As mentioned previously, Ivy Simons stated that her own two aunts came to New York seeking a better life. The two women lived together on 116th Street in Harlem, both working as domestic servants. They were influential in her own decision to immigrate to the United States. Simons recalls that her aunts were also indispensable in making her feel welcome when she first arrived in New York in the 1940s. They helped her secure housing and establish herself in the city by introducing her to the BBA and their networks of other Caribbean immigrants in New York. "I joined the Bermuda [Benevolent] Association soon after I came here [to New York]," said Ivy, "because that was just automatic; you had to be in the association. My aunts and uncles were all members . . . they knew everybody . . . they had a lot of activities."[23] In adjusting to American life, she credited her membership in a mutual aid society with giving her a built-in social network of other Caribbean immigrants, many whom had been in the United States for some time and had various levels of experience with American society. Mutual aid societies appealed to Caribbean women like Simons because they gave them a sense of home in their new city, and they were one of the few places where the women could address the specific issues they faced as Black female immigrants.

Within heavily male-dominated associations, women frequently organized their own auxiliary groups; they took on important executive positions and ran their own programs, ensuring that their views and interests were addressed.[24] Although it was originally a men's only organization, women played a major role in the development of the West Indian Social Club of Hartford, Connecticut. In 1954, some of the members' wives decided to form a Ladies Auxiliary comprised of women who were either West Indian or related to other members by birth, blood, or marriage. Connie Mills served as the West Indian

Social Club of Hartford's Ladies Auxiliary's first president.[25] Together, these women organized their own programs and assisted male members in their projects as well. In this capacity, women were able to wield full control and take on executive positions that might not have otherwise been open to them.

The West Indian Social Club of Hartford along with the Ladies Auxiliary was instrumental in establishing the West Indian Independence Celebration Committee, which hosted a week of cultural festivities that connected people from across Connecticut and the Caribbean. The groups also established the West Indian Foundation in 1978 to promote and encourage "the strong cultural, social and economic status of West Indians in the city [of Hartford]," by hosting a number of educational, cultural and civic activities.[26] Prominent female members of the group include former city councilwoman and deputy mayor of Hartford, Veronica Airey-Wilson, who served as the first female president of the West Indian Social Club in 1989. Subsequent female presidents of the group included: Alred Dyce, Phd; Doreth Flowers; and Doreen Forest.[27]

American West Indian Ladies Aid Society (AWILAS)

As we have seen, Caribbean women formed their own mutual aid societies and benevolent associations that catered specifically to their needs as immigrant women. One of the most successful women's organizations, spanning more than half a century, was the AWILAS. Founded in 1915 and active well into the 1960s, the AWILAS was a mutual aid society that later served as an umbrella organization for numerous Caribbean American women's organizations. The society's purpose was to establish camaraderie among Caribbean immigrant women. The organization—like others of its kind, both male and female—offered its members sick and death benefits, mutual assistance, and a meeting place to discuss their opinions and find their way in their new country. The society organized various social events such as teas, dances, and bid whist parties, as well as programs on child rearing and the naturalization process. However, most importantly, the AWILAS served as a home away from home for Caribbean women, where they could discuss the problems they faced as both immigrant and minority women in an unfamiliar city.

The AWILAS was an invaluable resource for Caribbean immigrant women navigating life in a new city. It functioned as an important community for its members, connecting a wide array of Caribbean women. As noted above, a sampling of the organization's membership records demonstrates

that Caribbean women of various ages and socioeconomic standing participated in the society. New applicants ranged in age from eighteen to forty-six
years, with various occupations, including students, housewives, and domestic workers. Additionally, both married and unmarried women joined the
AWILAS, reflecting the appeal this organization had for numerous Caribbean women. Through their memberships in the AWILAS, Caribbean women
formed very close relationships with one another and created intimate kinship
networks. Many early Caribbean women immigrated to the United States by
themselves, leaving behind family and friends in the Caribbean. Once in the
United States, they usually had one relative or close family friend who served
as their guide and helped them settle into their new homes, similar to Ivy
Simons and her two aunts.

Mutual aid societies and benevolent associations provided intimate networks for Caribbean immigrant women by establishing death and sick benefits for members, as well as visiting committees, which kept track of members'
well-being. The AWILAS provided members such as C. Simmonde two weeks
of sick benefits in 1928 and Maud McFarlane a sick benefit of $30 for five weeks
in 1929. Services such as this provided a great sense of relief and a safety net
for immigrants who fell sick and could not work.[28] In addition to monetary
benefits, the AWILAS had a visiting committee that made wellness checks and
brought flowers to ill members in the hospital to keep them in good spirits.
In this way, mutual aid societies helped members feel less alienated and more
connected, providing their members with a sense of community. This type
of kinship had a very powerful impact on members, as is illustrated by the
records of the AWILAS, which are littered with dozens of letters and cards
from members thanking the society for their compassion and generosity. In
one letter, AWILAS member Beatrice B. Matthews expressed her gratitude to
the AWILAS: "Please accept my sincere thanks and appreciation for your very
kind and thoughtful gift of flowers during my recent illness, also those members that called to see me. I feel deeply greatful [sic]."[29] Matthews's note, along
with a dozen others just like it, demonstrates the significance the AWILAS
and other mutual aid societies and benevolent associations had on the lives of
Caribbean immigrant women. Mutual aid societies like the AWILAS filled the
role that familial networks once played in immigrant women's lives.

Most notably, the AWILAS was forward-looking and served as a gateway
to collaborate and connect with other mutual aid societies, both Caribbean
and African American. AWILAS archives contain a great deal of correspondence between the society and other groups such as the United Brothers and

Sisters of the United Islands, Saint Benedict Ladies' Auxiliary No. 204 (an African American women's group), and the BSCP and its Ladies Auxiliary. These organizations sought to work with and for the social and political benefit of Caribbean immigrant women and their families. Members of the AWILAS invited Caribbean women to their organizational meetings as well as social activities. In the records of the AWILAS, there are invitations from other Caribbean mutual aid societies and benevolent associations, such as the American Virgin Islands Society, inviting the women of the AWILAS to one of their meetings where they had a presentation by a physician named Dr. Baker.[30] Collaboration among Caribbean women's groups was very common and is demonstrated in the high percentage of correspondence between Caribbean women's groups recorded in the AWILAS's records.

The AWILAS and other Caribbean women's mutual aid societies and benevolent associations worked extensively with American women's groups. The AWILAS often served as a point of connection between the two groups of women. In a 1934 letter, Sarah E. Mahoney-Messer, Chairlady of the Saint Benedict Ladies' Auxiliary No. 204, requested that the women of the AWILAS join the Ladies' Auxiliary's "Sunshine Club" for a social event. Members of the AWILAS were in attendance and later sent a thank-you letter to the "Sunshine Club" for having them at their event.[31] Other African American groups like the Eton Benevolence Society sought out the women of the AWILAS in order to forge connections between the two groups of Black women. In a letter addressed to the AWILAS, Eton Benevolence Society members wrote, "seeking to establish a bond of unity and friendship between your organisation [sic] and ours, [through this medium we] ask your permission to send a representative at your next meeting, who will make the request and as we hope establish soon."[32] Letters like these illustrate the value African American women saw in working with Caribbean women's mutual aid societies. Equally, Caribbean women in immigrant mutual aid societies and benevolent associations understood the importance of forging networks with African American organizations to their success in the United States.

Leadership Training Grounds

Caribbean immigrant mutual aid societies and benevolent associations served as leadership training grounds for Caribbean immigrant women. These groups gave Caribbean women, such as Elizabeth Hendrickson, a platform to discuss an array of issues ranging from social and political reform to transnational concerns. They empowered immigrant women to become involved in organizing and political activism, giving them a built-in audience and political base.

Women such as Elizabeth Hendrickson, who emerged from these organizations, used their positions and experience to venture into other endeavors. Utilizing the leadership skills and professional experience organizing and running mutual aid societies she had gained from the AWILAS, Hendrickson then went on to co-found the Harlem Tenants League in 1928, which advocated for improved housing conditions for Harlem residents. She also served as the treasurer and secretary general of the Community Progressive Painter's Union, Inc., an organization dedicated to fighting for labor issues affecting all Black New York workers. Hendrickson would eventually feel empowered enough to take her oratory skills to the street corners of Harlem, where she became a prominent soapbox speaker. She also used her platform in mutual aid societies and benevolent associations to mobilize support for various social justice campaigns. Many of her fellow society members would also serve as her soapbox audience, highlighting the fact that immigrant mutual aid societies provided female leaders with a built-in base of supporters.

Ivy Simons, similar to Hendrickson, used her involvement in Caribbean immigrant mutual aid societies and benevolent associations to gain leadership skills and experience. As mentioned earlier in this chapter, her aunts were responsible for introducing her to their network of Caribbean immigrants, which centered around the BBA.[33] Simons would eventually work her way up in the association, and in 1959 she was elected president of the BBA, serving three consecutive terms. Within the association, Simons held several other leadership positions, including chaplain, financial secretary, chair of the Forum Committee and House Committee, chair of the Board of Trustees, and she was elected a lifetime member of the Executive Board.[34] Simons did not limit her involvement to only the BBA; she was actively involved in multiple Caribbean social organizations and held various leadership positions, including serving as the vice president of the United Benevolent Societies of New York and the financial secretary of the UBS Holding Corporation. After being introduced to the Grace Congregational Church parishioners in Harlem through her involvement with the BBA, Simons joined the church in 1959 and would go on to serve on the Board of Directors of its Credit Union. She was also elected a deacon in the church and served as chair of the Board of Deacons.[35]

Simons was actively involved within the BBA and used her membership in the association to become politically active in her community. Through the BBA, she marched in demonstrations to advocate for reform in the New York City public school system, participated in worker's strikes, and became an active member in her local union. Many women similar to Hendrickson and Simons used their participation in Caribbean mutual aid societies and benevolent associations to take on leadership positions in their communities, such as Veronica Airey-Wilson who served as the first female president of the West Indian Social Club of Hartford in 1989. Five years later in 1994, Airey-Wilson was elected to the Hartford Court of Common Council as a councilwoman. In 2003, she became the first Jamaican to serve as the city's deputy mayor. Additionally, she served as co-chair of the Youth Workforce Development Task Force, an executive member of the Capital Region Council of Government Joint Policy Steering Committee, chair of the Republican State Convention, and an executive member of the Capital Region Council of Government Joint Policy Board.[36] Mutual aid societies and benevolent associations were often one of the few outlets in which Black immigrant women could hold positions of power and influence and many immigrant women used them to do just that.

Formal and Informal Networks

Caribbean immigrant mutual aid societies and benevolent associations allowed immigrants a way to highlight and celebrate their ethnic identities, create a community within the United States, and remain connected to their communities back home in the Caribbean. Female members of these associations played a significant role in this process, as they were the majority members of many of these organizations and played a large role in their daily operations, programming, and mutual aid organizing. Through mutual aid societies and benevolent associations' activities and social events, immigrant women created a system of formal and informal networks that brought together Caribbean immigrants from various socioeconomic backgrounds. Involvement in Caribbean mutual aid societies also helped to connect more established Caribbean immigrants with newly arrived immigrants, allowing them the opportunity to exchange their immigrant experiences and share advice for living in a new foreign country, particularly one that was extremely segregated. Moreover, they helped the children of Caribbean immigrants to connect to and learn about their heritage through their juvenile auxiliary groups. These groups provided a model for younger immigrant children, as well as the second generation of Caribbean immigrants, not only to continue the tradition of mutual aid societies and benevolent associations in the United States but to foster a sense of ethnic identity in children who were not born in the Caribbean. Through these mutual aid societies and benevolent associations, the children of Caribbean immigrants cultivated kinship networks that were essential to the survival of Caribbean immigrant groups in the United States. Caribbean women were at the forefront of these processes.

Female association members like Ivy Simons and Elizabeth Hendrickson organized events such as Bermuda Week.[37] Simons, who served on the BBA's executive board in various capacities, undoubtedly played a large role in establishing these types of cultural events. When Saint Lucia gained independence from the British in 1979, the St. Lucia United Association held celebrations to commemorate the historic moment. Annually, they continued to host events leading up to Saint Lucian independence in order to celebrate the history and culture of the island. Such occasions fostered strong bonds between Caribbean immigrants living in New York and effectively created a sense of community. They also helped immigrants maintain a connection to their home islands in the Caribbean.

Female members of immigrant mutual aid societies in New York were responsible for creating diasporic networks that helped keep them abreast of events occurring in the Caribbean through the relief efforts, charity work, and a constant stream of collaboration with groups in the Caribbean. For instance, when a hurricane hit the island of Saint Thomas in 1928, members of the BVIBA quickly organized to form an emergency relief committee under the suggestion of association president A. Waters and female member Z. Henly. Henly, along with other association members, proposed the idea of having an agent in Saint Thomas who could keep the organization abreast of news from the island as well as the immediate needs of residents on the island. Henly, along with several other women of the BVIBA, volunteered to spearhead the committee.[38] Women in Caribbean immigrant mutual aid societies and benevolent associations often had their eye on creating and maintaining transnational connections with their home islands. This is evident in the correspondence recorded in their organizational records.

Conclusion

In summary, an examination of the role female Caribbean immigrant women in mutual aid societies and benevolent associations in New York City is essential in shaping a more complex and diverse immigrant narrative. As the founders and often the majority of participants in these groups, immigrant women preserved Caribbean culture in the United States and played an important role in the formation of ethnically distinct Caribbean communities. Caribbean women used these associations to celebrate their ethnic identities within the larger American community of the United States, and to create new communities for themselves and their families while staying connected to the homeland. They acted collectively through these organizations, helping family members immigrate to the United States by raising money to pay for their relatives' passage, and also supported family back home through remittances. Women's involvement in mutual aid societies provided Caribbean immigrants with the community and kinship networks they needed to survive upon their arrival in the United States. Through their formal and informal social networks, Caribbean women helped pave the way for Caribbean immigration to the United States.

The following chapter explores the political turn that Caribbean American mutual aid societies and benevolent associations took as they moved into the latter part of the twentieth century and the aims of the members of these groups grew increasingly more political.

CHAPTER 5

Community Building and Political Mobilization

Forging a Caribbean and Black Identity

The beginning of the twentieth century was a turbulent time for Black people in America, a time that would ultimately result in widespread political engagement among men and women in the Black community, both native and foreign-born. Dubbed "the nadir of American race relations" by historian Rayford Logan, the period between 1880 and 1919 was characterized by racial discrimination and extreme violence toward Black populations. More than thirty violent and deadly race riots erupted in cities across the United States between the summer and early autumn of 1919—named the "Red Summer" by civil rights leader James Weldon Johnson—claiming the lives of hundreds of Black people. The lynching of Black people was also a common occurrence in this period. In 1919, the NAACP reported that an estimated 3,224 people had been lynched by white mobs throughout the United States between 1889 and 1918. While Black men made up the majority of victims, a small percentage of Black women were also lynched. Most lynchings occurred in the South, and Black Americans accounted for more than 70 percent of those deaths.[1] More recent estimates of the number of lynchings between 1889 and 1963 total more than four thousand.[2]

This period was also characterized by the passing of discriminatory immigration laws that severely curtailed the admission of nonwhite immigrants into the United States. In addition, segregationist voting laws robbed minority groups—especially people of African descent—of their voting rights. All in all, coupled with the numerous inequitable and segregationist laws that took away voting rights and oppressed minority groups in the United States, the early twentieth century was a period of great hardship for people of African descent.

The Black community in the United States mobilized politically in response to the racial antipathy, violence, and discriminatory laws that characterized this period, lobbying for civil rights that included anti-lynching laws, better housing, civil rights, voting rights, and educational and immigration reform. Some groups even proposed emigration as a solution to these issues, believing that there was no place and would never be a place for Black people in a structurally racist American society; some activists urged Black people to establish their own colonies in West Africa. Not surprisingly, radical ideas uniting Black Americans with those in Africa and the larger African Diaspora gained currency throughout the United States, striking a chord in many Black communities and gaining great popularity. In fact, this period was characterized by a deluge of intellectual and political ideas and conversation among Black communities throughout the world.

New York City, in particular, became a hotbed of Black radical politics, with West Indian immigrants taking the lead. Among these groups were the Universal Negro Improvement Association (UNIA), which established a New York City chapter in 1917 by Jamaican-born Marcus Garvey; the Liberty League, under the direction of Hubert Harrison of Saint Croix, founded in the same year; and the African Blood Brotherhood for African Liberation and Redemption (ABB), founded in 1919 by Cyril Briggs of Nevis. These leaders and their organizations advocated for Black self-determination and political equality. Caribbean mutual aid societies and benevolent associations, undoubtedly influenced by coetaneous radical Black organizations such as the UNIA, became more politically active, advocating not only for protection from discrimination and violence, but for full unfettered civil rights. These organizations hosted politicians and political activists at their meetings, held political rallies, and partnered with African American groups like the BSCP to find solutions to the injustices they faced. In doing so, members of Caribbean immigrant mutual aid societies and benevolent associations took a more diasporic view of the social injustices affecting Black people throughout the world. The welfare of people of African descent across the globe became a clear and pressing concern for many of these organizations in the twentieth century.

This era became a transitional period in which the objectives of Caribbean immigrant mutual aid societies and benevolent associations grew progressively more political and began to move beyond their initial goals of facilitating the adjustment of Caribbean immigrants to the United States and forming social networks with other Caribbean immigrants. As association members became

more settled in the United States, their concerns began to move beyond simple acclimation and their associations broadened their objectives to meet this
need. The Scottsboro trials of 1931, in particular, mark one of the poignant
junctures in the politicization of Caribbean American mutual aid societies.

Influenced by the idea of a unified Black identity, Caribbean American
mutual aid societies and benevolent associations joined together with African American organizations to fight racial discrimination and inequality.
Through their participation in these groups, Caribbean immigrants were
able to build on their existing social networks and mobilize politically with
African Americans to champion issues that affected the Black community as
a whole. As a result, their mutual aid societies' objectives—which had always
inherently been political—became more explicit in their actions and began to
address issues affecting the wider Black community. Members of Caribbean
immigrant mutual aid societies and benevolent associations frequently collaborated with African Americans with whom they shared the same neighborhoods, occupations, and common experiences. Caribbean mutual aid and
benevolent association members, in many cases, simultaneously developed
a Caribbean identity and a Black American identity. Consequently, mutual
aid societies' events and activities took on a more diasporic lens. They held
programs that reflected their new perceived identities as members of an African Diaspora and unleashed a political activism among immigrants to ensure
their equality in the tumultuous Jim Crow era.

Caribbean immigrants in New York were not only actively engaged with
the welfare of Black people in the United States, they were also deeply invested
in events occurring in the Caribbean. This chapter argues that these mutual
aid societies helped create a transnational space for Anglophone Caribbean
immigrants where they could engage with the political landscapes of their
home islands and the greater Caribbean region. Caribbean immigrants' growing political agenda is further highlighted by the transnational concerns of
their mutual aid societies and emphasized in the international initiatives
these organizations implemented to help people of African descent within the
Caribbean and throughout the world. Many mutual aid societies gave scholarships to students in the Caribbean, provided relief for islands hit by natural
disasters, and actively followed political elections and labor strikes occurring
in the Caribbean. Through their involvement with these mutual aid societies
and benevolent associations, which advanced clear international initiatives,
Caribbean immigrants demonstrated the belief that their own fate was closely
intertwined with the social, economic, and political welfare of the Black

international community. Investigating the political activities of Caribbean mutual aid societies and benevolent associations illuminates a strong link between mutual aid organizing and larger political movements. This chapter illustrates the ways in which "economics, politics, and culture [are] inextricably linked."[3] Caribbean immigrants through their memberships in Caribbean mutual aid societies utilized their ethnic identities and culture to create communities and ultimately a tool with which to engage in political activism in the United States and the wider African Diaspora. In hosting social events these mutual aid societies provided a platform for their members to forge the networks that would eventually culminate in political mobilization.

Political Landscape

By the beginning of the twentieth century, African Americans had long been living with the failure of Reconstruction that followed the U.S. Civil War (1861-1865). Although Reconstruction (1865-1877) was initially touted as a period of great hope and opportunity for Black people in America, its promises were far from ever being fully realized. During Reconstruction, the United States took progressive steps toward creating racial equality with the passage of the Fourteenth and Fifteenth Amendments, which respectively granted Black Americans full citizenship rights and equal protection under the Constitution, and Black men the right to vote. The Fifteenth Amendment, Section One, proclaimed that "the right of citizens of the United States to vote shall not be denied or abridged by the United States or by any State on account of race, color, or previous condition of servitude."[4]

Reconstruction saw Black men elected to state and local political positions, including Hiram R. Revels, the first Black man elected to the U.S. Senate, in 1870.[5] Historian Eric Foner notes that between 1869 and 1901, twenty Black men were elected to the House and two were elected to the Senate. In total, he estimates that around 1,500 Black men held official offices at the local, state, and federal level.[6] After Reconstruction ended, Black men and women lost nearly all the political, economic, and social gains of Reconstruction. In the South, the Jim Crow era saw increasing violence against Black populations and the loss of most of their civil rights. Black politicians elected during Reconstruction were voted out of office and replaced with white Democratic politicians, who enacted laws rescinding the Reconstruction rights and protections of Blacks Southerners.

In the North, Black people were not much safer than their compatriots in the South and were also threatened by racial antagonism and violence. New York City saw a major race riot between African Americans and white citizens in 1900, following the wrongful accusation of a Black woman, May Enoch, for loitering and prostitution by an off-duty white police officer. Enoch's husband, Arthur Harris, not knowing the man was a police officer, came to her defense and confronted him. The officer struck Harris with his billy club. Harris then drew a knife and fatally stabbed the officer, who died several days later. This event resulted in a wave of violent outbursts for several days throughout the city, with white mobs brutally attacking Black men. A news report from the Associated Press chronicled the chaos and violence: "Such a furious ebullition of race hatred as found vent in the rioting occurred here last night . . . has not been equaled in many years. There were about fifty persons injured by pistol balls, razors or knives, rocks, and clubs." The rioting took place between "the whole of the West Side from Twenty-eight street to Longacre Square, above Forty-second street, including Eighth and Ninth avenues," and more than forty arrests were made.[7] Large sections of Manhattan were in an uproar. The mainly white Irish police force did little to contain the disorder and violence and, in some cases, encouraged it. As a result, the mayor of the city was forced to call in military reserves to quell the violent clashes. The Black community in New York City feared for their safety and had little faith in the local police force.[8] The rioting left a great sense of tension among white and Black New Yorkers.

Racial antagonism continued to grow between 1916 and 1920, as the Great Migration brought half a million Black Southerners into already over-crowded urban centers in northern and midwestern cities; another one million followed in the 1920s.[9] Northward migration increased as the need for industrial labor grew, fueled by the First World War in 1914 and expanding the number of factory jobs available to Blacks. Black Southerners looking for better economic opportunities arrived in northern and midwestern cities to fill these vacancies. Black individuals from the South, however, found themselves competing with northern and midwestern white and Black populations and other recent immigrant groups for jobs. This competition for jobs, coupled with mass overcrowding and health concerns, led to even more tensions between Black and white communities, sparking a series of race riots throughout the nation, most notably the Red Summer riots that occurred during the summer and fall of 1919. These riots were some of the most violent and deadliest racial conflicts in U.S. history, with more than two hundred Black people killed and many more injured.

Further afield, international events wreaked havoc on Black populations on the African continent as European imperial powers fought the First World War and further divided the continent. Anticolonial feelings grew throughout the African Diaspora, as Black individuals in the Diaspora increasingly found themselves invested in events occurring in the larger Black world, especially the African continent. Leaders such as Jamaican-born Marcus Garvey were dedicated to "Africa's redemption, Africa's freedom, and Africa's liberty."[10]

In this period, Caribbean immigrants and African Americans alike leaned into a growing sense of Black internationalism, demonstrated by the concerted effort of members of the African Diaspora to forge transnational collaborations and solidarities with people of African descent around the world in response to imperialism and colonialism. Historian Keisha Blain describes Black internationalism as "the political and cultural ways in which Black communities collectively raised questions of struggle and liberation on a global scale; [it] captures the various ways Black people built relationships with other communities across the globe."[11] Moreover, she states that Black people in the Diaspora believed that freedom would come through a global political, intellectual, and artistic movement of African-descended people engaged in a collective struggle to overthrow global white supremacy in its many forms.[12] Caribbean immigrant mutual aid societies embraced an ideology of Black internationalism in their own organizational agendas.[13]

As the world moved into the 1930s and unknowingly toward another world war, people of African descent were deeply aware of events occurring globally and closely followed the Italian invasion of Ethiopia in 1935. Ethiopia had long been a bastion of Black freedom in the African Diaspora and seen as a symbol of hope and freedom from racial and colonial oppression.[14] So on October 3, 1935, when Italian troops under the direction of fascist dictator Benito Mussolini launched a full-scale attack and invaded the only independent African nation at the time, the Diaspora took notice. Italian forces defied international law and indiscriminately used the full force of their modern weaponry, including poisonous gas, on the country.[15] Many believed this to be direct retaliation for the first Italian invasion of Ethiopia in 1896, when Italian attempts at conquest were shut down by Ethiopian forces at the battle of Adwa.[16] In addition, Italy had a vested interest in furthering its stronghold in East Africa, having already occupied neighboring Eritrea, Libya, and Somalia. Ethiopian emperor Menelik II was regarded as a hero throughout the African Diaspora, as he was able to successfully defeat the Italian army and maintain Ethiopia's status as the only African nation free of European control.

Consequently, the Second Italo-Ethiopian War was a matter of great concern for members of the African Diaspora. Black populations in America, including Caribbean immigrants, saw the Italian invasion and eventual defeat of Ethiopia as a major setback in their collective struggle for freedom and equality, especially during the turbulent 1930s when racial injustice was prevalent in the United States. Leaders like George Padmore believed that Black individuals in the Diaspora must "unite with Ethiopia and declare a 'Holy War' against the whites [and] drive them out of Africa."[17] Arturo Schomburg served on the advisory board for the Ethiopian World Federation, Inc., a Harlem-based organization dedicated to "the cause of right, justice, and independence of Ethiopia."[18] The UNIA provided frequent updates on the war and called for people of African descent to provide aid to Ethiopia: "The hour of negro progress is here and every man and woman of the race must 'pitch in' and do their bit to bring everlasting success to the scattered children of Ethiopia."[19] Dominican poet and Pan-Africanist J. R. Ralph Casimir corresponded with Ethiopian minister Dr. Asaj Martin and even sent funds collected from his own Ethiopian Defense Fund. In a letter to Martin, Casimir expressed his sense of international Black solidarity: "I can assure you that the Negroes (Africans and people of African descent) throughout the world are prepared to help Ethiopia in her hour of distress through which I hope she will emerge victoriously to attain a glorious and progressive future."[20] The range of Black internationalism is also illustrated by buildings in Harlem named in honor of Ethiopian leaders; groups such as the ABB named their headquarters buildings in honor of Ethiopian leaders. Thus, buildings with names like Post Menelik and the Ethiopian Federation Hall were prevalent throughout Harlem.[21]

Members of Caribbean mutual aid societies and benevolent associations equally lent their support to Ethiopia during the war. They hosted several joint meetings of mutual aid societies to discuss a course of action they could take to aid the Ethiopian army. Additionally, members of the BBA attended meetings hosted by the editors of *The African: Journal of African Affairs*—which was the literary organ of the Universal Ethiopian Students' Association established in 1937—inviting their members to discuss the Italian occupation of Ethiopia. The Universal Ethiopian Students' Association (UESA), established in 1927 by Arnold Hodge, a Trinidadian immigrant in Harlem, mobilized the Black community to fight against imperialism, colonialism, and fascist Italy. The objectives of the group were greatly influenced by the ideals of Ethiopianism, Black Nationalism, the New Negro Movement, Garveyism, communism, and Pan-Africanism.[22] Members of the BBA also helped plan a Peace Parade Conference that met to discuss actions they could take to aid the Ethiopian people in their fight for independence.[23] They joined together with other Caribbean mutual aid societies and African American organizations such as the American League for Peace and Democracy. One resolution was to collect money to purchase surgical supplies for wounded Ethiopian soldiers.[24] They saw this as a tangible way they could lend their support to the embattled nation. Ethiopia and its fight against Italy remained a topic of discourse among mutual aid societies for months during the battle and Italian occupation, with Caribbean mutual aid societies giving updates on the war in every meeting.[25] The Italian invasion was one of a series of events occurring in the twentieth century that helped shape a Black international identity for many members of immigrant mutual aid societies who connected not only with other Caribbean mutual aid societies in support of Ethiopia, but with African American groups as well.

Other events that fueled a Black international identity included labor strikes that erupted across the British Caribbean between 1934 and 1939 and widespread feelings of anticolonial unrest and African nationalism expressed in labor strikes throughout West Africa. Caribbean mutual aid societies called for political action to be taken. In 1934, delegates from several Virgin Island mutual aid societies and benevolent associations came together as the Federation of American Virgin Islands Benevolent Societies. The group included members of the American West Indian Benevolent Society, the AWILAS, the American Virgin Islands Society, the Virgin Islands Prudential Society, and the Virgin Islands Mechanics' Association. They called a conference with other mutual aid societies in order "to formulate a program of mutual helpfulness, including adult education projects—study of 'political action, civics, history of the Virgin Islands and child care.'"[26] They believed that if "Virgin Islanders turn[ed] to organized political action, they, with their fellow citizens, w[ould] be able 'to bring the political power of the Negro in New York to have a greater influence on the political scene in the state and nation.'"[27] Caribbean mutual aid society members increasingly engaged with political actions affecting the larger African Diaspora, recognizing the strength that their collaborations with each other and African American organizations could have.

African Blood Brotherhood for African Liberation and Redemption

Black Americans, angered by frequent and persistent racial violence, organized and fought for Black self-determination and political equality. Leaders like Caribbean-born Cyril Valentine Briggs, through the ABB, advocated for the creation of a separate Black state outside the United States in which people of the African diaspora could settle. Briggs, born on the Caribbean island of Nevis, immigrated to the United States in 1905 at the age of seventeen, immediately throwing himself into the cause of African Americans. As editor for the *New York Amsterdam News*, Briggs wrote what many regarded as extremely radical articles that called for unity between Caribbean immigrants and African Americans, the right of self-determination for Blacks, as well as the end of Jim Crow laws throughout the United States. Because he was considered too militant and radical for the paper, the publishers of the *New York Amsterdam News* asked Briggs to tone down his work; Briggs, however, refused to be censored and eventually left his position with the newspaper in 1918. He soon established his own magazine called the *Crusader* with initial funding of $200 from a Caribbean importer named J. Anthony Crawford. A monthly periodical, the *Crusader* denounced lynching and race riots, and asserted that Black people had the right to defend themselves against such attacks. Many of Briggs's editorials endorsed "race patriotism," an idea stipulating that Black people should be proud of their race and prepared to make sacrifices for it. He criticized Black leaders who, in his view, espoused accommodation as opposed to self-determination.[28]

Briggs brought this same fervor to his establishment of the ABB in 1919, announcing it in a small advertisement in an October issue of the *Crusader*: "Membership by enlistment. No dues, fees or assessments. Those only need apply who are willing to go the limit."[29] Shrouded in secrecy, the aim of the group was to serve as a self-defense, Black liberation organization for Black people who were threatened by race riots and lynching; it advocated for race equality, racial pride, a united Negro front, worker's rights, and anti-imperialism ideals.[30] The local Black community immediately and enthusiastically responded to the ABB, with letters from around the nation pouring into the *Crusader* in support of the organization. Disillusioned by the violent attacks against Black people that continued to occur throughout the United States, Briggs soon concluded that the only way Black Americans could gain their rightful dignity was to create and emigrate to an autonomous Black state in Africa, South America, or the Caribbean where Black people could live freely. Briggs was in fact the first person to use the term "Africa for the Africans," which was the title of a letter he wrote to the *New York Globe* in 1918. In this letter, Briggs called on whites to support Black people in establishing a free native state under temporary international or American guidance. He argued that while the creation of such a state would not provide complete justice or full reparation for the injustices suffered by Black Americans, it would give millions of Black people in the United States the "opportunity for the enjoyment of genuine freedom, with free development and security of life."[31] This idea of Black liberation and the creation of a separate state for Black individuals soon became a popular objective for many Black leaders, including arguably the most famous Back to Africa proponent—Marcus Garvey and his UNIA. Garvey's movement is credited with arousing a deep mass interest in the challenges faced by people of African descent throughout the world and with uniting Caribbean immigrants with American-born Black groups.[32]

Universal Negro Improvement Association

Marcus Mosiah Garvey, born in St. Ann's Bay, Jamaica, on August 17, 1887, was the youngest of eleven children. Garvey became involved with politics when he first left Jamaica in 1910, at the age of twenty-three, to work in Costa Rica and Panama. There he experienced racism firsthand in the poor working conditions and overall mistreatment of Black laborers on United Fruit Company's banana plantations. Realizing that Black populations throughout the Diaspora suffered from similar oppression and politically radicalized, he became involved in local political protests in Central America. In 1914, he returned to Jamaica, establishing the UNIA on the belief that only by uniting would Black people be able to overcome the racism that hobbled their civil rights and economic ambitions. In 1916, Garvey undertook a short tour to the United States, looking for patrons to support a school he wanted to establish in Jamaica. After meeting with several African American leaders in the United States, he—along with several other Black American leaders—was inspired to found the first branch of the UNIA in New York City in 1917. The goals of the UNIA included repatriation, promoting racial pride, and developing more independent African states. The UNIA would eventually grow to a membership of six million with nine hundred branches by 1923.[33]

Although many of the early founders of the UNIA were largely of Caribbean descent—many were in fact also members of Caribbean immigrant mutual aid societies—its members comprised both Caribbean immigrants and African Americans. In fact, in some states, Garveyites, as the followers of Garvey were called, were predominantly African American. The UNIA movement, however, did not come without its naysayers, both Caribbean and American-born. Many scholars have accused Garvey's movement of being patriarchal and limiting women's leadership roles within the organization.[34] The facts, however, contradict these charges: women accounted for fifty percent of the membership and were heavily involved as leaders, fundraisers, and organizers in the association. Many women held high-level positions, such as Henrietta Vinton Davis, who served as the first assistant president general and then as president general of the UNIA, helping to establish several chapters throughout the Caribbean.[35] Two other women who played significant roles in the UNIA were Garvey's first and second wives, Amy Ashwood Garvey and Amy Jacques Garvey. Amy Ashwood Garvey brought her executive experience as the director of the Black Star Line shipping corporation to her work in the early development of the UNIA, serving as Garvey's chief aide and general secretary of the New York branch in 1919. She also was instrumental in the development of other UNIA branches and later organized a women's auxiliary for the association. Additionally, she helped to establish the UNIA's newspaper, the *Negro World*. Amy Ashwood Garvey, through her involvement with the UNIA, advocated for the repatriation of all people of African ancestry to Africa. Later in her life, she fought for the rights of African women, as well as for the liberation of the African continent, through the Nigerian Progress Union, which she co-founded in London with Nigerian law student Ladipo Solanke. The Nigerian Progress Union would go on to inspire other organizations such as the West African Students' Union.[36]

Amy Euphemia Jacques Garvey was Marcus Garvey's second wife and, like Ashwood, she played an important role in the UNIA. Born in Kingston, Jamaica, she immigrated to the United States in 1917. The following year, she began working at the UNIA as Garvey's personal secretary and office manager. Jacques served as the *Negro World*'s associate editor from 1924 to 1927 and created a column entitled "Our Women and What They Think." During her tenure as associate editor, she wrote over 150 editorials and articles.[37] While many women's journals of the time focused on fashion and good housekeeping, Jacques wrote about Pan-Africanism and resistance to racism, sexism, and imperialism. Her writings centered on "the struggle towards self-determination, the importance of motherhood, and the importance of education to the emergence of the 'New Negro Woman.'"[38]

Jacques was an adamant advocate of women's rights. She believed that women were equally as important to the movement as men, and that if their efforts were to succeed Black men and women had to work together for the greater cause. After her husband was incarcerated on charges of mail fraud in 1925, Jacques took over leadership of the UNIA and oversaw its continued growth. An effective public speaker and excellent administrator, Jacques is often described as the glue that held the UNIA together during Garvey's imprisonment. A Pan-Africanist from early adulthood, Jacques continued to advocate for the rights of Black people long after Garvey's death in 1940. A few years after his death, she toured West Africa for three and a half years, examining women's education in several countries, where she subsequently organized fifteen women's associations.[39] In her various writings, Jacques "challenged Blacks to have pride in their race and to look toward Africa for their future ... argu[ing] that Black empowerment could only occur by bringing together American Blacks, Caribbean people and Africans."[40]

Marcus Garvey's UNIA and the Back-to-Africa Movement mobilized large numbers of Black people. Garvey, with the help of his wives, was able to organize record numbers of ordinary people of African descent in the United States, Caribbean, and abroad, with six million UNIA members globally. He empowered the poor and disavowed by giving them leadership roles and, most significantly, hope.

While many Black people in the United States, both American and Caribbean-born, supported organizations like the UNIA that promoted repatriation, there were some in the Black community who did not. Some Black leaders criticized the UNIA's message because they believed it played into white supremacist thinking by removing the "Black problem" from the United States, instead of giving Black individuals their full rights as American citizens. Many African Americans identified primarily as American and could not see how a return to Africa would improve their lives.[41] Some members of the Black elite, such as A. Philip Randolph and W. E. B. Du Bois, distrusted Garvey and the UNIA's leadership, believing that true leadership of the Black race should come from the middle-class and the well-educated "Talented Tenth." Du Bois's articles in the NAACP's *Crisis* magazine criticized Garvey's leadership ability and the UNIA's overall aims. In one article, Du Bois called Garvey "without doubt, the most dangerous enemy of the Negro race in America and the world. He is either a lunatic or a traitor."[42] Du Bois believed that Garvey's movement was a capitulation to white supremacist notions that there was no place for Black people in American society. Du Bois felt that the Back-to-Africa Movement was a dangerous idea to propose in a racially divided America. While no direct evidence in the records of Caribbean immigrant mutual aid societies and benevolent associations links their members to the UNIA, we can reasonably assume that these organizations were directly influenced by many of the principles of the UNIA and the ABB, including the idea that Black individuals must join together in order to liberate the race. Additionally, the UNIA at its core relied on many of the principles of mutual aid organizing present in Caribbean friendly societies and later Caribbean immigrant mutual aid societies and benevolent associations.

Political Engagement

Racial tensions continued to grow as the United States suffered through the Great Depression in the 1930s. Members of Caribbean immigrant mutual aid societies and benevolent associations increasingly inserted themselves into the larger political debates occupying Black people in the United States, recognizing their shared oppression and the need for their organizations to expand their objectives. As journalist A. M. Wendell Malliet argued, "He [the West Indian] is gradually being swept into the whirling stream of American Negro life."[43] As a result, many mutual aid societies became radicalized, joining with Black Americans to tackle issues affecting the entire Black community in the United States. In essence these groups promoted Garvey's message that the Black community was stronger united, and only by working together would they be strong enough to throw off their subjugation and find their place in American society.

On July 28, 1917, the NAACP, church groups, and a coalition of benevolent associations in Harlem organized the Silent March Against Lynching. It is estimated that between 10,000 and 15,000 Black men, women, and children took to the streets to protest the lynching and racial violence that had been brewing that summer in cities such as Waco, Texas; East St. Louis, Missouri; and Memphis, Tennessee. The procession marched silently—with the exception of the sound of muffled drums—down Fifth Avenue from 56th Street to 23rd Street in Manhattan. Black women and children were dressed in white to illustrate the sobriety of the occasion, while men were dressed in black. Remaining silent, the protesters carried signs that loudly expressed their outrage and frustration at the senseless violence being inflicted upon the Black community. Caribbean social organizations such as the AWILAS, BBA, Danish West Indian Benevolent Society, and the Montserrat Benevolent Association came together with African American groups to fund and organize the protest.[44] New York Age declared, "for once the American Negro, [British] West Indian Negro and the Haitian worked in unison as Black men."[45] It is at this point that historian Winston James declares that Caribbean immigrants fully embraced their place in American Black society:

Without a doubt, then, the midnight darkness of the moment in which these migrants from the islands entered the country contributed to the speed and depth of their radicalization in America. That turn-of-the century conjuncture constitutes a point in the nation's history when the contrast between the United States and the Caribbean on the question of race must have been one of the sharpest and most disturbing for an islander in America. The contrast no doubt deepened the Caribbeans' [sic] discontent with the new country. It was, therefore, not just the place that contributed to their radicalization: the exceptional times—a veritable state of emergency for Black America—played their part. It is not surprising nor is it insignificant that Caribbeans [sic] in Harlem helped to organize and took part in the Silent Parade.[46]

A few years later, the miscarriage of justice in the Scottsboro case of 1931 was another significant incident that served to politicize members of Caribbean American mutual aid societies and benevolent associations and solidify their cooperation with African Americans throughout the United States. Black people throughout the nation were outraged by the failure of the justice system in this case. Multiple all-white juries in Alabama had sentenced nine Black teenagers to death; the young men had been accused of and tried for raping two white women, even though there was no evidence to support the claim, and during a retrial one of the accusers openly admitted she had fabricated the story. Both Caribbean and African American members of mutual aid societies joined together in hosting mass meetings to discuss what actions they could take to help the young boys. Organizations like the African American International Labor Defense petitioned Caribbean American mutual aid societies and benevolent associations to join with them in support of the Scottsboro boys: "Those of us who are Negro. We must protest. We must agitate. If we cannot fight in this manner ourselves we must come to the aid of those who will."[47] Building on the idea of a unified Black identity, mutual aid societies joined with African American groups to fight this and other injustices in the United States.

Leading the defense of the teenagers in the Scottsboro trials was the Communist Party. In the 1920s and 1930s, the Communist Party of the United States of America (CPUSA) actively recruited both Caribbean immigrants and African Americans. The CPUSA placed advertisements in Black periodicals such as *The Negro Champion*, inviting African Americans to "See

Russia for Yourself!" and declaring: "Here is your opportunity to visit the Soviet Russia, the home of the new social order, the first Workers' Republic. Leave lynching, Jim Crowism, etc. behind for awhile [sic]. Enjoy Full Equality and Racial Freedom in the first country in which the workers have kicked out the parasites and established their own rule. Visit the Negro tribes in the Caucasus. Enjoy yourself in the fatherland the oppressed peoples know! Total Cost $475!"[48] The appeal of the Communist Party was that it directly addressed the oppression that Black populations suffered in the United States and offered them an alternative solution. Multiple advertisements, like the one above, found a response in Black people who not only joined the Communist Party, but visited Russia.[49] Evidence for this is found in the records of the AWILAS, where countless letters from CPUSA members ask Caribbean women to join their organization or attend meetings. One such letter from Friends of the Soviet Union, for example, asked members of the AWILAS to join them for a conference to discuss the platform of the Communist Party.[50] Additional letters state that the Communist Party can help "Negroes secure social and political equality for the Negro worker in every phase of industry."[51]

The CPUSA's support of civil rights and its large role in the Scottsboro case resonated not only with Caribbean immigrants but also with native-born African Americans, with the result of a significant uptake in party membership. Historian Winston James argues that many Caribbean immigrants in New York City became involved with the Communist Party through Cyril Briggs's ABB, which was influential in recruiting African Americans into the party.[52] In reality, however, many Caribbean American immigrants such as Grace Campbell, Claudia Jones, Bonita Williams, Hubert Harrison, and Elizabeth Hendrickson already had ties to the Communist Party through various organizations and associations, and their involvement in the CPUSA attracted many more Black people to join the party.[53] Some Black leaders hoped that with the help of CPUSA they would be able to obtain equal rights for all people of African descent in the United States. There were tensions, however, with groups such as the NAACP, which had other ideas of how those rights could be obtained and denounced the actions of the CPUSA. Conversely, members of the CPUSA accused NAACP leadership of "'joining the lynching mob' and of betraying the 'Negro masses and . . . the Negro liberation struggle,'" as they argued the NAACP did not act quickly enough to come to the Scottsboro boys' defense.[54] A clear line delineated more radical members of the CPUSA from members of the NAACP.

One of the first issues that politicized mutual aid societies and benevolent associations in New York was the passage of federal laws (1910–1924) drastically limiting the number of immigrants admitted into the country each year. In response, social organizations hosted meetings and conferences to discuss how to stop Congress from passing additional legislation. In 1939, Congress passed the Dempsey Bill, which called for the exclusion or deportation of immigrants who advocated for or affiliated with groups in favor of "the making of any changes in the American form of government."[55] Mutual aid societies like the BBA partnered with the American Committee of Protection of the Foreign Born to distribute protest cards opposing the Dempsey Bill. These groups also asked community members to sign petitions demanding that President Roosevelt stop the bill from being passed.[56] Additionally, the BBA, along with eighteen other organizations, participated in a 1939 conference hosted by the Caribbean Union (an organization for civic betterment) on how to prevent the enactment of "anti–foreign born" bills pending in Congress at the time. The conference aimed to defeat the Dempsey Bill, along with several other bills, including the Reynolds-Starnes Bill that would deport all noncitizens who had been on relief in the preceding six months; the Reynolds-Starnes Bill, which required all noncitizens to register and be fingerprinted; the Pace Bill, which would stop all immigration to the United States and deport all noncitizens; and the Hobbs Bill, which would establish concentration camps for all deportable noncitizens. The conference brought together Caribbean immigrants and African Americans in a common effort to protect the interests of all Black immigrants affected by these proposed laws.[57]

In these efforts, Caribbean immigrants worked with African Americans to prevent laws that would negatively affect Caribbean immigration to the United States. Through mutual aid societies, Caribbean immigrants worked with such groups as the National Negro Congress, which placed immigration laws among the top issues of their platform. The membership of the National Negro Congress—founded in response to racial violence in the United States—was composed of prominent African American and Caribbean immigrant delegates. These delegates recognized the threat that discriminatory immigration laws posed to both Caribbean immigrants and Black people in the United States. At the first New York State Conference of the National Negro Congress, delegates deeply concerned with the rights of Caribbean immigrants in the United States, and also those back in the Caribbean, stated, "[Legislative] attacks against the foreign-born must be opposed. In our ranks there are thousands of Negroes from the West Indies, from

South and Central America, and from Africa. We must not permit those who would divide us to set us group against group. The struggle for full democratic rights for the Negro people is the same whether it is in Georgia, in Barbados, in British Guiana, or in New York."[58]

Organizers of the Second National Negro Congress also spoke out for the rights of Caribbean immigrants, arguing that all Black individuals, native and foreign-born, must be willing to fight for the economic and social justice of Black people everywhere, including the Caribbean. Congress organizers hosted a special session about foreign born Blacks, which resulted in a resolution that the congress "make an immediate determined attempt to consolidate and unify the work being done by various organizations dealing with problems of the foreign born so as to present a world-wide united front working in the interest of Negro peoples"; the resolution also urged "that every effort be made to clarify the misunderstandings which surround relationships between American and West Indian Negroes."[59] These resolutions highlight the importance African American leaders placed on aligning their organizations with Caribbean immigrant groups. Other African American–led groups such as the NAACP were also deeply concerned with the rights of Caribbean immigrants and frequently collaborated with immigrant associations, such as the AWILAS and the APS. Members of associations like the BBA and the Jamaica Associates maintained lifetime memberships in the NAACP, illustrating their common commitment to work toward the goals of these organizations.[60] Caribbean immigrants and African Americans shared both professional and personal spaces and, in many cases, saw the great benefit of uniting their efforts.

In addition to hosting meetings to discuss the issues facing the Black community, members of Caribbean mutual aid societies and benevolent associations invited local politicians and activists to speak at their monthly meetings, illustrating how important it was to these associations that their members be politically well-informed.[61] For instance, the Jamaica Associates often hosted speakers, ambassadors from Caribbean islands, and state and local government officials at their meetings and events.[62] The BVIBA, BBA, and the APS did so as well.[63] In addition, members of mutual aid societies and benevolent associations campaigned for candidates who supported their political agenda, such as Democratic assemblyman David Paris from the 21st Congressional District, which included Harlem and parts of the Bronx. Paris wrote to the women of the AWILAS, thanking them for their support in his recent election.[64]

Caribbean mutual aid societies campaigning for a Democratic candidate was a watershed moment for the Black community in early twentieth-century electoral politics. Until the 1932 election of Democratic presidential nominee Franklin Delano Roosevelt, Black Americans were staunchly Republican. However, in 1932 Roosevelt garnered more than 70 percent of the Black vote. Roosevelt's New Deal programs, with their promise to create jobs for disadvantaged and minority groups, appealed to oppressed Black populations nationally.[65] Members of Caribbean immigrant mutual aid societies such as the AWILAS were major players in the transfer of political allegiance to the Democratic Party, as demonstrated by their attendance at political meetings like those held by the Chicopee Democratic Club. In 1933, members of the Chicopee Democratic Club thanked the AWILAS for attending meetings where prominent speakers addressed matters pertaining to "the welfare of the community."[66] Politicians quickly recognized the potential power of Caribbean immigrant mutual aid societies and benevolent associations and reached out to these groups to solicit their vote. For instance, a letter dated October 10, 1933, from New York politician A. C. Burnes encouraged AWILAS members to go out and vote in the November 7 election, as their vote would "greatly affect decisions being made in the Virgin Islands."[67] By 1930, almost a quarter of the Black population of Harlem was of Caribbean heritage and 23.5 percent of the foreign-born Black population were naturalized citizens.[68] In 1938 the *New York Amsterdam News* reported that British West Indians outnumbered all other groups in Harlem, and proclaimed that with the exception of Kingston, Jamaica, Harlem was "'the largest West Indian city in the world.' And if the children of West Indian parents were classified with the West Indian group, Kingston would be a small city when compared with Harlem."[69] Historian Lara Putnam adds that in cities such as Cambridge, Massachusetts, and Miami, Florida, Caribbean immigrants and their children made up two-fifths of the Black population.[70] Looking to secure this large voting bloc, politicians frequently looked for opportunities to connect with Caribbean groups.

Politicians such as African American Democrat William T. Andrews, who ran for assembly in the 21st District, asked the AWILAS executive board for an invitation to speak to their members at one of their general body meetings, as he was about to enter into the general election and wanted to solicit their support.[71] Highly endorsed by prominent Jamaican journalist and author J. A. Rogers, Andrews supported himself as a court reporter for the *New York Amsterdam News* while he attended Columbia University Law School.[72] He later became an attorney for the NAACP. In the election of 1934,

Andrews promoted more effective laws to prevent discrimination by the public utility agencies and advocated that New York hire more Black workers as
motormen, train conductors, and porters, as well as workers in the electric,
gas, and telephone industries. Andrews also wanted to amend various New
York state civil rights laws in order to protect Black patrons against discrimination. Finally, he called for a 5 percent freeze in public transportation fares
and a reduction in electric, gas, and telephone rates; an improvement in ten-
ement housing conditions; and the creation of unemployment insurance.[73]
Andrew's platform and proposed changes in the law would directly benefit
Caribbean voters.

Twentieth-century politicians saw the benefits of winning the support of
the growing number of Caribbean immigrant voters, whom they saw as an
influential subsection of the Black community and key to securing the Black
vote in New York City. As a result, they frequently canvassed their meetings
and included their interests in their platforms. The late 1920s and 1930s witnessed a surge in Caribbean mutual aid societies' involvement in mainstream
politics. As we have seen, this surge in political involvement was greatly influenced by prior and contemporaneous radical movements of the early twentieth century, as Caribbean immigrant mutual aid societies' networks merged
with those of African American organizations, which had longer-term experience with U.S. society and politics. Caribbean immigrants wanted to ensure
their equality in a racially divided nation and understood the positive impact
their involvement in politics could have for their members.

In addition to changing immigration laws, Caribbean mutual aid societies and benevolent associations advocated for anti-lynching laws, housing
and renting laws, as well as educational reform.[74] In 1937, the BBA collaborated with the Washington Heights Improvement Council, Inc., to help fight
poor housing conditions on behalf of tenants' rights.[75] Established in 1928,
the Harlem Tenants League advocated on behalf of Harlem tenants against
oppressive rent hikes and unsanitary conditions.[76] As seen in Chapter 4,
Elizabeth Hendrickson, president of the AWILAS for several years, was also
one of the founders and secretary of the Tenants League, and thus there was
much collaboration between the AWILAS and the Tenants League, as members of the AWILAS were heavily involved in the activities of the group. The
Harlem Tenants League held mass meetings that appealed to all Black tenants as well as domestic workers, calling on them "to organize, to demand
rent ceiling prices; ceiling prices on all foods; and [to draw] the attention of
the OPA [Office of Price Administration] official to the mismanagement of

food dealers."[77] They picketed, demanding that federal, state, and municipal authorities construct livable housing facilities for local residents, in addition to the "immediate abolition of the slums and fire-traps that is [sic] a social danger and a thorough disgrace in the Negro communities." Additionally, they sent a delegation to Washington, DC, to lobby Congress and bring awareness to the social, economic, and industrial problems Black people faced in the United States. The delegation also attended meetings of the OPA, the American Federation of Labor, the National Youth Administration, and the War Production Board.[78] Hendrickson was a regular speaker at Harlem Tenants League meetings and conferences, encouraging members of Caribbean immigrant mutual aid societies to join together with African Americans in order to fight against the deplorable conditions in which Black residents in New York were forced to live.

The Harlem riots of March 19, 1935, were another significant event that mobilized Caribbean immigrant mutual aid societies politically. Lino Rivera, a sixteen-year-old Puerto Rican of African descent, stole a penknife from a store on 125th Street in Harlem. The store owner caught him and called the police. However, he decided not to press charges and asked the police to let Rivera go. A crowd gathered outside the store, and rumors rapidly spread that Rivera had been killed. There was an uproar, and five thousand Harlemites looted businesses up and down Harlem's avenues with the rallying cry "Down with the ofay stores!" Black leaders, weary of the racism and oppression they faced, urged mass picketing of stores in Harlem and an open boycott of the public utility agencies and larger corporations who discriminated against Black workers in employment. The *New York Amsterdam News* estimated property damage at $500,000 and that a hundred people had been injured.[79] Many Black Harlem residents, including members of Caribbean mutual aid societies, supported the rioting. For instance, in a letter to the editor of the *New York Amsterdam News*, a reader wrote: "Dear Sir—The riot in Harlem was one of the best things that could have happened. The Negroes have been silent long enough about their social and economic ills given them by white people."[80] Other Black people in Harlem shared the same sentiments, as stated in a letter written to the New York City newspaper *Daily Mirror*: "It took such an occurrence [the riots] to bring local authorities to the realization that the theory that all men are created equal includes Negroes—who have hurts desires and aspirations. They must come to realize that the Negro in Harlem is being trampled upon, that he is being discriminated against in Federal and municipal projects, in business ventures setup right here in Harlem and in every other quarter where he is entitled to equal recognition—and, too, that he resents such treatment."[81] As devastating as the 1935 Harlem riots were, many Black people, including members of Caribbean mutual aid societies and benevolent associations, agreed with these sentiments, and as a result, Caribbean mutual aid societies emphasized even more the importance of working together with African American organizations to fight the racial oppression they suffered. They had hoped some good would come out of the attention that was now on Harlem.

Through their efforts in mutual aid societies, Caribbean immigrants came together with African American groups to fight for common causes. As a result, there was a lot of correspondence between African American and Caribbean immigrant organizations, as is illustrated in the files of the BBA, BVIBA, APS, and AWILAS. One African American group that frequently reached out to collaborate with Caribbean immigrant mutual aid societies was the BSCP. Founded in New York in 1925, the BSCP was one of the first Black labor unions in the United States. The organization grew out of the unhappiness of Black Pullman porters and maids with long working hours, low wages, and very little job security, who joined together to form the BSCP with the help of A. Philip Randolph and Milton Price Webster. The BSCP, with chapters throughout the United States, handled employee labor disputes. In addition, the BSCP supported larger Black workers' movements and civil rights for people of African descent, including Caribbean immigrants.[82] Significantly, many Caribbean immigrant men worked as Pullman porters, including Jamaican-born Harlem Renaissance writer Claude McKay, journalist J. A. Rogers, and activist and union organizer Frank Crosswaith.[83]

The BSCP's close involvement with Caribbean mutual aid societies was related to the fact that Ashley L. Totten, national secretary-treasurer of the BSCP, was himself a Caribbean immigrant from the Virgin Islands, and a member of Caribbean immigrant mutual aid societies and benevolent associations, such as the Virgin Islands Civic and Industrial Association. Totten insisted on the serious contributions Caribbean immigrants could offer African American organizations in helping to lift up Black people as a whole. He articulated the racial and cultural pride he felt members of Caribbean mutual aid societies shared with African Americans: "Since we are apart [sic] of the United States and new [to] enjoy its political and other rights, it is my contention that our natives resident in New York and so well represented in our established organizations should take advantage of every opportunity to show in larger measure that dignity and culture of which we are especially proud."[84] Totten called for Caribbean immigrants to join African American organizations for the purpose of working together.

Totten made sure that the BSCP supported issues that pertained to events going on in the Caribbean. For instance, in 1934, the BSCP protested a commission appointed by President Roosevelt to advise on the rehabilitation of the Virgin Islands. The BSCP took issue with the commission because it did not have any Virgin Islanders on its board. In a letter to the AWILAS, Totten, as the national secretary-treasurer of the BSCP, wrote: "The Brotherhood is essentially concerned about this matter since it regards the major problems of the Virgin Islands as being essentially labor, and therefore requires, along with labor experience, and a record of sacrifice, to advise with President Roosevelt and the government of the Virgin Islands on the expenditures of the million dollars and the general method and program for the rehabilitation of the islands."[85] Totten announced a mass meeting that year and declared that the presence of the AWILAS was imperative to find solutions to address this oversight by President Roosevelt.

Further demonstrating the importance African American organizations placed on collaborating with members of Caribbean immigrant mutual aid societies, many similar letters exist between the AWILAS, the BSCP, and the Ladies Auxiliary of the Brotherhood of Sleeping Car Porters (LABSCP) requesting AWILAS members collaborate with their organizations. For example, in one letter dated July 21, 1933, the ladies of the LABSCP appealed to the women of the AWILAS to join their cause: "The Brotherhood of the [sic] Sleeping Car Porters will stage a monster parade and demonstration throughout the length and breadth of Harlem [on] Saturday, August 5th 4 P.M. for the purpose of creating public sentiment to help Pullman Porters get back their jobs that have been taken by 1,000 Filipinos, Japanese and Chinese. It will arouse sentiment in behalf of the Negroes of Harlem receiving a just and fair share of relief and employment."[86] Additional letters invited AWILAS members to other political rallies and social events hosted by the BSCP, once again illustrating the importance African American organizations placed on cooperation with Caribbean associations. Some of the insistence on collaborating with Caribbean immigrant organizations may have also partly been due to the fact that some of the members and even leadership of "African American" organizations might have had West Indian heritage, much like Totten.

The women of the LABSCP, as well as other predominantly African American organizations, built connections with Caribbean immigrant mutual aid societies and would later solicit their help for larger political objectives, such as educational reform and the fight against unfair housing laws. For instance, a letter from the Eton Benevolence Society, dated December 10, 1933, states, "seeking to establish a bond of unity and friendship between your organization and ours, [we] ask your permission to send a representative at your next meeting, who will make the request and as we hope [to] establish soon."[87] Other African American organizations did the same. For example, the Saint Benedict Ladies' Auxiliary No. 204 and the Excelsior Literary Club invited AWILAS members to various social events in the hope of fostering bonds between Caribbean and African American women.

Social networking, however, was not just for women's organizations. Coed groups such as the BVIBA and the BBA also attended social functions hosted by predominantly African American groups, such as the NAACP, Oddfellows' Lodges, the United Sons of Georgia, and the Associated Clubs of Harlem. Later groups, like the League of Struggle for Negro Rights, would use these connections to call on all Black workers to unite to fight "Negro oppression and Jim Crow for the ultimate freedom of the masses of all races."[88] Similarly, the American League Against War and Fascism extended invitations to the AWILAS and urged their members to join forces.[89] By interacting with each other through their mutual social events, Caribbean immigrants and African Americans were slowly but steadily building a collective community. This community grew closer as Caribbean immigrant mutual aid societies became more politicized and advocated for laws that aligned with the political goals of African Americans.

Caribbean immigrant political engagement did not stop with the United States. In fact, the roots of this engagement go back to labor disputes and strikes beginning as early as the nineteenth century, as immigrants were very cognizant of labor unrest taking place in the Caribbean. Caribbean immigrants in the United States kept abreast of these labor disturbances occurring in their home islands and often sent support to striking family members and friends. Concern for the welfare of Black individuals not only in the United States but throughout the world became a very important aim of mutual aid societies and benevolent associations. Organizations such as the APS believed "that we [APS members] in America should help those in the islands to obtain and enjoy the same privileges which we have and enjoy here ... we should fight for better conditions in the islands." Amended to the 1926 constitution of the BVIBA is the group's overwhelmingly diasporic objective: "Whereas we the people of the British Virgin Islands joined ourselves together for the purpose of having an organization to assist in giving alms to the needy among our people; not only here but to the homeland also."

Worker disturbances occurred throughout the Caribbean in the early twentieth century as the region experienced a period of economic depression. In 1921, Jamaica in particular was suffering a severe financial depression caused by the decline in commodity prices in both in England and United States. The price of export items, such as sugar, rum, ginger, pimento, coconuts, and other tropical products, sharply declined and caused great stress on Jamaica's labor industry, resulting in lowered salaries and a reduction in the labor force.[90] That same year, the employees of the Jamaica Government Railway, including station masters, locomotive engineers, firemen, mechanics, clerks, and running staff, threatened to strike for the restoration of Sunday and holiday overtime pay. The strike could have caused great financial losses among fruit and other planters in Jamaica, and since there was only one railroad system on the island, estates held by small planters in the interior of the island would especially be affected. However, the strike never occurred, as the railway came to an agreement with their employees.[91]

In 1922, Jamaica experienced its highest unemployment rate in a number of years, and on the island the cost of food sharply increased and residents could barely find enough meat, cereal foods, and grain to sustain themselves. These factors, coupled with the gross mistreatment of the Jamaican labor force, led to unrest among the population.[92] On September 15, 1925, in Kingston, Jamaica, around six hundred dock workers called a general strike demanding a wage increase. Their demands were not met and the strikers were replaced with four hundred laborers brought in from other districts of the island. The labor strike, however, did have an effect on operations and prevented some of the United Fruit Company's steamer ships from being loaded.[93]

Jamaica had a history of labor strikes. The Jamaican newspaper the *Gleaner* recounts multiple workers' strikes as early as 1918 occurring in Jamaica and on other islands in the region. Laborers in nearly every industry, including match factory laborers, farm workers on banana and sugar plantations, dock workers, and railway laborers, demanded better wages, improved working conditions, and shorter workdays.[94] Labor strikes also took place in Central American countries. For instance, in Guatemala, Black West Indian migrants working for the railroad, on the docks, and in banana plantations held massive strikes in 1898, 1909, 1913, 1915, 1918, and 1919, for higher wages and better working conditions.[95]

A series of particularly violent strikes in 1938 resonated with Caribbean mutual aid societies and benevolent associations, which came to the aid of their compatriots in the Caribbean. In the spring of 1938, Jamaican dock workers, sugar plantation workers, and farm laborers went on a collective work stoppage, nearly crippling production in these industries. Striking workers held large public meetings, mass rallies, and demonstrations. One such demonstration ended in the brutal shooting of Jamaican protesters by the police. Four people were killed, dozens wounded, and 103 jailed. In response, the British-Jamaican Benevolent Association of New York held a mass meeting to discuss how Caribbean immigrant mutual aid societies in New York could support not only the injured but those still striking. Associations like the BBA and the Jamaica Associates attended the British-Jamaican Benevolent Association's meeting, demonstrating their solidarity with a Pan–West Indian movement calling for fair work practices in the Caribbean.[96]

The direct involvement of Anglophone Caribbean mutual aid societies with events occurring in the Caribbean demonstrates the ways in which Caribbean immigrant mutual aid societies and benevolent associations helped create a transnational space for political engagement with their home islands and the greater Caribbean region. This idea is further bolstered by the 1940 participation of members of Caribbean immigrant mutual aid societies in a mass meeting of mutual aid society leaders in New York. On the meeting's agenda was a discussion of a conference of Pan-American nations, in which official representatives from twenty-one countries were meeting in Havana, Cuba. Mutual aid societies and benevolent associations hosted an urgent conference of all Caribbean organization leaders in New York in order to alert Caribbean immigrant leaders that they were "facing the most serious Emergency in the life history of the Caribbean people. . . . It is vitally necessary for us all to sit down and put our heads together, to support the cause of freedom for our people in the homelands as well as for ourselves . . . and demonstrate our unity and strength."[97] Mutual aid societies such as the APS attended the conference and lent their support.

On the meeting's agenda was a discussion of the "plans and proposals being acted upon to decide the fate of all our brothers in the West Indies, the Guianas, and British Honduras." In response, members of Caribbean mutual aid societies and benevolent associations sent their own representatives to advocate for "the right of self-determination" for people of African descent in the Diaspora, illustrating their desire to create transnational social fields that kept members closely connected to the Caribbean by updating them on

Caribbean current events, and actively involved in different situations affecting the region.[98] In this way, mutual aid societies and benevolent associations in New York helped Caribbean immigrants create a transnational identity that extended to concerns for people of African descent around the world.

Associations such as the BBA and the APS embraced a Pan-African identity and were invested in the affairs of people of African descent not only in the Caribbean, but throughout the world. Newspaper clippings preserved by these organizations demonstrate the importance members placed on keeping abreast of new and current events taking place within the African Diaspora. As mentioned previously, groups such as the BVIBA even had representatives throughout the Caribbean in order to remain well informed of events occurring on the islands. Representatives frequently updated members of the BVIBA in New York with news from the islands. Furthermore, mutual aid societies and benevolent associations even expressed interest in traveling to the African continent in order to reconnect with their African heritage, as African travel agency pamphlets found in their association records reveal.[99] In addition, the BBA housed a lending library for its members, named the Library of Negro History, with collections of works pertaining to Africa and the African Diaspora, thus giving members an opportunity to learn about their African heritage.[100] As mentioned earlier in this chapter, Caribbean immigrant mutual aid societies and benevolent associations took great interest in the Second Italo-Ethiopian War. The Italian invasion was one of a series of events occurring in the twentieth century that helped to shape a Black international identity, as Caribbean immigrants recognized that their fate was closely intertwined with the social, political, and economic welfare of the Black international community.[101]

Conclusion

Although the early twentieth century was marked by racial antipathy, violence, and discriminatory laws, the Black community in the United States was resilient. They mobilized politically, lobbying for anti-lynching laws, better housing, and educational and immigration reform. Embracing the idea that the struggle against racial oppression connected all Black people in the United States with those in Africa and the African Diaspora, African Americans and Caribbean immigrants in the United States engaged in a wider conversation with Black communities globally. The welfare of people of African descent internationally became a clear and pressing concern of immigrant mutual aid societies, as international unrest and threats of violence to people of African descent reached a fever pitch and New York City became a hotbed of Black radical politics. Having experienced American structural racism firsthand, members of Caribbean immigrant mutual aid societies and benevolent associations engaged in political action, fighting not only the oppression of Black people in the United States but also the racial and social injustices facing Black people throughout the world. Through their participation in these mutual aid societies, Caribbean immigrants were able to mobilize politically with African Americans and championed issues that affected the wider Black community in an effort to ensure their equality in the tumultuous Jim Crow era.

Caribbean mutual aid societies came to serve not only as a means to create community among fellow compatriots, but also as a base for political activism both within the United States and in the wider African Diaspora. Immigrant mutual aid societies and benevolent associations were influential in helping Caribbean immigrants create multiple identities for themselves—be they transnational, Pan-Caribbean, Pan-African, or Black.

Conclusion

In every field of our American life we find the West Indian
pushing ahead and doing all in his power to uphold the
dignity of the Negro race. In every industry, in every
profession, in every trade, we find this son of the islands.

—Fenton Johnson

In 2006, then U.S. president George W. Bush signed a proclamation officially
making June National Caribbean-American Heritage Month in the United
States in order to "recognize the historic relationship between the people
of the Caribbean and the people of the United States, as well as to recognize
the many contributions of Caribbean immigrants and their descendants to
the well-being of America."[1] Documented and examined in this book are the
major influences Caribbean immigrants, through their work in mutual aid
societies, have had on American history since the nineteenth century, including such prominent Caribbean-born leaders as Elizabeth Hendrickson, Ashley Totten, and Hubert Harrison. Caribbean immigrants have been among
the most influential members of Black society, serving as religious leaders,
educators, politicians, and businesspeople and leaving an indelible mark on
the history of the United States by changing the political and social landscape
for Black people in America.

While the impact of Caribbean immigrants on the United States has
not always been recognized or acknowledged in U.S. or African American historiography, *A Home Away from Home* identifies the achievements
of Caribbean immigrants in the early twentieth century by exploring their
participation in Caribbean American mutual aid societies and benevolent
associations. These organizations helped to combat the invisibility that

Anglophone Caribbean immigrants felt as Black immigrants in the United States and ensured the preservation and celebration of their various ethnic backgrounds. Additionally, these mutual aid societies paved the way for future Caribbean immigration to the United States through their system of formal and informal social networks, providing members with a community to draw on for social and economic support. Additionally, as has been illustrated, these groups were essential in the political formation and mobilization of Caribbean immigrants. Through their mutual aid organizing Caribbean immigrants were able to collectively create political strategies for self-preservation and communal welfare in an often hostile new home. They used these groups to pool resources, monetary and otherwise, in order to bring the traditions of home to the United States and create "a home away from home."

Even for Caribbean immigrants who did not formally belong to a Caribbean American mutual aid society or benevolent association, their lives were in many ways still affected by these organizations. Take the case of Beatrice Beach, who, throughout her almost sixty years of living in New York City, was bound to have had friends and even relatives who were members of mutual aid societies and benevolent associations. Additionally, she may have attended a meeting or gone to a social event, such as one of the frequent dances or church services that were organized by these mutual aid societies. She may have even possibly rented a room in a building secured by funds garnered through Caribbean immigrant rotating credit unions. Needless to say, she certainly benefited from the accomplishments of Caribbean immigrant mutual aid societies. The influence of Caribbean immigrant mutual aid societies and benevolent associations was pervasive in New York City in the early twentieth century, so much so that even people who were not directly members were still affected by and often benefited from their initiatives. Beach, and other Caribbean immigrants like her, undoubtedly benefited from the advances that these mutual aid societies made in securing a place for Caribbean immigrants within the United States.

Caribbean immigrant mutual aid societies and benevolent associations continue to play an important role in the Caribbean American community to this day, albeit not as significantly as they did in the twentieth century. Founded in 1920 by newly arrived St. Lucian immigrants, the St. Lucia United Association continues to operate from its headquarters, Saint Lucia House in Brooklyn, New York, and holds meetings once a month. In November 2022, members celebrated the association's 102nd anniversary, and they continue to engage with both the Saint Lucian community in New York as well as the community back in Saint Lucia.[2] The association's membership numbers have declined greatly since its founding, but the efforts and the relevance of the association to Saint Lucian communities on the island and abroad, and the larger Black community in the United States, still remain. The group continues to host social and cultural events in New York, such as dances, Independence Day galas, and creole festivals, which highlight traditional Saint Lucian customs, cultural wear, music, and dance. The association annually participates in the American Cancer Society's Making Strides Against Breast Cancer walk each October in order to raise awareness in the Black community, which suffers the highest mortality rates among those affected by breast cancer. Breast cancer is also one of the leading forms of cancer among African American women. The St. Lucia United Association has also held several successful blood drives for local hospitals within members' communities in New York. Finally, the association is still actively involved with the Union of Overseas Associations, which is a union of St. Lucian Associations from London, Saint Croix, Barbados, Canada, and Saint Lucia. Several St. Lucian United Association members also serve on the board of the Union of Overseas Associations, which meets biannually to "discuss ways in which we (collectively) can help those in St. Lucia."[3]

Another early twentieth-century association that continues to operate in the twenty-first century is the APS. The APS was founded on August 22, 1934, under the direction of Antiguan-born Reverend James P. Roberts, along with twenty-two other Antiguan immigrants. The APS later merged with another organization and renamed themselves the Antigua and Barbuda Progressive Society (ABPS). In 1964, the society with the help of founder Salome Drysdale purchased a headquarters building in Harlem, located at 12 West 122nd Street, and named it the Antigua and Barbuda House.[4] The society continues to operate from this building today, eighty-eight years after its founding. In 2012, the society donated its records to the Manuscripts, Archives, and Rare Books Division at the Schomburg Center for Research in Black Culture. The following year, it held a public exhibit at the Schomburg Center titled "A Lighthouse in New York," which showcased the records of the society and its accomplishments for the first fifty years of its existence.[5] The society continues to host meetings and is actively engaged with the Harlem community; members organize local book drives for children to promote literacy, among other events. Additionally, the society holds annual blood drives at Mount Saint John Medical Centre in Antigua.

The APBS continues to hold relevance to not only Caribbean immigrants in New York, but West Indians in the Caribbean as well, as is witnessed by the society hosting Antiguan dignitaries, such as the Governor General of Antigua and Barbuda, Sir Rodney Williams, at its meetings and working in conjunction with the New York Consulate General of Antigua and Barbuda. In April 2015, the Consulate announced that it would begin to provide mobile services at the Antigua and Barbuda House in Harlem every third Saturday of the month, offering "easier accessibility to consular services such as passport processing, precinct letters, emergency travel documents, and advice on national services."[6]

In 2019, the organization undertook the process to have the street where its headquarters is located co-named "Bishop James P. Roberts Sr. Way," after the founder of the organization. As part of the co-naming application, the organization had to submit a petition demonstrating community support. The petition had to include a minimum of 60 percent of the total residents and businesses on the designated block, including the names, addresses, phone numbers, email addresses, and signatures of the residents. The society was easily able to gain support from its neighbors. In its co-naming application letter to Manhattan Community Board 10, the society stated:

> The APBS has a strong connection with the local Harlem community and actively helps to foster transnational connections with communities back in Antigua. More importantly, the society has been able to successfully engage younger members and encourage their participation within the society, which has ultimately led to the growth of its membership. To maintain the legacy of service to the Harlem community for future generations of the Antigua and Barbuda Progressive Society, Inc., the current members of the Society request to co-name the corner of 122nd Street and Lenox as the "Bishop James P. Roberts Sr. Way." . . . As our Society works to preserve the achievements of our ancestors, co-naming 122nd Street and Lenox Avenue would serve as an everlasting reminder of Bishop Roberts' commitment to serve God and community and would inspire all those who traverse on the corner of 122nd Street and Lenox Avenue to do the same.[7]

The Community Board voted unanimously to approve the APBS's street co-naming application on March 4, 2020. Two years later, on June 25, 2022, the APBS held a street co-naming ceremony at 122nd Street Malcolm X Boulevard, solidifying its place in Harlem history.[8]

The APBS and the St. Lucia United Association serve as two examples of Caribbean immigrant mutual aid societies and benevolent associations that continue to thrive well into the twenty-first century; however, not many Caribbean mutual aid societies have shared the same fate. In fact, many of the associations that continue to operate in the United States have witnessed dwindling membership numbers, as younger generations have not taken the same interest in these social organizations. Some groups, like the BBA, were forced to stop operating altogether. In discussing the fissure of the association, former BBA member Ivy Simons stated that the association was forced to sell its headquarters building in 1989 because it had only twenty active members remaining. The association was finally forced to dissolve in 1996, because many of the remaining members had moved out of state or passed away, or their increasing age prevented them from taking part in the association's activities. Simons went on to state that younger generations were simply no longer interested in these kinds of groups.[9] This trend of declining membership can be observed among many Caribbean immigrant mutual aid societies and benevolent associations in the twenty-first century.

Within the Caribbean, friendly societies reached their height during the 1940s and 1950s, and then began to rapidly decline. By the 1970s, friendly societies had considerably less influence on West Indian populations than they had in the past.[10] The decline in friendly societies is due to numerous factors, including "changes in the level of income, modernization, urbanization, emigration, and such government-initiated programs and policies as old age pension, minimum wage, and health insurance."[11] These factors have decreased the demand for the economic services provided by friendly societies. In turn, societies lost their members (and their membership dues) and became financially weak. Friendly societies could no longer afford to provide social and ameliorative services in order to attract new members and were forced to dissolve. Modern economic institutions, economic growth, and modernization have indirectly created an important vacuum in the social infrastructure. Adding to these factors was the large number of Caribbean immigrants who left the Caribbean to immigrate to cities in the United States and the United Kingdom, leaving behind their memberships in societies.

As the twentieth century progressed, cooperative societies, credit unions, and loan agencies began to replace friendly societies. For the first time in decades, West Indians no longer found friendly societies beneficial. The same factors contributed to the decline of mutual aid societies and benevolent associations in the United States. Additionally, it appears that many of the organizations in the United States lessened their political activity in the twenty-first century and focused their programming mainly on cultural and social events. As a result, later generations may not have been able to connect with these associations, especially given the rising political activism among young people in the last several years with the rise of the Black Lives Matter movement.[12]

Nonetheless, an examination of Caribbean mutual aid societies and benevolent associations is essential in shaping complex and diverse immigrant narratives, without which we are left with an inadequate analysis of how Caribbean American identity and community developed, how a Caribbean American transnational identity formed, and the relationship between culture and politics. In examining the number of these organizations, their membership, and the functions they served, this monograph argues that mutual aid societies and benevolent associations not only fostered a West Indian American ethnic identity among Caribbean immigrants in the United States, but also strengthened kinship networks among immigrants in the United States and those back home in the Caribbean. Immigrants' involvement with mutual aid associations and benevolent societies demonstrated their strong desire to stay connected to their communities back home in the Caribbean. Furthermore, through their involvement with these mutual aid societies, which pushed international initiatives, Caribbean immigrants demonstrated their belief that their own fate was closely intertwined with the social, economic, and political welfare of the Black international community.

A Home Away from Home contends that immigrant mutual aid societies and benevolent associations played a vital role in the formation of transnational identities and more importantly facilitated community building. Caribbean immigrants did not initially perceive themselves as a collective group upon arrival in the United Sates. Many early immigrant associations were organized by specific islands, highlighting the fact that these groups primarily saw themselves as nationals from their own individual islands, not as the collective group in which they were categorized by default. Consequently, it is in the context of U.S. social and cultural organizations that Caribbean immigrants first saw themselves as Caribbean or West Indian as opposed to Saint Lucian or Antiguan.

Moreover, this book challenges the historiographical tendency to normalize the male experience of immigrants by highlighting the prominent role of women in Caribbean immigrant mutual aid societies and benevolent associations. Immigrant women played a vital role as founders of and participants in many mutual aid societies and benevolent associations in the early twentieth century. Associations became a training ground for female leaders in which Caribbean immigrant women were able to gain professional experience in managing and organizing groups. Examining women's roles in immigrant mutual aid societies provides an important voice to an often-neglected aspect of the Caribbean immigrant experience and highlights the inextricable links between notions of gender, race, and class in shaping complex and diverse immigrant narratives. Finally, *A Home Away from Home* demonstrates a strong link between mutual aid organizing and larger political movements. As mutual aid societies and benevolent associations became more invested in their newly adopted homes, their aims grew progressively more political. Building on the idea of a unified Black identity, Caribbean mutual aid societies would eventually join together with African American organizations like the BSCP to fight racial inequality and social injustice within the United States.

A Home Away from Home sheds light on the process of transnational identity formation and the subsequent creation of community that occurs among immigrants. Neither the development of modern American history nor the African American community at the turn of the twentieth century can be understood without an examination of Caribbean immigrants in the United States, nor can we adequately comprehend how issues of immigration, such as transnational communities, globalization of labor, global capitalism, and the influx of immigrant women and children, are currently shaping American life. As immigration and transnational communities continue to be hot-button issues in the twenty-first century, studies featuring Caribbean immigration are crucial.

NOTES

INTRODUCTION

1. Interview with former Bermuda Benevolent Association President Ivy Simons, September 2014.

2. Ira Philip, "Ivy Simons Earns a Declaration in the US Congress as She Marks Her 90th Birthday," *Royal Gazette*, August 31, 2013, https://www.royalgazette.com/other/lifestyle/article/20130831/ivy-simons-earns-a-declaration-in-the-us-congress-as-she-marks-her-90th-birthday/.

3. Interview with former Bermuda Benevolent Association President Ivy Simons, September 2014.

4. See Irma Watkins-Owens, *Blood Relations: Caribbean Immigrants and the Harlem Community, 1900–1930* (Bloomington & Indianapolis: Indiana Press, 1996), Winston James, *Holding Aloft the Banner of Ethiopia: Caribbean Radicalism in the Early Twentieth Century America* (New York: Verso Publishers, 1998), Violet Showers Johnson, *The Other Black Bostonians: West Indians in Boston, 1900–1950* (Bloomington: Indiana University Press, 2006), and Lara Putnam, *Radical Moves: Caribbean Migrants and the Politics of Race in the Jazz Age* (Chapel Hill: University of North Carolina Press, 2013).

5. Dean Spade, *Mutual Aid Building Solidarity During This Crisis (and the Next)*, (New York: Verso Books, 2020) and "Solidarity Not Charity: Mutual Aid for Mobilization and Survival," *Social Text 142*, 38, no. 1 (March 2020), 131–151.

6. Tyesha Maddox, "Can Mutual Aid Withstand Pandemic Fatigue?," *Bloomberg CityLab*, April 16, 2021, https://www.bloomberg.com/news/articles/2021-04-16/new-yorkers-need-mutual-aid-groups-more-than-ever.

7. Tyesha Maddox and Daniel Joslyn, "The History and Impact of Mutual Aid in America," YouTube, February 9, 2022, educational video, 0:54–1:06, https://youtu.be/wFqOLHsj6nE.

8. With the exception of Martin Summers, *Manliness & Its Discontents: The Black Middle Class & the Transformation of Masculinity, 1900–1930* (Chapel Hill: University of North Carolina Press, 2004) and Keisha Blain, *Set the World on Fire: Black Nationalist Women and the Global Struggle for Freedom* (Philadelphia: University of Pennsylvania Press, 2018).

9. See Watkins-Owens, *Blood Relations*; James, *Holding Aloft the Banner of Ethiopia*; Violet Showers Johnson, *The Other Black Bostonians*–; Lara Putnam, *Radical Moves*;

and Tammy L. Brown, *City of Islands: Caribbean Intellectuals in New York* (Jackson: University Press of Mississippi, 2015).

10. Nina Mjagkij, *Organizing Black America: An Encyclopedia of African American Associations* (New York: Garland Publishing, Inc., 2001); Paul Lawrence Dunbar, "Hidden in Plain Sight: African American Secret Societies and Black Freemasonry," *Journal of African American Studies* 16, no. 4 (December 2012): 622–637; David Beito, *From Mutual Aid to the Welfare State: Fraternal Societies and Social Services, 1890–1967* (Chapel Hill: University of North Carolina Press, 2000).

11. David Beito, *From Mutual Aid to the Welfare State*, 1–2.

12. Notable exceptions include several works within the historiography of the Hispanophone Caribbean that explore the participation of immigrants in mutual aid societies and benevolent associations, such as Susan D. Greenbaum's *More Than Black: Afro-Cubans in Tampa* (Gainesville: University Press of Florida, 2002) and Frank Guridy's *Forging Diaspora: Afro-Cubans and African Americans in a World of Empire and Jim Crow* (Chapel Hill: University of North Carolina Press, 2010).

13. Nina Mjagkij's encyclopedic work *Organizing Black America: An Encyclopedia of African American Associations* (New York: Garland Publishing, Inc., 2001) provides a detailed look at over five hundred historical and contemporary African American organizations, yet does not highlight any Caribbean American groups, with the exception of the Universal Negro Improvement Association (UNIA)

14. See Lawrence Schulman, *The Skills of Helping Individuals, Families, Groups, and Communities* (Chicago, Illinois: F.E. Peacock Publishers, Inc., 1979); Alex Gitterman and Lawrence Schulman, *Mutual Aid Groups, Vulnerable and Resilient Populations, and the Life Cycle* (New York: Columbia University Press, 2005); Peter Gelderloos, *Anarchy Works: Examples of Anarchist Ideas in Practice* (San Francisco: Ardent Press, 2010); Dominique Moyse Steinberg, *A Mutual-Aid Model for Social Work with Groups* (London: Routledge Taylor & Francis, 2014); Spade, *Mutual Aid*; Mariame Kaba and Alexandria Ocasio-Cortez, *Mutual Aid 101*, Tool Kit (2020).

15. Peter Kropotkin, *Mutual Aid: A Factor in Evolution* (New York: McClure Phillips & Co., 1902).

16. See Daniel Soyer, *Jewish Immigrant Associations and American Identity in New York, 1880–1939* (Cambridge: Harvard University Press, 1997); Beito, *From Mutual Aid to the Welfare State*; Him Mark Lai, *Becoming Chinese American: A History of Communities and Institutions* (New York: AltaMira Press, 2004); Jessica Gordon Nembhard, *Collective Courage: A History of African American Cooperative Economic Thought and Practice* (State College: Pennsylvania State University Press, 2014).

17. See Watkins-Owens, *Blood Relations*; and James, *Holding Aloft the Banner of Ethiopia*.

18. Caribbean immigrants in the nineteenth and twentieth century traveled extensively throughout the Caribbean basin, most notably to Costa Rica and Panama, to work on the construction of the International Railways of Central America and later the Panama Canal. British West Indians from Jamaica, Barbados, and smaller Windward

and Leeward islands came together for the first time in Central America and developed communities and sociocultural infrastructure. They built churches and schools, and established associations and social clubs that would help them begin to foster a sense of British West Indian identity. However, while the beginnings of a unified Caribbean or West Indian identity may have been seen in these early Central American communities, it is through Anglophone Caribbean immigrant mutual aid societies and benevolent associations in the United States that a more fully developed and unified Caribbean identity emerged. Anglophone Caribbean immigrants in the United States worked extensively with each other not only to create a shared sense of Caribbean identity, but also to foster an identity that was transnational and very much still connected to the Caribbean. Caribbean laborers in the nineteenth century traveled to Central America often for seasonal and long-term work projects. However, many returned home to their native islands or moved on to other locations such as Cuba for work. The communities that formed in New York City between 1890 and 1940 were less transient than communities in areas such as the Canal Zone, where workers regularly arrived and departed. Conversely, Caribbean immigration to New York was more permanent and thus immigrants were able to strengthen any existing ideas of West Indian identity that they may have had prior to arrival in New York.

19. Some scholars of Caribbean immigration who write against these male-centered narratives include Watkins-Owens, *Blood Relations*; Showers-Johnson, *The Other Black Bostonians*; Putnam, *Radical Moves*; Michelle Stephens, *Black Empire: The Masculine Global Imaginary of Caribbean Intellectuals in the United States, 1914 to 1962* (Durham: Duke University Press, 2005); Blain, *Set the World on Fire*; and J. Flores-Villalobos, "'Freak Letters': Tracing Gender, Race, and Diaspora in the Panama Canal Archive," *Small Axe: A Caribbean Journal of Criticism* 23, no. 2 (2019): 34–56, and "Gender, Race, and Migrant Labor in the 'Domestic Frontier' of the Panama Canal Zone," *International Labor and Working-Class History* 99 (2021): 96–121.

20. The turn of the twentieth century saw the rise of the African American women's club movement, in which African American women advocated for social and political reform and stepped into important leadership roles. See Beverly Washington Jones, "Mary Church Terrell and the National Association of Colored Women: 1896–1901," *Journal of Negro History* 67, no. 1 (Spring, 1982): 20–33; and *Quest for Equality: The Life and Writings of Mary Eliza Church Terrell* (New York: Carlson Publishing, Inc., 1990); Evelyn Brooks Higginbotham, *Righteous Discontent: The Women's Movement in the Black Baptist Church, 1880–1920* (Cambridge: Harvard University Press, 1993); Deborah Gray White, *Too Heavy a Load: Black Women in Defense of Themselves, 1894–1994* (New York: W.W. Norton & Co., 1999); Brittney C. Cooper, *Beyond Respectability: The Intellectual Thought of Race Women* (Urbana: University of Illinois Press, 2017) for some works that discuss the club women movement.

21. See Guridy, *Forging Diaspora*, Jesse Hoffnung-Garskof, *Racial Migrations: New York City and the Revolutionary Politics of the Spanish Caribbean* (Princeton: Princeton University Press, 2019), and Craig Steven Wilder, *In the Company of Black Men: The*

African Influence of African American Culture in New York City (New York: New York University Press, 2001) for other works that highlight this connection between social organizations and political activism.

22. "Letter dated March 27, 1934," AWILAS General Correspondence 1933–1935, American West Indian Ladies Aid Society Records, 1915–1965, Box 1, Folder 4. MARBD, SCRBC.

23. Nancy Foner, *Islands in the City: West Indian Migration to New York* (Berkeley: University of California Press, 2001), 47; Louis J. Parascandola (ed.), *Look for Me All Around: Anglophone Caribbean Immigrants in the Harlem Renaissance* (Detroit: Wayne State University Press, 2005), 39.

24. Interview with former Bermuda Benevolent Association President Ivy Simons, September 2014.

25. James, *Holding Aloft the Banner of Ethiopia.*

26. 17th Census of the United States, 1950 Population Volume IV Special Reports, Part 3 origins Table 25, 3B-82.

27. A. M. Wendell Malliet, "British West Indians Outnumber all Other Groups in Harlem; Immigration More than 100 Years Old," *New York Amsterdam News*, March 05, 1938, 13.

28. U.S. Census of Population, 1930; 17th Census of the United States, 1950 Population Volume IV Special Reports; and James, *Holding Aloft the Banner of Ethiopia*, 364.

29. Tina Campt and Deborah A. Thomas, "Gendering Diaspora: Transnational Feminism, Diaspora and Its Hegemonies," *Feminist Review* 90, no. 1 (October 2008): 2.

30. See Brandon R. Byrd, *The Black Republic: African Americans and the Fate of Haiti* (Philadelphia: University of Pennsylvania Press, 2019) and Mamyrah Dougé-Prosper, "An Island in the Chain," *NACLA Report on the Americas* 53, no. 1 (2021): 32–38.

31. For a larger discussion on seasoning see Michael A. Gomez, *Exchanging Our Country Marks: The Transformation of African Identities in the Colonial and Antebellum South* (Chapel Hill: University of North Carolina Press, 1998):154–185.

CHAPTER 1

1. "Saint Vincent Handbook, Directory, and Almanac—1844," RBK 737, National Archives of St. Vincent and the Grenadines.

2. 4/77/194 *Friendly Societies in the West Indies: A Report on a Survey* by Alan Frank and D. Wells, Colonial Office, 1949, 6, Jamaica National Archives.

3. Leonard P. Fletcher, "The Friendly Societies in St. Lucia and St. Vincent," *Caribbean Studies* 18, no. 3/4 (Oct 1978-Jan. 1979): 100.

4. Bridget Brereton, "The Development of an Identity: The Black Middle Class of Trinidad in the Later Nineteenth Century," in *Caribbean Freedom: Economy and Society from Emancipation to the Present*, ed. Hilary Beckles and Verene Shepherd (Kingston: Ian Randle Publishers, 1993), 274–276.

5. Beverley Joy Anderson, The Decline of Friendly Societies of Jamaica: A Traditional Voluntary Association in a Developing Society (PhD diss., Boston College, 1985), 75.

6. Anderson, *The Decline of Friendly Societies of Jamaica*, 75.

7. Woodville K. Marshall, "'We Be Wise to Many More Things': Blacks' Hopes and Expectations of Emancipation," in *Caribbean Freedom: Economy and Society from Emancipation to the Present*, ed. Hilary Beckles and Verene Shepherd (Kingston: Ian Randle Publishers, 1993), 15.

8. 333,027 enslaved Africans were brought to the British Caribbean from the Bight of Benin, 132,111 from Sierra Leone, 870,041 from the Bight of Biafra, 704,922 from the Gold Coast, and 147,455 from Senegambia. Estimates Database. 2009. Voyages: The Trans-Atlantic Slave Trade Database, accessed October 22, 2014, http://www.slavevoyages.org/tast/assessment/estimates.faces?yearFrom=1501&yearTo=1866&flag=2.

9. These scholars include Maureen Warner-Lewis, *Central Africa in the Caribbean: Transcending Time, Transforming Cultures* (Kingston: University of the West Indies Press, 2003); Craig Steven Wilder, *In the Company of Black Men: The African Influence of African American Culture in New York City* (New York: New York University Press, 2001); Alan Gregor Cobley and Alvin Thompson (eds.), *The African-Caribbean Connection: Historical and Cultural Perspectives* (Bridgetown: University of the West Indies, National Cultural Foundation, 1990); and Mervyn Alleyne, *Roots of Jamaican Culture* (London: Pluto Press, 1988).

10. Warner-Lewis, *Central Africa in the Caribbean*, xxii–xxvi, 57, 65.

11. Wells and Wells, *Friendly Societies in the West Indies*, 46.

12. Anita J. Glaze, *Art and Death in a Senufo Village* (Bloomington: University of Indiana Press, 1981), 149.

13. Glaze, *Art and Death in a Senufo Village*, 149.

14. Glaze, *Art and Death in a Senufo Village*, 196.

15. Howard Johnson, "Friendly Societies in the Bahamas 1834–1910," *Slavery & Abolition: A Journal of Slave and Post-Slave Studies* 12, no. 3 (December 1991): 185.

16. Michael Gomez, *Exchanging Our Country Marks: The Transformation of African Identities in the Colonial and Antebellum South* (Chapel Hill: University of North Carolina Press, 1998), 95.

17. Kenneth Little, *The Mende of Sierra Leone: A West African People in Transition* (Oxford: Alden Press, 1969), 248.

18. Gomez, *Exchanging Our Country Marks*, 97.

19. Melville Herskovits, *Dahomey: An Ancient West African Kingdom* (New York: J.J. Augustin, 1938), 63–65, 70, 72.

20. Melville Herskovits, *Myth of the Negro Past* (New York: Harper Brothers, 1941), 165.

21. George Eaton Simpson, "The Acculturative Process in Jamaican Revivalism," in *Men and Cultures: Selected Papers*, ed. Anthony F.C. Wallace (Philadelphia: University of Pennsylvania Press, 1960), 335.

22. Johnson, "Friendly Societies in the Bahamas," 184–185.

23. Wells and Wells, *Friendly Societies in the West Indies*, 6.

24. The apprentice system was ubiquitous in all but two of the colonies in the British Caribbean, Antigua and the Bahamas, where laws were passed abolishing the apprenticeship clause of the 1833 Slavery Abolition Act. Thereby, enslaved Black people in these islands were granted full emancipation rights with no labor restrictions on August 1, 1834.

25. Cyril Hamshere, *The British in the Caribbean* (Cambridge: Harvard University Press, 1972), 147–149.

26. Marshall, "We Be Wise to Many More Things," 17–18.

27. Marshall, "We Be Wise to Many More Things," 13.

28. Thomas Holt, *The Problem of Freedom: Race, Labor, and Politics in Jamaica and Britain, 1832–1938* (Baltimore: John Hopkins University Press, 1992), 56; *Saint Vincent Witness*, January 21, 1864, Vol. II, No. 7; *Palladium: Saint Lucia Free Press*, April 18, 1840.

29. *Port of Spain Gazette*, September 2, 1834, American Antiquarian Society.

30. Throughout the period of enslavement in the British Caribbean, the enslaved did in fact demonstrate many acts of self-reliance. For instance, in many locations, the enslaved were in charge of their own provision grounds and by these unofficial means were able to feed themselves, nurture their families, and establish kinship networks. Additionally, money earned from the huckstering of these provisions provided the enslaved with the means to build and maintain homes in many cases.

31. Anderson, *The Decline of Friendly Societies of Jamaica*, 64.

32. 4/77/194 (Jamaica National Archives) *Friendly Societies in the West Indies: A Report on a Survey by Alan Frank and D. Wells*, Colonial Office, 1949, 6.

33. Anderson, *The Decline of Friendly Societies of Jamaica*, 66.

34. Anderson, *The Decline of Friendly Societies of Jamaica*, 6–7.

35. Howard Johnson, "Friendly Societies in the Bahamas"; Leonard P. Fletcher, "The Friendly Societies in St. Lucia and St. Vincent," 89.

36. Wells and Wells, *Friendly Societies in the West Indies, 50.*

37. Wells and Wells, *Friendly Societies in the West Indies, 10.*

38. Anderson, *The Decline of Friendly Societies of Jamaica*, 65–66, 77–78.

39. Johnson, "Friendly Societies in the Bahamas," 183–199.

40. Wells and Wells, *Friendly Societies in the West Indies,* 1–11.

41. Anderson, *The Decline of Friendly Societies of Jamaica*, 75.

42. Johnson, "Friendly Societies in the Bahamas," 186.

43. Wells and Wells, *Friendly Societies in the West Indies,* 6.

44. "Friendly Societies," 1844 St. Vincent Handbook, Directory, and Almanac, RBK 737, National Archives of St. Vincent and the Grenadines. Other friendly societies connected to religious affiliations include: The St. George's Friendly Society and the St. Andrews Friendly Society, both established in 1840 with a respective membership of 476 members, (1887 Blue Books of St. Vincent, National Archives of St. Vincent and the Grenadines); The Catholic Fellowship established July 19, 1896, with 195 members ("St. Lucia Blue Books—1900," National Archives Authority of Saint Lucia); St. Patrick's Friendly Society of Barbados founded in 1907 (Pam A 107, "St. Patrick's Friendly

Society," National Archives of Barbados); St. John's Friendly Society in Antigua founded by the Rector of St. John's in 1829 (Wells and Wells, *Friendly Societies in the West Indies*, 9); and the St. Joseph's Friendly Society connected to the RC Church in St. Vincent (*The Sentry*, March 19, 1897). Additionally, an ecclesiastical return for the Diocese of Barbados and the Leeward Islands and dated July 1841 highlights the existence of five friendly societies connected with the Anglican Church in Trinidad with a membership of 656.

45. James A. Thome and J. Horace Kimball, *Emancipation in the West Indies: A Six Months' Tour in Antigua, Barbados, and Jamaica in the Year 1837* (New York: American Anti-Slavery Society, 1838), 28.

46. Oliver W. Furley, "Moravian Missionaries and Slaves in the West Indies," *Caribbean Studies* 5, no. 2 (July 1965): 15.

47. S. U. Hastings and B. L. MacLeavy, *Seedtime and Harvest: A Brief History of the Moravian Church in Jamaica, 1754–1979* (Barbados: Cedar Press, 1979), 17.

48. Hastings and MacLeavy, *Seedtime and Harvest*, 33.

49. Oliver W. Furley, "Moravian Missionaries and Slaves in the West Indies," 5.

50. Furley, "Moravian Missionaries and Slaves in the West Indies," 11.

51. Furley, "Moravian Missionaries and Slaves in the West Indies," 11–12.

52. Furley, "Moravian Missionaries and Slaves in the West Indies," 12.

53. Furley, "Moravian Missionaries and Slaves in the West Indies," 12.

54. Mary Prince, *The History of Mary Prince, a West Indian Slave* (London: F. Westley and A.H. Davis, 1831):1, 17.

55. Furley, "Moravian Missionaries and Slaves in the West Indies," 16.

56. "Amended Rules of the Chateaubelair Provident Friendly Society," Financial Services Authority in Saint Vincent, accessed July 2014, 9.

57. "Amended Rules of the Chateaubelair Provident Friendly Society," 9.

58. "Amended Rules of the Chateaubelair Provident Friendly Society," 28.

59. "Amended Rules of the Chateaubelair Provident Friendly Society," 19.

60. "Amended Rules of the Chateaubelair Provident Friendly Society," 19.

61. Johnson, "Friendly Societies in the Bahamas," 186.

62. "Amended Rules of the Chateaubelair Olive Society," Financial Services Authority in Saint Vincent, accessed July 2014.

63. "Trinidad," *Port of Spain Gazette*, Tuesday August 28, 1838 Vol XIII no. 69, 1, National Archives of Trinidad.

64. Johnson, "Friendly Societies in the Bahamas," 184.

65. CO 23/94 "Grant's Town Letter dated 14th August 1835," British National Archives.

66. Thome and Kimball, *Emancipation in the West Indies*, 13.

67. CO 23/93 Despatch [sic] from WM. M. G. Colebrooke dated 13th August 1835. British National Archives

68. RBK 737 1844 "Saint Vincent Handbook, Directory, and Almanac," 35, National Archives of Saint Vincent and the Grenadines.

69. Thome and Kimball, *Emancipation in the West Indies*, 48.

164

Notes to Pages 33–38

70. Johnson, "Friendly Societies in the Bahamas," 183–185.

71. Johnson, "Friendly Societies in the Bahamas," 185, 190.

72. "St. Lucia Handbook," Directory & Almanac 1903, National Archives Authority of Saint Lucia; Working Men's Friendly Society, National Archives Authority of Saint Lucia.

73. Wells and Wells, *Friendly Societies in the West Indies*, 34, 37.

74. "St. Patrick's Friendly Society," Pam A 107, National Archives of Barbados.

75. Pam A 662, "British Order of the Ancient Free Gardeners Friendly Society—Myrtle E Flower," no. 149, Pam A 1498, "Amended Rules of the Saint Lucia Mutual Benefit Association," National Archives of Barbados, "Amended Rules of the Chateaubelair Provident Friendly Society," Financial Services Authority in Saint Vincent, accessed July 2014, 10.

76. "Amended Rules of the Chateaubelair Provident Friendly Society," accessed July 2014, 10.

77. The objective, aims, and goals of more than forty West Indian friendly societies have all had a provision allowing for death and/or funeral benefits upon the death of one of their members.

78. "Amended Rules of the Saint Lucia Mutual Benefit Association," Pam A 1498.

79. Vincent Brown, *The Reaper's Garden: Death and Power in the World of Atlantic Slavery* (Cambridge: Harvard University Press, 2008), 61–62.

80. Brown, *The Reaper's Garden*, 61–62.

81. Brown, *The Reaper's Garden*, 65.

82. "Amended Rules of the Chateaubelair Provident Friendly Society," accessed July 2014.

83. "Amended Rules of the Chateaubelair Provident Friendly Society," accessed July 2014.

84. Thome and Kimball, *Emancipation in the West Indies*, 13.

85. Wells and Wells, *Friendly Societies in the West Indies*, 12.

86. *St. Lucia Guardian*, June 13, 1901.

87. "British West Indies," *National Era* (March 23, 1848) Vol. II, no. 64, 46. "Letter to the Editor," *Palladium: Saint Lucia Press* (December 22, 1838) no. 27.

88. Barry B. Levine, *The Caribbean Exodus* (New York: Praeger, 1987), 19.

89. Johnson, "Friendly Societies in the Bahamas," 193.

90. Wells and Wells, *Friendly Societies in the West Indies*, 22.

91. Johnson, "Friendly Societies in the Bahamas," 193.

92. Johnson, "Friendly Societies in the Bahamas," 189

93. Wells and Wells, *Friendly Societies in the West Indies*, 7.

94. Brereton, "The Development of an Identity," 274–276, 278.

95. Brereton, "The Development of an Identity," 274–276, 278.

96. OP 12, "Annual Colonial Report for 1891," No. 38, National Archives of St. Vincent and the Grenadines, *Handbook of the America Republics* (Washington, DC: Bureau of the American Republics, 1893), 280.

97. Thome and Kimball, *Emancipation in the West Indies*, 10; see Footnote 34 about Antigua's exemption from the Apprenticeship Clause.

98. Wells and Wells, *Friendly Societies in the West Indies*, 11–12.

99. Johnson, "Friendly Societies in the Bahamas," 186–187, 195.

100. CO 23/94 "Grant's Town Letter dated 14th August 1835," British National Archives; Trinidad," *Port of Spain Gazette*, Tuesday August 28, 1938 Vol XIII, no. 69, 1, National Archives of Trinidad.

101. Johnson, "Friendly Societies in the Bahamas," 189.

102. Johnson, "Friendly Societies in the Bahamas," 187–188.

103. CO 23/93 "Bahamas Friendly Society dispatch dated March 31, 1835," British National Archives.

104. Johnson, "Friendly Societies in the Bahamas," 194.

105. Liberated Africans were Africans who were on illegal slave ships headed to the Americas intercepted by the British navy as part of the British campaign against the foreign slave trade. The British role in suppression of the slave trade was large, and by the mid-1840s, more than sixty British, French, American, and Portuguese warships were patrolling the African coast. Between 1848 and 1850, 12,000 liberated Africans reached the Caribbean. In the twenty-five years after 1841, 36,000 arrived in the region, with the majority going to Trinidad, British Guiana, and Jamaica, and 16,000 going to the French Caribbean. Once in the Caribbean, they were initially given indentureship contracts for one year, but that quickly changed to three years after government officials realized that as soon as their contracts were done they immediately would leave the plantations. For more on Liberated Africans see Daniel Domingues da Silva, David Eltis, Philip Misevich, and Olatunji Ojo's "The Diaspora of Africans Liberated from Slave Ships in the Nineteenth Century," *Journal of African History* 55, no. 3 (2014): 347–369.

106. Domingues da Silva, "The Diaspora of Africans Liberated from Slave Ships in the Nineteenth Century," 195.

CHAPTER 2

1. Barbadoan [*sic*] servant; File #54,5955–39, Box #3291; Records of the Immigration and Naturalization Service [INS], Record Group 85, Entry 9, National Archives at College Park, MD (NACP).

2. Velma Newton, *The Silver Men: West Indian Labour Migration to Panama 1850–1914* (Bridgetown: Institute of Social and Economic Research University of the West Indies), 7.

3. Lara Putnam, *The Company They Kept: Migrants and the Politics of Gender in the Caribbean Costa Rica, 1870–1960* (Chapel Hill: University of North Carolina Press, 2002), 7.

4. Putnam, *The Company They Kept*, 11, 35.

5. "Panama silver," as it came to be known, was held in high regard as it trickled into the West Indian economy. "Panama silver" was named such due to the segregated pay system established by Americans in 1904, when white canal workers were paid on a

Gold Roll in gold American dollars and Black Americans and Black West Indian laborers were paid in silver American dollars. The Gold Roll also referred to higher pay, better health benefits, amenities, and standard of living for white canal workers.

6. Newton, *The Silver Men*, 21–23.

7. U.S. Census of Population, 1930; 17th Census of the United States, 1950 Population Volume IV Special Reports; and James, *Holding Aloft the Banner of Ethiopia*, 364.

8. Holt, *The Problem of Freedom*, 144.

9. Edith Clarke, "Land Tenure and the Family in Four Selected Communities in Jamaica," *Social and Economic Studies* 1, no. 4 (August 1953): 82–85; Christine Barrow, *Family Land and Development in St. Lucia* (Cave Hill: Institute of Social and Economic Research [Eastern Caribbean], University of the West Indies, 1992), 1, 12–14.

10. Putnam, *The Company They Kept*, 24, 28–29, 33.

11. "Reports on the Present State of her Majesty's Colonial Possessions," AA7.1.92, 1859, 63, National Archives of St. Vincent and the Grenadines.

12. Newton, *The Silver Men*, 7.

13. Newton, *The Silver Men*, 7.

14. "British West Indies," *National Era*, March 23, 1848, II, no. 64, 46.

15. Barry B. Levine, *The Caribbean Exodus* (New York: Praeger, 1987), 19.

16. Fredrick Douglass Opie, *Black Labor Migration in Caribbean Guatemala, 1882–1923* (Gainesville: University Press of Florida, 2009), 1, 4–5. An estimated 2,500–5,000 Black Americans from U.S. cities such as New Orleans and Mobile, Alabama, also arrived in Guatemala between 1863 and 1923. They were also contracted to work on various foreign projects along the Caribbean coast, including the International Railways of Central America.

17. Newton, *The Silver Men*, 21–23.

18. The number of West Indian women working in the Canal Zone and its surrounding cities is hard to estimate, as Canal records often did not acknowledge their daily social reproduction labor or even their presence. The 1910 census does affirm that more than six thousand West Indian women lived inside the Canal Zone.

19. Despatches [*sic*] to the Department of State: January 1, 1870–July 31, 1886, Despatch [*sic*] 51—July 30, 1886; UD 182 Box 40; Bridgetown, Barbados BWI Consular Posts; Records of the Foreign Service Posts, Record Group 84, National Archives at College Park, MD (NACP).

20. "March 7, 1934—Letter from the British Legation in Panama to British Ambassador in DC," 1B/5/79/551, The Jamaica Archives and Records Department.

21. "February 2, 1934 Letter from the British Legation in Panama to British Ambassador in DC," The Jamaica Archives and Records Department.

22. Newton, *The Silver Men*, 26.

23. See note 5.

24. *1890 St. Lucia Colonial Reports*, 17, National Archives Authority of Saint Lucia.

25. Irma Watkins-Owens, *Blood Relations*, 13–14, 18.

26. Newton, *The Silver Men*, 170.

27. Putnam, *The Company They Kept*, 11, 35.

28. Putnam, *The Company They Kept*, 44.

29. "December 26, 1928 Letter from the British Legation in Havana to the Governor of Jamaica," 1B/5/77/48, The Jamaica Archives and Records Department.

30. Jorge L. Giovannetti, "Black British Caribbean Migrants in Cuba: Resistance, Opposition, and Strategic Identity in the Early Twentieth Century" in *Regional Footprints: The Travels and Travails of Early Caribbean Migrants*, ed. Annette Insanally, Mark Clifford, and Sean Sheriff (Kingston: Latin American-Caribbean Centre, University of the West Indies, 2006), 105–113.

31. Ada Ferrer, *Freedom's Mirror: Cuba and Haiti in the Age of Revolution* (New York: Cambridge University Press, 2014), 9.

32. Giovannetti, "Black British Caribbean Migrants in Cuba," 105.

33. "December 12, 1928 Memorandum in regards to West Indian emigration to foreign countries (mostly Cuba) to the Governor of Jamaica Sir, R.E. Stubbs GCMG from the colonial office," 1B/5/77/140, The Jamaica Archives and Records Department.

34. Opie, *Black Labor Migration in Caribbean Guatemala*, 2.

35. Glenn A. Chambers, *Race, Nation, and West Indian Immigration to Honduras, 1890–1940* (Baton Rouge: Louisiana State University Press, 2010).

36. "October 16, 1933 Memorandum from Mr. Vice Consul Rundal," 1B /5/79/551, The Jamaica Archives and Records Department.

37. Chambers, *Race, Nation, and West Indian Immigration to Honduras*, 13.

38. Opie, *Black Labor Migration in Caribbean Guatemala*, 52, 55, 60–65.

39. Giovannetti, "Black British Caribbean Migrants in Cuba," 113.

40. Newton, *The Silver Men*, 7.

41. "State of the West Indies," *National Era*, May 12, 1859, XIII, no. 645, 76.

42. "British West Indies," *National Era*, March 23, 1848, II, no. 64, 46.

43. "The West Indies as They Were and Are," *National Era*, June 2, 1859, XIII, no. 648, 86.

44. OP12 1890–1906, *Colonial Reports*—Annual, No 212 Report for 1896, 16; National Archives of St. Vincent and the Grenadines.

45. AA7.1.90, 1882–1883, *Reports on the Present State of Her Majesty's Colonial Possessions*, 197; National Archives of St. Vincent and the Grenadines.

46. OP3.1887, 1887, Notice—November 26, 1887, *Government Gazettes-Saint Vincent*, p. 386.

47. OP3.1880, 1880, Circular Dispatch—November 28, 1878, *Government Gazettes-Saint Vincent*, p. 141.

48. CO, British National Archives.

49. In the years 1875, 1880, 1884, 1889, 1892, 1896, 1901, 1905, 1911, and 1912 we see a spike in East Indian immigration to Trinidad with more than three thousand migrants coming in these respective years. *Trinidad Blue Books*, 1874–1912, National Archives of Trinidad and Tobago.

50. AA7.1.92, 1859, Reports on the Present State of her Majesty's Colonial Possessions, p. 27; National Archives of St. Vincent and the Grenadines.

51. Lomarsh Roopnarine, "East Indian Indentured Emigration to the Caribbean: Beyond the Push and Pull Model," *Caribbean Studies* 31, no. 2 (Jul–Dec 2003), 101, 107.

52. It is interesting to note that colonial officials recorded, to their dismay, that many West Indian laborers were migrating throughout the Caribbean to other British colonies, but they seldom kept official records of the number of immigrants migrating. More important, at least in record keeping, was recording the number of Indian indentured workers being shipped to the colonies annually. There are very detailed records of the number of Indian laborers that came annually to the colonies and how many stayed on after their indentureship was complete. Additionally, much of the legislature passed between 1860 and 1880 focused on this East Indian immigration and making sure there were rules set in place for these immigrants, including their healthcare and general wellbeing, minimum wage, and housing.

53. Major G. St. J. Ore. Browne, *Great Britain Colonial Office Report: Labour Conditions in the West Indies* (London: H.M. Stationery Office, 1939), 13.

54. Rioting in Trinidad, Despatch [*sic*] 431—December 5, 1919, 844F.612/8—844G.5123/15, Box 8898, RG 85, NACP.

55. "Earthquake Disasters in the Eastern Caribbean over the Past 300 Years," University of the West Indies, Seismic Research Unit 2006.

56. "The West Indies as They Were and Are," *National Era*, June 2, 1859, XIII, no. 648, 86.

57. Despatch [*sic*] 23—November 17, 1879, June 3, 1863—January 21, 1882, Roll 5, NACP.

58. Despatch [*sic*] 162—November 29, 1902, Box 0030 Despatched [*sic*] from State Department 1902.

59. Most recently the Soufrière volcano explosively erupted on April 9, 2021, after lying dormant for forty-two years. An estimated 20,000 residents were forced to evacuate their homes, and the neighboring islands of Saint Lucia, Barbados, Antigua, and Grenada took in evacuees. Fortunately, no casualties were reported.

60. Op12; No 403 Report for 1902–1903, *Annual Colonial Reports 1890–1906*, National Archives of St. Vincent and the Grenadines; TP33.1.1, Register of Co-operative Societies Report (annual), May 18, 1902, Volcanic Eruption in St Vincent, National Archives of St. Vincent and the Grenadines.

61. TP33.1.1, Register of Co-operative Societies Report (annual), May 11, 1902, Volcanic Eruption in St Vincent, National Archives of St. Vincent and the Grenadines.

62. Despatch [*sic*] 153—October 18, 1902, Box 0030 Despatched [*sic*] from State Department 1902.

63. Despatch [*sic*] 174—March 24, 1903; Letter Book, UD 182, Box 0037; Bridgetown, Barbados BWI Consular Posts; Records of the Foreign Service Posts, Record Group 84; NACP.

64. Newton, *The Silver Men*, 7.

65. Newton, *The Silver Men*, 7.

66. It is important to note that this number of Caribbean immigrants is inclusive of those immigrants coming from Cuba, Puerto Rico, and the Dutch Caribbean, and may reflect non-Black immigrants from the Caribbean.

67. Between 1918 and 1940, Caribbean women were a significant immigrant group outnumbering Caribbean males in the United States. The pattern is consistent. Between 1918 and 1922, for instance, 17,504 Caribbean immigrant women arrived in the United States compared to 17,320 Caribbean men. Between 1923 and 1927, 12,283 Caribbean women arrived in the United States while 10,154 Caribbean men arrived. From 1928 to 1931, again, arriving Caribbean immigrant women outnumbered Caribbean men each year. Data taken from the U.S. Census of Population, 1930; 17th Census of the United States, 1950 Population Volume IV Special Reports; and James, *Holding Aloft the Banner of Ethiopia*, 364.

68. Jeffery B. Perry, *Hubert Harrison: The Voice of Harlem Radicalism, 1883–1918* (New York: Columbia University Press, 2009), 55–56.

69. Nancy Foner, *Islands in the City: West Indian Migration to New York* (Berkeley: University of California Press, 2001), 26.

70. Beach-Thomas Family Papers, 1888–1973. Manuscripts, Archives, and Rare Books Division, Schomburg Center for Research in Black Culture.

71. Foner, *Islands in the City*, 4.

72. HT a/c aliens dpt to Unilda Gooding [Nov-1911], File #53,369–113, Box #1397, RG 85, Entry 9, NACP.

73. Putnam, *Radical Moves*, 31.

74. 17th Census of the United States, 1950 Population Volume IV Special Reports, Part 3 origins Table 25, 3B-82.

75. A. M. Wendell Malliet, "British West Indians Outnumber all Other Groups in Harlem; Immigration More than 100 Years Old," *New York Amsterdam News*, March 05, 1938, 13.

76. "September 1, 1928 Letter," Box 1, Folder 13, Beach-Thomas Family Records, 1888–1973. Manuscripts, Archives, and Rare Books Division, Schomburg Center for Research in Black Culture.

77. U.S. Department of Justice, Immigration and Naturalization Service. Yearbook of Immigration Statistics, "1983 Statistical Yearbook of the Immigration and Naturalization Service," Washington, DC: U.S. Department of Homeland Security, Office of Immigration Statistics, 2002, 2–5. Again, it is important to note that this number of Caribbean immigrants is inclusive of those immigrants coming from Cuba, Puerto Rico, and the Dutch Caribbean, and may reflect non-Black immigrants from the Caribbean.

78. "Immigration Act of 1924," United States Department of State Website, http://www.state.gov/r/pa/ho/time/id/87718.htm.

79. Ira De A. Reid, *The Negro Immigrant: His Background, Characteristics and Social Adjustments, 1899–1937* (New York: AMS Press, 1939), Appendix A, Table VII, 239. See also Table 2.1.

80. Winston James, *Holding Aloft the Banner of Ethiopia*, 155.

81. U.S. Bureau of the Census, *Historical Statistics of the United States Colonial Times to 1957*, Washington, DC, 1961.

82. File #003933/000, Box #14771–484 Nationality Reports; Records of the INS, Record Group 85, Entry 9, NACP.

83. March 6, 1913, Ships Daily Journal; Kingstown, St. Vincent Consular Post; UD 468, Box 0009; Records of the Foreign Service Posts, Record Group 84, National Archives at College Park, MD (NACP).

84. Stowaway-illegal ex NY October 15, 1906; File #51,384–86, Box #16; Records of the Immigration and Naturalization Service [INS], Record Group 85, Entry 9, National Archives at College Park, MD (NACP).

85. File #54670–362, Box #3416; Records of the INS, Record Group 85, Entry 9, NACP.

86. File #54670–362, Box #3416; Records of the INS, Record Group 85, Entry 9, NACP.

87. Erika Lee, historian of immigration and Asian American History, details in her work *At America's Gates Chinese Immigration During the Exclusion Era, 1882–1943* (2014) the ways in which Chinese immigrants, due to the exclusionary immigration laws of the early twentieth century, also found alternative ways or the "crooked path" to enter the United States and evade detection from immigration officials.

88. Alien Enemies, 1917–1918 June-August, Nov 1917-Feb 1918; File #54297/1, Box #2915, 118pp; Records of the Immigration and Naturalization Service [INS], Record Group 85, Entry 9, National Archives at College Park, MD (NACP).

89. "Mortimer S. Gordon re smuggling of Bermudians, Jamaicans & Spaniards via Puerto Rico," File #55607–457, Box #7590; RG 85, Entry 9; Records of the INS, Record Group 85, Entry 9, NACP.

90. "Mortimer S. Gordon re smuggling of Bermudians, Jamaicans & Spaniards via Puerto Rico," File #55607 -457, Box #7590; RG 85, Entry 9; Records of the INS, Record Group 85, Entry 9, NACP.

91. Dowridge-Challenor Family Letters, 1904–1917. Manuscripts, Archives, and Rare Books Division, Schomburg Center for Research in Black Culture. Dowridge's letters were donated to the Schomburg Center by her daughter Dorothy Challenor Burnham.

92. Nancy Foner, *Islands in the City: West Indian Migration to New York* (Berkeley: University of California Press, 2001) 5.

93. Barbadoan [*sic*] servant; File #54,595–539, Box #3291; Records of the Immigration and Naturalization Service [INS], Record Group 85, Entry 9, National Archives at College Park, MD (NACP).

94. Watkins-Owens, *Blood Relations*, 2.

95. Perry, *Hubert Harrison*, 56.

96. "September 22, 1925 Letter," Box 1, Folder 2, Beach-Thomas Family Records, 1888–1973. Manuscripts, Archives, and Rare Books Division, Schomburg Center for Research in Black Culture.

97. Watkins-Owens, *Blood Relations*, 1, 40–42.

98. Paule Marshall, *Brown Girl, Brownstones* (Old Westbury: Feminist Press, 1981).

99. Marshall, *Brown Girl, Brownstones*, 223–230.

100. Reid, *The Negro Immigrant*, 244.

101. "Letter dated March 12, 1926," Box 1, Folder 6. George Padmore Collection, University of the West Indies St. Augustine (Trinidad); "Letter dated September 15, 1925," Box 1, Folder 6. George Padmore Collection, University of the West Indies St. Augustine (Trinidad); "William H. Gore of Antigua, British West Indies got a scholarship to Howard University," September 24, 1934; File #55,853–732; Records of the Immigration and Naturalization Service [INS], Record Group 85, Entry 9, National Archives at College Park, MD (NACP).

102. James, *Holding Aloft the Banner of Ethiopia*, 89.

103. Interview with former Bermuda Benevolent Association President Ivy Simons, September 2014.

104. Interview with former Bermuda Benevolent Association President Ivy Simons, September 2014.

105. James, Holding Aloft the Banner of Ethiopia, 89–90.

106. Charles Diggs, *Kin Meets Kin: An Analysis of Afro-American and Afro-Caribbean Relations in Harlem During the 1920's*. Master's thesis, Cornell University, 1988, 44.

107. American West Indian Ladies Aid Society Records, 1915–1965. Manuscripts, Archives, and Rare Books Division, Schomburg Center for Research in Black Culture.

108. Beach-Thomas Family Records, 1888–1973. Manuscripts, Archives, and Rare Books Division, Schomburg Center for Research in Black Culture.

109. W. A. Domingo, "The Tropics in New York," *Survey* 53, March 1, 1925, 649. Roach is often referred to as African American, but he was born in the British West Indian island of Montserrat.

110. Kia Gregory, "In Harlem, Renaissance Theater Is at the Crossroads of Demolition and Preservation," *New York Times*, December 19, 2014; Gray, Christopher. "A Harlem Landmark in All but Name," *New York Times*, February 18, 2007.

111. "Despatch [*sic*] 373—May 3, 1906," Miscellaneous Official 1906–1908, Box 0049, INS, RG 85, NACP.

112. James, *Holding Aloft the Banner of Ethiopia*, 88.

113. Beach-Thomas Family Records, 1888–1973. Manuscripts, Archives, and Rare Books Division, Schomburg Center for Research in Black Culture.

114. American West Indian Ladies Aid Society Records, 1915–1965. Manuscripts, Archives, and Rare Books Division, Schomburg Center for Research in Black Culture.

115. Table XXI, "Gainful Workers 10 years old and over, by general divisions of occupations and sex, for the United States, 1870 to 1930," 100; Table XXII, "Percentage Distribution, by general divisions of occupations, of Gainful Workers 10 years old and over, by sex, for the United States, 1870 to 1930," 101. *Sixteenth Census of the United States: 1940, Population, Comparative Occupation Statistics for the United States, 1870 to 1940*, Washington, DC: United States Government Printing Office, 1943. Alba M. Edwards.

116. Foner, *Islands in the City*, 52–53.

117. Beach-Thomas Family Papers, 1888–1973. Manuscripts, Archives, and Rare Books Division, Schomburg Center for Research in Black Culture.

118. "August 2, 1929," "November 14, 1929," "October 28, 1930" Letter to the British Colonial Office, 1B/5/77/24, The Jamaica Archives and Records Department.

119. Foner, *Islands in the City*, 19.

120. "Appropriation to assist alien Mrs. Corbin and family to the US," July 1910, File #53,007–43, Box #973, RG 85, Entry 9; NACP.

121. Leon F. Litwack, *Trouble in My Mind: Black Southerners in the Age of Jim Crow* (New York: Alfred A. Knopf, Inc. 1998), 487.

122. "Finds Negro Exodus from South Gaining," *New York Times*, May 27, 1923.

123. "Harmful Rush of Negroes to the North," *New York Times*, June 3, 1917.

124. "Harmful Rush of Negroes to the North," *New York Times*, June 3, 1917.

125. Diggs, *Kin Meets Kin*, 40.

126. Watkins-Owens, *Blood Relations*, 53.

127. Watkins-Owens, *Blood Relations*, 40.

128. "The St. Thomas Treaty: A Series of Letters to the Boston Daily Advertiser," Andrews, Sidney, 1837–1880; Box 1869, 22–23; Massachusetts Historical Society.

129. Arturo Schomburg, Hubert Harrison, Ashley L. Totten, Frank Crosswaith, Edward Blyden, Elizabeth Hendrickson, and J. Raymond Jones are several of the numerous Virgin Islanders that aligned themselves with British West Indians once they had migrated to the United States.

130. "American West Indian Ladies Aid Society Records, 1915–1965," Manuscripts, Archives, and Rare Books Division, Schomburg Center for Research in Black Culture.

131. "Citizenship status of Inhabitants of the Virgin Islands," Opinion Solicitor—October 20, 1925, File #79–2, Box #1279, Records of the Immigration and Naturalization Service [INS], Record Group 85, Entry 26, National Archives at College Park, MD (NACP).

132. "Convention Between the United States and Denmark," Treaty Series, No. 629, Cession of the Danish West Indies, Article 6, August 4, 1916. U.S. Department of the Interior, http://www.doi.gov/index.cfm.

133. C. Gerald Fraser, "J. Raymond Jones, Harlem Kingmaker, Dies at 91," Obituary, *New York Times*, June 11, 1991, accessed October 2014, https://www.nytimes.com/1991/06/11/obituaries/j-raymond-jones-harlem-kingmaker-dies-at-91.html.

134. Records of the Immigration and Naturalization Service [INS], Record Group 85, Entry 26, National Archives at College Park, MD (NACP).

CHAPTER 3

1. Bermuda Benevolent Association Records, 1898–1969, Boxes 1,2,8. Manuscripts, Archives, and Rare Books Division, Schomburg Center for Research in Black Culture; "Bermudans Give a Ball," *New York Times*, April 7, 1899, 2.

2. 100th Anniversary of the Bermuda Benevolent Association, 1987–1997 program booklet, donated by former member Ivy Simons.

3. Bermuda Benevolent Association Records, 1898–1969, Boxes 1,2,8. Manuscripts, Archives, and Rare Books Division, Schomburg Center for Research in Black Culture; "Bermudans Give a Ball," *New York Times*; 100th Anniversary of the Bermuda Benevolent Association, 1987–1997 program booklet; Interview with former Bermuda Benevolent Association President Ivy Simons, September 2014.

4. See pages 158–159, note 18 on the complexities of early West Indian identity.

5. This is not to dismiss the connections that many Caribbean immigrants made in the nineteenth and early twentieth centuries, when large numbers of Caribbean immigrants traveled to Central America to work on the International Railways of Central America and the Panama Canal, but the communities that formed in New York City between 1890 and 1940 were less transient than communities in areas such as the Canal Zone, and thus immigrants were able to strengthen any existing ideas of West Indian identity that they may have had prior to arrival in New York. See pages 158–159, note 18 on the complexities of early West Indian identity.

6. Bermuda Benevolent Association Records, 1898–1969, Box 8. MARBD, SCRBC.

7. St. Lucia United Association history from Danette O. Sampson, former St. Lucia United President, May 2011.

8. I argue that these organizations can be viewed as "proto-Pan-African," because their ideas of Pan-Africanism were not as developed as the Pan-African ideology and movement that emerged in the 1950s and 1960s. However, they genuinely expressed concern for the well-being and uplift of people of African descent around the world. They also recognized the connection between themselves and the shared fate of other Black people.

9. I use the contemporary terms *African Diaspora* and *diasporic* throughout this and proceeding chapters in order to understand the way in which Caribbean immigrants conceptualized themselves as part of the larger Black world. However, immigrants in the twentieth century did not use this term to classify their international politics.

10. File #27671/17681, "Revision of Suggestions for Americanization Work Among Foreign Born Women"; File #27671/4720, "The Woman Citizen," Record Group 85—Entry 30 Box 187. National Archives at College Park, MD.

11. Bert J. Thomas, "Historical Functions of Caribbean-American Benevolent/ Progressive Associations," *Afro-Americans in New York Life and History* 12, no. 2 (July 1988): 45.

12. Interview with former Bermuda Benevolent Association President Ivy Simons, September 2014.

13. "How to Be a Good American Booklet," Beach-Thomas Family Records, 1888–1973, Box 1, Folder 14. MARBD, SCRBC.

14. Constitution and By-laws of the West Indian Benevolent Association [Amended and republished, June 1, 1891], F128.9.W54 W47 1891, New York Historical Society.

15. Similar patterns can be seen among Caribbean immigrant mutual aid societies and benevolent associations founded in Boston in the early twentieth century. Groups

such as the West India Aid Society formed in 1915 (Showers Johnson, *The Other Black Bostonians*, 59).

16. Showers Johnson, *The Other Black Bostonians*, 59.

17. This list comprises mutual aid societies and benevolent associations that could be found in archival records. It is quite possible that the number of immigrant social organizations founded between 1890 and 1940 is much larger than this preliminary list. It is also important to note that while some associations had island-specific names, such as the British-Jamaican Benevolent Association, Incorporated, they still had Pan–West Indian objectives and their membership was open to anyone from the Caribbean.

18. U.S. Department of Justice, Immigration and Naturalization Service. Yearbook of Immigration Statistics, "1983 Statistical Yearbook of the Immigration and Naturalization Service," Washington, DC: U.S. Department of Homeland Security, Office of Immigration Statistics, 2002, 2–5. See Chart 4 in Chapter 2.

19. Letter dated February 6, 1938 from C.A. Fausett, Chairman of the Advisory Board," Antigua and Barbuda Progressive Society, ABPS Folder—Membership Correspondence 1935–1970. MARBD, SCRBC.

20. Antigua Progressive Society, ABPS: Admin Box. MARBD, SCRBC.

21. Montserrat Progressive Society of New York, Inc., Constitution and By-Laws donated by Alan Pinado to Irma Watkins-Owens.

22. Montserrat Progressive Society of New York, Inc., Constitution and By-Laws donated by Alan Pinado to Irma Watkins-Owens.

23. Richard B. Moore Papers, Sc MG 397, Folder 7—Caribbean Organizations and Activities, MARBD, SCRBC.

24. American West Indian Ladies' Aid Society, MARBD, SCRBC. Constitution and By-laws of the West Indian Benevolent Association [Amended and republished, June 1, 1891], F128.9.W54 W47 1891, New York Historical Society.

25. Membership Applications (AWILAS) Folder 12, Box 1. MARBD, SCRBC.

26. Interview with former Bermuda Benevolent Association President Ivy Simons, September 2014.

27. Montserrat Progressive Society of New York, Inc., Constitution and By-Laws donated by Alan Pinado to Irma Watkins-Owens, 252–6.

28. Bermuda Benevolent Association Records, 1898–1969, Box 2. MARBD, SCRBC.

29. "August 14, 1933 Letter," British Virgin Islands Benevolent Association, Folder 1|1, Box 1. MARBD, SCRBC.

30. "BVIBA Juvenile Society Bylaws," British Virgin Islands Benevolent Association, Folder 1|1, Box 1. MARBD, SCRBC.

31. Bermuda Benevolent Association Records, 1898–1969, Box 1. MARBD, SCRBC.

32. American West Indian Ladies Aid Society Records, 1915–1965, Box 2, Folder 3. MARBD, SCRBC.

33. Montserrat Progressive Society of New York, Inc., Constitution and By-Laws donated by Alan Pinado to Irma Watkins-Owens, 21.

34. Montserrat Progressive Society of New York, Inc., Constitution and By-Laws donated by Alan Pinado to Irma Watkins Owens, 3, 20.

35. Constitution and By-laws of the West Indian Benevolent Association [Amended and republished, June 1, 1891], F128.9.W54 W47 1891, New York Historical Society.

36. Montserrat Progressive Society of New York, Inc., Constitution and By-Laws donated by Alan Pinado to Irma Watkins-Owens, 17.

37. American West Indian Ladies Aid Society Records, 1915–1965, Box 1, Folder 4. MARBD, SCRBC.

38. Bermuda Benevolent Association Records, 1898–1969, Box 2, 8 and "October 24, 1933 Letter," The Virgin Islands Civic and Industrial Association, American West Indian Ladies Aid Society, Folder 9, Box 1. MARBD, SCRBC.

39. "November 27, 1934—Minutes," American West Indian Ladies Aid Society Records, 1915–1965, Box 1, Folder 1. MARBD, SCRBC.

40. British Virgin Islands Benevolent Association Records, 1926–1989, Box 8, Folder 10. MARBD, SCRBC.

41. St. Lucia United Association history from Danette O. Sampson, former St. Lucia United President, May 2011.

42. St. Lucia United Association history from Danette O. Sampson, former St. Lucia United President, May 2011.

43. "Letter dated February 6, 1938 from C.A. Fausett, Chairman of the Advisory Board," Antigua and Barbuda Progressive Society, ABPS Folder—Membership Correspondence 1935–1970. MARBD, SCRBC.

44. Antigua Progressive Society, ABPS: Admin Box. MARBD, SCRBC.

45. AWILAS General Correspondence 1928–1936, Folder 4, Box 1. MARBD, SCRBC

46. AWILAS General Correspondence 1928–1936, Folder 2, Box 1. MARBD, SCRBC.

47. British Virgin Islands Benevolent Association Records, 1926–1989, Box 9, Folder 1. MARBD, SCRBC

48. Asian American immigrants also pooled financial resources to help one another because, like many other immigrant groups, they faced obstacles to participating in mainstream banking and financial institutions. In some cases, they did not have access to financial information needed by banks to open accounts, encountered strong language barriers, were distrustful of banks, or simply did not have enough money to save. These informal banking systems functioned as a collective savings plan in which members could pool their money and distribute it among themselves periodically. The Chinese call this rotating credit line practice hui or ko, the Japanese called it *tanomoshi* or *mujin*, Koreans: *kyes*, Indonesians: *arisan*, and Indians: *chits* or *kuries*. Yvonne Yen Liu, "For Asian Immigrants, Cooperatives Came from the Home Country," *Yes! Magazine* (May 22, 2018), accessed August 3, 2020, https://www.yesmagazine.org/democracy/2018/05/22/for-asian-immigrants-cooperatives-came-from-the-home-country/; and Shirley Ardener, "The Comparative Study of Rotating Credit Associations," *Journal of the Royal Anthropological Institute of Great Britain and Ireland* 94, no. 2 (July–December 1964).

49. Bermuda Benevolent Association Records, 1898–1969, Box 8. MARBD, SCRBC.

50. Paule Marshall, *Brown Girl, Brownstones*.

51. Antigua and Barbuda Progressive Society, ABPS Folder—Membership Correspondence 1935–1970; MARBD, SCRBC.

52. British Virgin Islands Benevolent Association, Folders 8|3 and 8|5, Box 2. Antigua and Barbuda Progressive Society, ABPS Folder—Admin General Office Files. MARBD, SCRBC.

53. Bermuda Benevolent Association Records, 1898–1969; Box 8. MARBD, SCRBC.

54. AWILAS Folder 8 Printed Materials, Box 2. MARBD, SCRBC.

55. American West Indian Ladies Aid Society Records, 1915–1965, MARBD, SCRBC.

56. AWILAS Folder 8 Printed Materials, Box 2. MARBD, SCRBC.

57. Antigua and Barbuda Progressive Society, ABPS Folder—Membership Correspondence 1935–1970. MARBD, SCRBC.

58. Montserrat Progressive Society of New York, Inc., Constitution and By-Laws donated by Alan Pinado to Irma Watkins-Owens, 13.

59. Bermuda Benevolent Association Records, 1898–1969, Boxes 1 and 2. MARBD, SCRBC.

60. "British Official Is Guest of Islanders: Benevolent Association Founded to Aid West Indians in New York," *New York Amsterdam News* (April 10, 1929).

61. "British Official Is Guest of Islanders: Benevolent Association Founded to Aid West Indians in New York," *New York Amsterdam News*.

62. Virgin Islands Congressional Council (VICC), 1927–1939, AWILAS, Folder 7 Box 1. MARBD, SCRBC

63. AWILAS American Virgin Island Correspondence, 1925–1935, American West Indian Ladies Aid Society Records, 1915–1965, Folder 6 Box 1. MARBD, SCRBC.

64. "American West Indian Ladies Aid Society Records, 1915–1965," Box 1, Folder 1. MARBD, SCRBC.

65. October 24, 1933 Letter from Ashley L. Totten, AWILAS, The Virgin Islands Civic and Industrial Association Folder 9 Box 1. MARBD, SCRBC.

66. Montserrat Progressive Society of New York, Inc., Constitution and By-Laws donated by Alan Pinado to Irma Watkins-Owens.

67. Richard B. Moore Papers, Sc MG 397, Folder 7—Caribbean Organizations and Activities, MARBD, SCRBC.

68. Montserrat Progressive Society of Boston, accessed July 2015, www.mpsofboston.org.

69. St. Lucia United Association history from Danette O. Sampson, former St. Lucia United President, May 2011.

70. American West Indian Ladies' Aid Society, MARBD, SCRBC. Constitution and By-laws of the West Indian Benevolent Association [Amended and republished, June 1, 1891], F128.9.W54 W47 1891, New York Historical Society.

71. Cameron McWhirter, *Red Summer: The Summer of 1919 and the Awakening of Black America* (Henry Holt and Company: New York, 2011), 13.

72. "Meeting notes—dated May 28, 1939," Antigua Progressive Society. MARBD, SCRBC.

73. Antigua and Barbuda Progressive Society, ABPS Folder—Membership Correspondence 1935–1970. MARBD, SCRBC.

74. Antigua Progressive Society, Folder—Admin Correspondence Political Concerns, MARD, SCRBC.

75. "April 14, 1935," British Virgin Islands Benevolent Association Records, 1926–1989, Box 1, Folder 1. MARBD, SCRBC.

76. "November 5, 1927 Letter," British Virgin Islands Benevolent Association, Folder 9|1, Box 9. MARBD, SCRBC.

77. "Report of the Development and Planning Committee," February 9, 1949, Bermuda Benevolent Association Records, 1898–1969, Box 8, Folder 2. MARBD, SCRBC.

78. St. Lucia United Association history from Danette O. Sampson, former St. Lucia United President, May 2011.

79. "May 16th, 1938—Letter from the British Jamaican Progressive League," Bermuda Benevolent Association Records, 1898–1969, Box 2. MARBD, SCRBC.

80. "January 6, 1939 Letter," Bermuda Benevolent Association Records, 1898–1969, Box 2. MARBD, SCRBC.

81. Bermuda Benevolent Association Records, 1898–1969, Box 8. MARBD, SCRBC.

CHAPTER 4

1. Hendrickson's exact year of birth is unknown. It is reported between 1883 to 1886 in multiple U.S. census records.

2. Thirteenth Census of the United States, 1910 (NARA microfilm publication T624, 1,178 rolls). Records of the Bureau of the Census, Record Group 29, National Archives, Washington, DC.

3. "New Harlem Tenants League to Sponsor Great Mass Meeting," *New York Age*, March 20, 1943.

4. "Plan Preventions to Increase Rents," *Chicago Defender*, May 5, 1925; A. Elizabeth Hendrickson, "The Man in the Street," *New York Amsterdam News*, Jan. 8, 1930.

5. Watkins-Owens, *Blood Relations*, 92.

6. "Working Women Asked to Attend Celebration," *New York Age*, April 7, 1928.

7. Tina Campt and Deborah A. Thomas, "Gendering Diaspora," 2.

8. Bermuda Benevolent Association Records, 1898–1969; Box 8. MARBD, SCRBC.

9. St. Lucia United Association history from Danette O. Sampson, former St. Lucia United President, May 2011.

10. Bermuda Benevolent Association Records, 1898–1969, Box 8. MARBD, SCRBC.

11. Bermuda Benevolent Association Records, 1898–1969, Box 2. MARBD, SCRBC.

12. Interview with former Jamaican Associates President Dr. Doreen Wilkinson, April 2016.

13. 80th Anniversary of the Jamaican Associates, Inc., 2014 program booklet, donated by member and former president Dr. Doreen Wilkinson.

14. Antigua Progressive Society MARBD, SCRBC.

15. New York State Archives; Albany, New York; State Population Census Schedules, 1925; Election District: 28; Assembly District: 13; City: New York; County: New York: 12.

16. Interview with ABPS President Mona Wyre-Manigo, August 6, 2019.

17. "'A Lighthouse in NY' at the Shomberg [sic]," *New York Amsterdam News*, October 10, 2013, accessed May 31, 2020, http://amsterdamnews.com/news/2013/oct/10/caribbean-lingo-lighthouse-ny-shomberg/.

18. "1911 Constitution Book," British Virgin Islands Benevolent Association Records, 19261–989, Box 1, Folder 1. MARBD, SCRBC.

19. Montserrat Progressive Society of New York, Inc., Constitution and By-Laws donated by Alan Pinado to Irma Watkins Owens, 5.

20. "Pamphlet—December 12, 1938," Folder—Admin Correspondence Political Concerns, Antigua Progressive Society. MARBD, SCRBC.

21. Between 1915 and 1919, Caribbean women made up 17.6 percent of arriving immigrants with Caribbean men making up 16.8 percent. Between 1920 and 1924, Caribbean women made up 29 percent of arriving immigrants with Caribbean men making up 23.1 percent. In 1925, Caribbean women were 7.8 percent of arriving immigrants with Caribbean men making up 6.6 percent. Data taken from the U.S. Census of Population, 1930, and 17th Census of the United States, 1950 Population Volume IV Special Reports.

22. Official Report 1921; File#844E.114/3—844F.612/7, Box #8897; General Records of the Department of State, Record Group 59, National Archives at College Park, MD (NACP).

23. Interview with former Bermuda Benevolent Association President Ivy Simons, September 2014.

24. "History," taken from the West Indian Social Club, Inc (http://www.westindiansocialclubinc.org/history.html) April 13, 2011.

25. "History," taken from the West Indian Social Club, Inc.

26. "History," taken from the West Indian Social Club, Inc.

27. "West Indian Social Club 60th Anniversary," *Hartford News*, April 15, 2010, accessed March 2, 2020, http://www.hartfordinfo.org/issues/documents/history/htfd_news_041510.asp.

28. AWILAS General Correspondence 1928–1936, Folder 3, Box 1. MARBD, SCRBC.

29. "Letter—dated February 28, 1928," AWILAS General Correspondence, 1928–1936, Folder 2, Box 1. MARBD, SCRBC.

30. "November 27th 1934 Minutes," Minutes AWILAS and Related Correspondence, 1928–1936, Folder 1, Box 1, MARBD, SCRBC.

31. AWILAS General Correspondence, 1928–1936, Folder 2, Box 1. MARBD, SCRBC.

32. "Letter—dated December 10, 1933," AWILAS General Correspondence, 1933–1935, Folder 4, Box 1. MARBD, SCRBC.

33. Interview with former Bermuda Benevolent Association President Ivy Simons, September 2014.

34. 100th Anniversary of the Bermuda Benevolent Association, 1987–1997 program booklet, donated by former member Ivy Simons.

35. 100th Anniversary of the Bermuda Benevolent Association, 1987–1997 program booklet.

36. "Jamaican Eyes US Senate Seat," *Jamaica Gleaner*, July 3, 2008, accessed March 2, 2020, https://jamaica-gleaner.com/power/2588; and "Veronica Airey-Wilson," *History Makers*, February 17, 2005, accessed March 2, 2020, https://www.thehistorymakers.org/biography/veronica-airey-wilson-40.

37. Bermuda Benevolent Association Records, 1898–1969, Box 8. MARBD, SCRBC.

38. "September 23, 1928 Minutes," Box 2, BVIBA Records. MARBD, SCRBC.

CHAPTER 5

1. National Association for the Advancement of Colored People, *Thirty Years of Lynching in the United States* (New York: Negro University Press, 1919), 7.

2. Christopher Waldrep (Ed.), *Lynching in America: A History in Documents* (New York: New York University Press, 2006).

3. Carole Boyce Davies, *Left of Karl Marx: The Political Life of Black Communist Claudia Jones* (Durham: Duke University Press, 2008), 174–175, 177.

4. The 15th Amendment of the U.S. Constitution. National Constitution Center–The 15th Amendment of the U.S. Constitution, accessed September 4, 2019, https://constitutioncenter.org/interactive-constitution/amendments/amendment-xv.

5. Philip Dray, *Capitol Men: The Epic Story of Reconstruction Through the Lives of the First Black Congressmen* (Houghton Mifflin: New York, 2008).

6. Eric Foner, *Reconstruction: America's Unfinished Revolution, 1863–1877* (Harper Collins: New York, 2002).

7. "War on the Blacks: Most Serious Race Riots at New York," *Los Angeles Times*, Aug 17,1900, I5.

8. "Capture of Arthur Harris," *New York Times*, Aug 17, 1900, 2.; "Policeman's Death a Murder," *New York Tribune*, Aug 14, 1900, 14; "Negroes Attacked in New York," *Independent*, Aug 23, 1900; "War on the Blacks: Most Serious Race Riots at New York," *Los Angeles Times*, Aug 17,1900, I5.

9. Litwack, *Trouble in My Mind*, 487.

10. Speech by Marcus Garvey, Liberty Hall, New York, March 6, 1920, March 13, 1920, reprinted in *The Marcus Garvey and the Universal Negro Improvement Association Papers*, vol. 1 (Berkeley: University of California Press, 1983), 141.

11. Keisha Blain and Tiffany Gill, *To Turn the Whole World Over: Black Women and Internationalism* (Chicago: University of Illinois Press, 2019), 2–4.

12. Blain and Gill, *To Turn the Whole World Over*, 2–4.

13. Though it may be anachronistic to say Caribbean immigrant mutual aid societies and benevolent associations called the work they did "Black Internationalism," this

ideology is demonstrated in their policies and initiatives at the time. These initiatives are examined in more detail later in the chapter.

14. Fikru Gebrekidan, "In Defense of Ethiopia: A Comparative Assessment of Caribbean and African American Anti-Fascist Protests, 1935–1941," *Northeast African Studies* 2, no. 1 (1995): 145–147.

15. William R. Scott, "Black Nationalism and the Italo-Ethiopian Conflict 1934–1936," *Journal of Negro History* 63, No. 2 (April 1978): 118.

16. Edward O. Erhagbe and Ehimika A. Ifidon, "African-Americans and the Italo–Ethiopian Crisis, 1935–1936: The Practical Dimension of Pan-Africanism," *Aethiopica* 11, no. 1 (2008): 68.

17. "Letter from George Padmore to Cyril Ollivierre dated July 28, 1934," George Padmore Letters, MARBD, SCRBC.

18. "Letter dated September 22, 1938 from the Ethiopian World Federation, Inc.," J. R. Casimir Papers, 1919–1981, Sc MG 110, MARBD, SCRBC.

19. "Pamphlet dated April 1920," J. R. Casimir Papers, 1919–1981, Sc MG 110, MARBD, SCRBC.

20. "Letter dated October 17, 1935," J. R. Casimir Papers, 1919–1981, Sc MG 110, MARBD, SCRBC.

21. "Letter dated May 16, 1939," Membership Correspondence 1935–1970, Antigua and Barbuda Progressive Society Records. MARBD, SCRBC.

22. TaKeia N. Anthony, *The Universal Ethiopian Students' Association, 1927–1948: Mobilizing Diaspora* (Cham, Switzerland: Palgrave Macmillan, 2019), 1, 15, 16, 37.

23. "African Journal of African Affairs Letter dated 1936," Bermuda Benevolent Association Records, 1898–1969, Box 2. MARBD, SCRBC; "Letter dated July 12, 1938 from the American League for Peace and Democracy," Bermuda Benevolent Association Records, 1898–1969, Box 2. MARBD, SCRBC.

24. "November Notes," Bermuda Benevolent Association Records, 1898–1969, Box 8. MARBD, SCRBC.

25. Bermuda Benevolent Association Records, 1898–1969, Box 8. MARBD, SCRBC.

26. V.I. Program Adopted Here: Federation Calls for Political Action Here and Abroad," *New York Amsterdam News*, October 20, 1934: 2.

27. "V.I. Program Adopted Here: Federation Calls for Political Action Here and Abroad," *New York Amsterdam News*, October 20, 1934: 2.

28. Louis J. Parascandola, *Look for Me All Around: Anglophone Caribbean Immigrants in the Harlem Renaissance* (Detroit: Wayne State University Press, 2005), 199.

29. Cyril V. Briggs, *Crusader* 2, no. 2 (October 1919): 27.

30. Parascandola, *Look for Me All Around*, 22.

31. Cyril V. Briggs, "Africa for the Africans," *New York Globe*, January 23, 1918: 10.

32. Reid, *The Negro Immigrant*, 153.

33. Ula Taylor, *The Veiled Garvey: The Life and Times of Amy Jacques Garvey* (Chapel Hill: University of North Carolina Press, 2003), 41.

34. Barbara Bair, "True Women, Real Men: Gender Ideology and Social Roles in the Garvey Movement," in *Gendered Domains: Rethinking Public and Private in Women's History*, ed. Dorothy O. Helly and Susan M. Reverby (Ithaca: Cornell University Press, 1992); Honor Ford-Smith, "Unruly Virtues of the Spectacular: Performing Engendered Nationalisms in the UNIA in Jamaica," *Interventions* 6, no.1 (2004); Rhonda Reddock, "The First Mrs. Garvey: Pan-Africanism and Feminism in the Early 20th Century British Colonial Caribbean," *Feminist Africa* 9 (March 2015), 59–77.

35. "Henrietta Vinton New Garvey Head," *Pittsburgh Courier*, May 19, 1934: 13; "Henrietta Vinton Davis Elected Leader of Garvey Supporters at Convention," *New York Amsterdam News*, August 11, 1934: 15.

36. Tony Martin, *Amy Ashwood Garvey: Pan-Africanist, Feminist and Mrs. Marcus Garvey No. 1 or A Tale of Two Amies* (Dover: The Majority Press, 2007), 47, 86.

37. Jinx Coleman Broussard, *Giving a Voice to the Voiceless: Four Pioneering Black Women Journalists* (New York: Routledge, 2004), 105–106.

38. Parascandola, *Look for Me All Around*, 108.

39. Hillal H. Nadji, "A Garvey Comes Home to Africa," *Chicago Defender*, August 6, 1949: 19.

40. Broussard, *Giving a Voice to the Voiceless*, 132–133.

41. Litwack, *Trouble in My Mind*, 484.

42. W. E. B. Du Bois, "A Lunatic or a Traitor," *Crisis* 28, no. 1 (May 1924), 8.

43. Malliet, "British West Indians Outnumber All Other Groups in Harlem; Immigration More Than 100 Years Old," 13.

44. Watkins-Owens, *Blood Relations*, 60; James, *Holding Aloft the Banner of Ethiopia*, 95–96; Wilder, *In the Company of Black Men*, 194.

45. Wilder, *In the Company of Black Men*, 194.

46. James, *Holding Aloft the Banner of Ethiopia*, 96.

47. "Letter dated March 27, 1934," AWILAS General Correspondence 1933–1935, American West Indian Ladies Aid Society Records, 1915–1965, Box 1, Folder 4. MARBD, SCRBC.

48. "Advertisement in *The Negro Champion* April 20, 1929, 7," Richard B. Moore Papers, Box 1, Folder 10—Personal Communist Party Years, Sc MG 397. MARBD, SCRBC.

49. Richard B. Moore Papers, Box 6, Folder 7, Sc MG 397. MARBD, SCRBC.

50. AWILAS General Correspondence 1933–1935, Folder 4, Box 1. MARBD, SCRBC.

51. "Letter dated August 30, 1929 from the Worker's School to the AWILAS," AWILAS General Correspondence 1928–1936, American West Indian Ladies Aid Society Records, 1915–1965, Box 1, Folder 2. MARBD, SCRBC.

52. James, *Holding Aloft the Banner of Ethiopia*, 155.

53. Foner, *Islands in the City*, 47; Parascandola, *Look for Me All Around*, 39.

54. Manfred Berg, *The Ticket to Freedom: The NAACP and the Struggle for Black Political Integration* (Gainesville: University Press of Florida, 2005), 63.

55. "Anti-Alien Bill Fought: Protests Are Urged on 'Threat to Democratic Rights,'" *New York Times*, July 1, 1939: 3.

56. "Letter dated August 23, 1939 from The American Committee of Protection of Foreign Born," Bermuda Benevolent Association Records, 1898–1969, Box 2. MARBD, SCRBC; "Anti-Alien Bill Fought: Protests Are Urged on 'Threat to Democratic Rights,'" *New York Times*.

57. "May 19, 1939 Letter," Bermuda Benevolent Association Records, 1898–1969, Box 2. MARBD, SCRBC; "Caribbean Union in Move to Defeat Bills," *New York Amsterdam News*, May 20, 1939: 4.

58. Richard B. Moore Papers, Box 6—International Labor Defense and National Negro Congress, Sc MG 397. MARBD, SCRBC.

59. Flyer for the Second National Negro Congress, October 15–17, 1937, Richard B. Moore Papers, Box 6—International Labor Defense and National Negro Congress, Sc MG 397. MARBD, SCRBC.

60. Bermuda Benevolent Association Records, 1898–1969, Box 1. MARBD, SCRBC; Interview with former Jamaican Associates President Dr. Doreen Wilkinson, April 2016; "Letter from the NAACP dated March 21, 1934," AWILAS General Correspondence 1933–1935, Box 1, Folder 4. MARBD, SCRBC.

61. "May 19, 1939 Letter," Bermuda Benevolent Association Records, 1898–1969, Box 2. MARBD, SCRBC; "November 12, 1931 letter from David Paris, from the Assembly Chamber State of New York," AWILAS General Correspondence 1928–1936, Box 1, Folder 2. MARBD, SCRBC.

62. Interview with former Jamaican Associates President Dr. Doreen Wilkinson, April 2016.

63. "Letter from Honorable Walter F. James to the BVIBA dated November 5, 1927," Box 9, Folder 1, British Virgin Islands Benevolent Association Records. MARBD, SCRBC.

64. "November 12, 1931 letter from David Paris, from the Assembly Chamber State of New York," AWILAS General Correspondence 1928–1936, Box 1, Folder 2. MARBD, SCRBC

65. "56 Contests Mark Primary on Tuesday," *New York Times*, September 14, 1930: 33.

66. "Letter from the Chicopee Democratic Club, Inc. dated August 31, 1933," AWILAS General Correspondence 1933–1935, Box 1, Folder 4. MARBD, SCRBC.

67. "Letter from A.C. Burnes dated October 10, 1933," AWILAS General Correspondence, 1933–1935, Box 1, Folder 4. MARBD, SCRBC.

68. 15th Census of the United States, 1930 Population Volume II Special Reports, Chapter 9, Table 18, 446.

69. Winston James, "Explaining Afro-Caribbean Social Mobility in the United States: Beyond the Sowell Thesis," *Comparative Studies in Society and History* 44, no. 2 (2002): 222–223; Malliet, "British West Indians Outnumber All Other Groups in Harlem; Immigration More Than 100 Years Old," 13.

70. Putnam, *Radical Moves*, 31.

71. "Letter dated October 18, 1934 from William T. Andrews," AWILAS General Correspondence, 1933–1935, Box 1, Folder 4. MARBD, SCRBC.

72. Jamaican-born Joel Augustus Rogers was a prominent journalist, historian, and author. His articles for newspapers such as *New York Amsterdam News*, *Crisis*, and *Negro World* were widely cited in both the Caribbean and West Indian communities. A great proponent of Pan-Africanism, he also served as the sub-editor of Marcus Garvey's *Daily Negro Times* in 1922. He is noted for popularizing African and African American history in the twentieth century and challenging discourse of the time that diminished and even omitted the historical contributions of people of African descent.

73. J. A. Rogers, "Ruminations: William T. Andrews Aspirant for Office," *New York Amsterdam News*, September 8, 1934: 8.

74. "October 28, 1927 Letter," AWILAS General Correspondence, 1928–1936, Box 1, Folder 2; "October 28, 1927; "August 31, 1933 Letter from the Tammany Hall Organization," AWILAS General Correspondence, 1933–1935, American West Indian Ladies Aid Society Records, 1915–1965, Box 1, Folder 4; "Letter from the NAACP, April 1, 1939," Box 2. Bermuda Benevolent Association Records, 1898–1969; "1939 Letter," Bermuda Benevolent Association Records, 1898–1969, Box 8. MARBD, SCRBC.

75. "Letter from Washington Heights Improvement Council, Inc. dated April 1937," Bermuda Benevolent Association Records, 1898–1969, Box 8. MARBD, SCRBC.

76. "Plan Preventions to Increase Rents," *Chicago Defender*, May 5, 1925; A. Elizabeth Hendrickson, "The Man in the Street," *New York Amsterdam News*, January 8, 1930.

77. "New Harlem Tenants League to Sponsor Great Mass Meeting," *New York Age*, March 20, 1943: 2.

78. "Plan Fight on Rental Raises: New Tenant's League Mass Meeting Next Tuesday," *New York Amsterdam Star-News*, September 30, 1941: 26.

79. "Damage Put at $500,000," *New York Amsterdam News*, March 23, 1935.

80. *New York Amsterdam News*, March 1935.

81. *Daily Mirror*, April 2, 1935.

82. Beth Tompkins Bates, *Pullman Porters and the Rise of Protest Politics in Black America, 1925–1945* (Chapel Hill: University of North Carolina Press, 2001).

83. Melinda Chateauvert, *Marching Together: Women of the Brotherhood of Sleeping Car Porters* (Chicago: University of Illinois Press, 1997) 17; John C. Walter, "Frank R. Crosswaith and the Negro Labor Committee," *Afro-Americans in New York Life and History* 3, no. 2 (July 31, 1979): 35.

84. "Letter from Ashley Totten to AWILAS dated February 17, 1930," Brotherhood of Sleeping Car Porters (AWILAS), 1930–1934, Box 1, Folder 8, American West Indian Ladies Aid Society Records, 1915–1965, Box 1, Folder 4. MARBD, SCRBC.

85. "March 30, 1934 Letter BSCP to AWILAS," Brotherhood of Sleeping Car Porters (AWILAS), 1930–1934, Box 1, Folder 8. American West Indian Ladies Aid Society Records, 1915–1965. MARBD, SCRBC.

86. "July 21, 1933 Letter," Brotherhood of Sleeping Car Porters (AWILAS), 1930–1934, Box 1, Folder 8. American West Indian Ladies Aid Society Records, 1915–1965. MARBD, SCRBC.

87. "December 10, 1933 Letter," AWILAS General Correspondence, 1933–1935, American West Indian Ladies Aid Society Records, 1915–1965, Box 1, Folder 4. MARBD, SCRBC.

88. Letter dated 1938, AWILAS Folder 8, printed Materials American West Indian Ladies Aid Society Records, 1915–1965, Box 1, Folder 4. MARBD, SCRBC.

89. "Letter dated June 21, 1934 from American League Against War and Fascism," AWILAS General Correspondence, American West Indian Ladies Aid Society Records, 1915–1965, Box 1, Folder 4. MARBD, SCRBC.

90. Despatch [sic] September 7, 1918, Despatch [sic] May 3, 1921; Despatch [sic] February 9, 1922; File #844D.123311/10—844D.52/9, Box #8895; General Records of the Department of State, Record Group 59, National Archives at College Park, MD (NACP).

91. Despatch [sic] on July 30, 1921, Despatch [sic] July 28, 1922; File #844D.123311/10—844D.52/9, Box #8895; General Records of the Department of State, Record Group 59, NACP.

92. Despatch [sic] September 7, 1918, Despatch [sic] May 3, 1921; Despatch [sic] February 9, 1922; File #844D.123311/10—844D.52/9, Box #8895; General Records of the Department of State, Record Group 59, National Archives at College Park, MD (NACP).

93. *Gleaner*, September 19, 1925.

94. "Strike News," *Gleaner*, "Strike on at Match Factory," *Gleaner*, April 29, 1919; Despatch [sic] 304 -July 17, 1918; File #844D.123311/10—844D.52/9, Box #8895; General Records of the Department of State, Record Group 59, NACP; Despatch [sic] August 20, 1924; File #844E.114/3—844F.612/7, Box #8897; General Records of the Department of State, Record Group 59, NACP.

95. Opie, *Black Labor Migration in Caribbean Guatemala*, 52, 55, 60–65; O. Nigel Bolland, *On the March: Labour Rebellions in the British Caribbean, 1934–39* (Kingston: Ian Randle Publishers, 1995), 20–23, 92––95.

96. "May 16th, 1938—Letter from the British Jamaican Progressive League," Bermuda Benevolent Association Records, 1898–1969, Box 2. MARBD, SCRBC.

97. "Letter dated July 26, 1940," Folder—Admin Correspondence Political Concerns, ABPS: Admin Box, Antigua and Barbuda Progressive Society. MARBD, SCRBC.

98. "Letter dated July 26, 1940," Folder—Admin Correspondence Political Concerns, ABPS: Admin Box, Antigua and Barbuda Progressive Society. MARBD, SCRBC.

99. British Virgin Islands Benevolent Association, Folder 9|6. MARBD, SCRBC.

100. Bermuda Benevolent Association Records, 1898–1969, Boxes 1, 2, 8. MARBD, SCRBC; 100th Anniversary of the Bermuda Benevolent Association, 1987–1997 program booklet, donated by former member Ivy Simons.

101. "November Notes," Bermuda Benevolent Association Records, 1898–1969, Box 8. MARBD, SCRBC.

CONCLUSION

Note to epigraph: Fenton Johnson, "Credit Is Due the West Indian," *Favorite Magazine* (December 1919), Vol. 3, 209.

1. Robert Beatty, "Caribbean Crossroads: June Is Caribbean-American Heritage Month!" *South Florida Times*, June 20, 2008.

2. St. Lucia United Association. "102nd Anniversary Celebration." Facebook, October 28, 2022. www.facebook.com/profile.php?id=100072237595282.

3. St. Lucia United Association history from Danette O. Sampson, former St. Lucia United President, May 2011.

4. Antigua Progressive Society, MARBD, SCRBC.

5. Having used the records of the ABPS extensively in my research, I was asked by the Schomburg Center to speak on this panel—where I met many of the members of the ABPS, including president Mona Wyre-Manigo.

6. "Consulate General in New York Announces Mobile Services," *Caribbean Times: Antigua & Barbuda* (March 25, 2015), http://www.caribbeantimes.ag/consulate-general -in-new-york-announces-mobile-services/.

7. At the request of ABPS President Mona Wyre-Manigo, I helped the organization to draft their co-naming application letter to highlight the history of the organization.

8. "NYC Street Renamed in Honour [*sic*] of Late Antiguan," *Antigua Observer*, June 26, 2022, antiguaobserver.com/nyc-street-renamed-in-honour-of-late-antiguan %EF%BF%BC/

9. Interview with former Bermuda Benevolent Association President Ivy Simons, September 2014.

10. Fletcher, "The Friendly Societies in St. Lucia and St. Vincent," 89.

11. Anderson, The Decline of Friendly Societies of Jamaica, 218.

12. Founded in 2013, after the acquittal of George Zimmerman for the murder of seventeen-year-old Black teenager Trayvon Martin, the Black Lives Matter (BLM) movement began with the use of the social media hashtag #BlackLivesMatter by organizers Alicia Garza, Patrisse Cullors, and Opal Tometi. It has since gone on to become an international activist movement that is also a Black-centered political will and movement building project with a global network of more than forty member-led chapters. BLM members protest violence and systemic racism toward Blacks, racial profiling, police brutality, and racial inequality in the United States' criminal justice system, regularly holding rallies and speaking out against these issues. See https://Blacklivesmatter .com/herstory for the movement's mission statement and Eddie Glaude Jr., *Democracy in Black: How Race Still Enslaves the American Soul* (New York: Broadway Books, 2017) for more historical context around the creation of BLM.

BIBLIOGRAPHY

Archives and Manuscript Collections

American Antiquarian Society

Newspapers from the Caribbean and Bermuda, 1718 to 1876

Barbados National Archives

Barbados Blue Book, 1870–1920
Friendly Societies Act of 1905

Jamaica Archives and Record Department: Spanish Town, Jamaica

"August 2, 1929," "November 14, 1929," "October 28, 1930." Letter to the British Colonial Office, 1B/5/77/24

December 12, 1928. Memorandum in regards to West Indian emigration to foreign countries (mostly Cuba) to the Governor of Jamaica Sir, R.E. Stubbs GCMG from the colonial office, 1B/5/77/140,

December 26, 1928. Letter from the British Legation in Havana to the Governor of Jamaica, 1B/5/77/48

February 2, 1934. Letter from the British Legation in Panama to British Ambassador in DC

Handbook of Jamaica,1881–1919

Island Records Office – I.R.O (1B/11)

March 7, 1934. Letter from the British Legation in Panama to British Ambassador in DC, 1B/5/79/551

October 16, 1933. Memorandum from Mr. Vice Consul Rundal, 1B/5/79/551

Manuscripts, Archives, and Rare Books Division,
Schomburg Center for Research in Black Culture

American West Indian Ladies Aid Society Records, 1915–1965
Antigua Barbuda Progressive Society Records
Beach-Thomas Family Records, 1888–1973
Bermuda Benevolent Association Records, 1898–1969
British Virgin Islands Benevolent Association Records, 1926–1989
Dowridge-Challenor Family Letters, 1904–1917
George Padmore Letters

GAYAP
J. R. Casimir Papers
Richard B. Moore Papers
St. Philip's Church Records
Universal Negro Improvement Association Miscellaneous Collection

Massachusetts Historical Society

The St. Thomas Treaty: A Series of Letters to the Boston Daily Advertiser," Andrews,
  Sidney, 1837–1880; Box 1869

National Archives Authority of St. Lucia

1890 St. Lucia Colonial Report
Friendly Societies Ordinances, 1896 No. 11
St. Lucia Blue Books, 1896–1902

National Archives of Barbados

St. Patrick's Friendly Society, Pam A 107
Amended Rules of the Saint Lucia Mutual Benefit Association, Pam A 1498
British Order of the Ancient Free Gardeners Friendly Society—Myrtle E Flower, no. 149,
  Pam A 662

National Archives in New York City

Records of the Government of the Virgin Islands [Record Group 55], 1672–1957

National Archives of St. Vincent and the Grenadines

Blue Books of St. Vincent, 1854–1910
St. Vincent Despatches [sic] of Government 1862–1870, 1877–1880, 1886–1896
Annual Colonial Reports, 1890–1906
Saint Vincent Government Gazette, 1868–1906
Register of Co-operative Societies Report (annual), May 11–18, 1902, Volcanic Eruption
  in St Vincent, TP33.1.1
Reports on the Present State of Her Majesty's Colonial Possessions 1859, 1861, 1868
Saint Vincent Handbook, Directory, and Almanac, 1844
Government Gazettes-Saint Vincent, 1878, 1887

National Archives of Trinidad and Tobago

Trinidad Blue Book, 1874–1925
Tobago Blue Book, 1857–1887

The National Archives (United Kingdom)

CO 23/94 Grant's Town Letter dated August 14, 1835
CO 23/93 Despatch [sic] from WM. M. G. Colebrooke dated August 13, 1835
CO 23/93 Bahamas Friendly Society Dispatch dated March 31, 1835

The New York Historical Society Library
The West Indian Benevolent Association of New York City Records

The Tamiment Library and Robert F. Wagner Labor Archives,
New York University
Communist Party of the United States of America Records TAM.132

The University of the West Indies at St. Augustine: Trinidad
"Earthquake Disasters in the Eastern Caribbean over the Past 300 Years," The University
of the West Indies, Seismic Research Unit 2006.

The University of the West Indies Library: Mona, Jamaica
West Indies and Special Collection: Colonial Office Records

U.S. National Archives: Washington, DC
Records of the Immigration and Naturalization Service [Record Group 85], 1787–1950
Records of the Immigration and Naturalization Service [Record Group 85]: Communist
Labor Party Membership as Grounds for Deportation, 1920
Information Regarding Alien Seamen: Laws, Regulations, Lists, and Statistics, 1926–1933
Thirteenth Census of the United States, 1910 (NARA microfilm publication T624, 1,178
rolls). Records of the Bureau of the Census, Record Group 29

U.S. National Archives: College Park, MD
Alien Enemies, 1917–1918 June-August, Nov 1917–Feb 1918; File# 54297/1, Box #2915,
118 pp; Records of the Immigration and Naturalization Service [INS], Record
Group 85, Entry 9
Appropriation to assist alien Mrs. Corbin and family to the US," July 1910, File #53,007–
43, Box #973, RG 85, Entry 9 Barbadoan [*sic*] servant; File #54,595–539, Box #3291;
Records of the Immigration and Naturalization Service [INS], Record Group 85,
Entry 9
Citizenship status of Inhabitants of the Virgin Islands," Opinion Solicitor—October 20,
1925, File #79–2, Box #1279, INS, Record Group 85, Entry 26
Despatch [*sic*] 23—November 17, 1879, June 3, 1863—January 21, 1882, Roll 5
Despatch [*sic*] 51—July 30, 1886; UD 182 Box 40; Bridgetown, Barbados BWI Consular
Posts; Records of the Foreign Service Posts, Record Group 84
Despatch [*sic*] 153—October 18, 1902, Box 0030 Despatched [*sic*] from State Depart-
ment 1902
Despatch [*sic*] 162—November 29, 1902, Box 0030
Despatch [*sic*] 174—March 24, 1903; Letter Book, UD 182, Box 0037; Bridgetown, Bar-
bados BWI Consular Posts; Records of the Foreign Service Posts, Record Group 84
Despatch [*sic*] 373—May 3, 1906," Miscellaneous Official 1906–1908, Box 0049, INS,
RG 85

Despatches [sic] to the Department of State: January 1, 1870–July 31, 1886, UD 182 Box 40; Bridgetown, Barbados BWI Consular Posts; Records of the Foreign Service Posts, Record Group 84

File #54670–362, Box #3416; Records of the INS, Record Group 85, Entry 9

File #844D.123311/10—844D.52/9, Box #8895; General Records of the Department of State, Record Group 59

HT a/c aliens dpt to Unilda Gooding [Nov-1911], File #53,369–113, Box #1397, RG 85, Entry 9

March 6, 1913, Ships Daily Journal; Kingstown, St. Vincent Consular Post; UD 468, Box 0009; Records of the Foreign Service Posts, Record Group 84

"Mortimer S. Gordon re smuggling of Bermudians, Jamaicans & Spaniards via Puerto Rico," File #55607–457, Box #7590; RG 85, Entry 9; Records of the INS, Record Group 85, Entry 9

Official Report 1921; File #844E.114/3—844F.612/7, Box #8897; General Records of the Department of State, Record Group 59

Rioting in Trinidad, Despatch [sic] 431—December 5, 1919, 844F.612/8—844G.5123/15, Box 8898, RG 85

Stowaway-illegal ex NY October 15, 1906; File #51,384–86, Box #16; INS, Record Group 85, Entry 9 "William H. Gore of Antigua, British West Indies got a scholarship to Howard University," September 24, 1934; File #55,853–732; INS, Record Group 85, Entry 9

Unofficial Archives

80th Anniversary of the Jamaican Associates, Inc., 2014 Program Booklet, donated by member and former president Dr. Doreen Wilkinson

100th Anniversary of the Bermuda Benevolent Association, 1987 1997 Program Booklet, donated by former member Ivy Simons

Financial Services Authority in Saint Vincent

Montserrat Progressive Society of New York, Inc., Constitution and By-Laws donated by Alan Pinado to Irma Watkins-Owens

"St. Lucia United Association History" from Danette O. Sampson, former St. Lucia United President, May 2011

Unpublished Interviews

Simons, Ivy. Interview by author. New York, NY. September 10, 2014.
Sampson, Danette O. Email correspondence with author. Brooklyn, NY. May 7, 2011.
Wilkinson, Doreen. Interview by author. Boston, MA. April 1, 2016.
Wyre-Manigo, Mona. Interview by author. New York, NY. August 6, 2019.

Databases and Websites

"Convention Between the United States and Denmark," Treaty Series, No. 629, Cession of the Danish West Indies, Article 6, August 4, 1916. U.S. Department of the Interior, http://www.doi.gov/index.cfm.

Maddox, Tyesha and Daniel Joslyn, "The History and Impact of Mutual Aid in America," YouTube, February 9, 2022, educational video, 0:54–1:06, https://youtu.be/wFqOLHsj6nE.

New York State Archives; Albany, New York; State Population Census Schedules, 1925; Election District: 28; Assembly District: 13; City: New York; County: New York: 12.

The Trans-Atlantic Slave Trade Database. Accessed October 22, 2014. http://www.slavevoyages.org/tast/assessment/estimates.faces?yearFrom=1501&yearTo=1866&flag=2.

"Immigration Act of 1924," United States Department of State Website, http://www.state.gov/r/pa/ho/time/id/87718.htm.

West Indian Social Club, Inc. Accessed April 13, 2011. http://www.westindiansocialclubinc.org/history.html.

Periodicals and Journals

Articles

Ardener, Shirley. "The Comparative Study of Rotating Credit Associations," *Journal of the Royal Anthropological Institute of Great Britain and Ireland* 94, no. 2 (July–December 1964): 201–229.

Briggs, Cyril V. *Crusader* 2, no. 2 (October 1919).

Campt, Tina and Deborah A. Thomas. "Gendering Diaspora: Transnational Feminism, Diaspora and Its Hegemonies," *Feminist Review* 90, no. 1 (October 2008): 1–8.

Clarke, Edith. "Land Tenure and the Family in Four Selected Communities in Jamaica," *Social and Economic Studies* 1, no. 4 (August 1953): 81–118.

Corinealdi, Kaysha. "A Section for Women: Journalism and Gendered Promises of Anti-Colonial Progress in Interwar Panama," *Caribbean Review of Gender Studies*, no. 12 (2018): 95–120.

———. "Envisioning Multiple Citizenships: West Indian Panamanians and Creating Community in the Canal Zone Neocolony," *Global South* 6, no. 2 (2013): 87–106.

Dougé-Prosper, Mamyrah. "An Island in the Chain," *NACLA Report on the Americas* 53:1 (2021): 32–38.

Dunbar, Paul Lawrence. "Hidden in Plain Sight: African American Secret Societies and Black Freemasonry," *Journal of African American Studies* 16, no. 4 (December 2012): 622–637.

Erhagbe, Edward O. and Ehimika A. Ifidon. "African-Americans and the Italo–Ethiopian Crisis, 1935–1936: The Practical Dimension of Pan-Africanism," *Aethiopica* 11, no. 1 (2008): 68–84.

Fletcher, Leonard P. "The Friendly Societies in St. Lucia and St. Vincent," *Caribbean Studies* 18, no. 3/4 (Oct 1978–Jan 1979): 89–114.

Flores-Villalobos, J. "'Freak Letters': Tracing Gender, Race, and Diaspora in the Panama Canal Archive," *Small Axe: A Caribbean Journal of Criticism* 23, no. 2 (2019): 34–56.

———. "Gender, Race, and Migrant Labor in the 'Domestic Frontier' of the Panama Canal Zone," *International Labor and Working-Class History* 99 (2021): 96–121.

Furley, Oliver W. "Moravian Missionaries and Slaves in the West Indies," *Caribbean Studies* 5, no. 2 (July 1965): 3–16.

Gebrekidan, Fikru. "In Defense of Ethiopia: A Comparative Assessment of Caribbean and African American Anti-Fascist Protests, 1935–1941." *Northeast African Studies* 2, no. 1 (1995): 145–173.

Harris, Lashawn. "Running with the Reds: African American Women and the Communist Party During the Great Depression." *Journal of African American History* 94, no. 1 (2009): 21–43.

Harris, Robert L. "Early Black Benevolent Societies, 1780–1830." *Massachusetts Review* 20, no. 3 (1979): 603–625.

James, Winston. "Explaining Afro-Caribbean Social Mobility in the United States: Beyond the Sowell Thesis," *Comparative Studies in Society and History* 44, no. 2 (2002): 218–262.

Johnson, Howard. "Friendly Societies in the Bahamas 1834–1910," *Slavery & Abolition: A Journal of Slave and Post-Slave Studies* 12, no. 3 (December 1991): 183–199.

Johnson, Fenton. "Credit Is Due the West Indian," *Favorite Magazine*, no. 3 (December 1919), 209–210.

Johnson, Violet Showers. "When Blackness Stings: African and Afro-Caribbean Immigrants, Race, and Racism in Late Twentieth-Century America," *Journal of American Ethnic History* 36, no. 1 (2016): 31–62.

Josiah, Barbara P. "After Emancipation: Aspects of Village Life in Guyana, 1869–1911," *Journal of Negro History* 82, no. 1 (1997): 105–121.

Maddox, Tyesha. "More Than Auxiliary: Caribbean Women and Social Organizations in the Interwar Period," *Caribbean Review of Gender Studies* no. 12 (2018): 67–94.

———, "Can Mutual Aid Withstand Pandemic Fatigue?," *Bloomberg CityLab*, April 16, 2021, https://www.bloomberg.com/news/articles/2021-04-16/new-yorkers-need-mutual-aid-groups-more-than-ever.

Putnam, Lara. "Borderlands and Border-Crossers: Migrants and Boundaries in the Greater Caribbean, 1840–1940," *Small Axe* 18, no 1 (March 2014): 7–21.

Roopnarine, Lomarsh. "East Indian Indentured Emigration to the Caribbean: Beyond the Push and Pull Model," *Caribbean Studies* 31, no. 2 (Jul–Dec 2003): 97–134.

Silva, Daniel Domingues da, David Eltis, Philip Misevich, and Olatunji Ojo. "The Diaspora of Africans Liberated From Slave Ships in the Nineteenth Century," *Journal of African History* 55, no. 3 (2014): 347–369.

Scott, William R. "Black Nationalism and the Italo-Ethiopian Conflict 1934–1936," *Journal of Negro History* 63, no. 2 (April 1978): 118–134.

Spade, Dean. "Solidarity Not Charity: Mutual Aid for Mobilization and Survival," *Social Text* 142, Vol. 38, No. 1 (March 2020): 131–151.

Thomas, Bert J. "Historical Functions of Caribbean-American Benevolent/Progressive Associations," *Afro-Americans in New York Life and History* 12, no. 2 (July 1988): 19–53.

Vecoli, Rudolph J. "Contadini in Chicago: A Critique of the Uprooted," *Journal of American History* 51, Issue 3 (December 1964): 404–417.

Walter, John C. "Frank R. Crosswaith and the Negro Labor Committee," *Afro-Americans in New York Life and History* 3, no. 2 (Jul 1979): 35–49.

—— and James H. Rigali. "The Anglophone Caribbean immigrant and Partisan Politics in New York City, 1900–1972." *Afro-Americans in New York Life and History* 30, no. 1 (2006): 19–75.

Weisbord, Robert G. "British West Indian Reaction to the Italian-Ethiopian War: An Episode in Pan-Africanism," *Caribbean Studies* 10, no. 1 (April 1970): 34–41.

——. "Black America and the Italian-Ethiopian Crisis: An Episode in Pan-Negroism," *Historian* 34, no. 2 (February 1972): 230–241.

Yen Liu, Yvonne. "For Asian Immigrants, Cooperatives Came from the Home Country," *Yes! Magazine* (May 22, 2018). Accessed August 3, 2020, https://www.yesmagazine .org/democracy/2018/05/22/for-asian-immigrants-cooperatives-came-from-the -home-country/.

Newspapers

Afro-American Red Star
Antigua Free Press and Gazette
Antigua Observer
Bermudian
Caribbean Times: Antigua & Barbuda
Chicago Daily Tribune
Chicago Defender
Daily Mirror (UK)
Hartford News
Los Angeles Times
New York Age
New York Amsterdam News
New York Tribune
Palladium: Saint Lucia Free Press (Castries, Saint Lucia)
Port of Spain Gazette, 1838–1839 (Port of Spain, Trinidad)
Saint Lucia Gazette
South Florida Times (Fort Lauderdale, Florida)
St. George Chronicle and Grenada Gazette, 1835
The Bermuda Recorder
The Gleaner (Kingston, Jamaica)
The Grenada Free Press and Public Gazette
The Independent
The Jamaica Journal
The National Era
The New York Times

The North Star
The Pittsburgh Courier
The Royal Gazette (Hamilton, Bermuda)
The Royal Gazette (Kingston, Jamaica)
The Saint Vincent Witness
The Sentry (Saint Vincent)
The St. Lucia Guardian (Castries, Saint Lucia)
The Voice (Castries, Saint Lucia)

Published Primary Sources

"1983 Statistical Yearbook of the Immigration and Naturalization Service," Washington, DC: U.S. Department of Homeland Security, Office of Immigration Statistics, 2002.

Broussard, Jinx Coleman. *Giving a Voice to the Voiceless: Four Pioneering Black Women Journalists.* New York: Routledge, 2004.

Browne, Major G. St. J. Ore. *Great Britain Colonial Office Report: Labour Conditions in the West Indies.* London: H.M. Stationery Office, 1939.

Domingo, W. A. "The Tropics in New York," *Survey* 53, (March 1, 1925).

Dray, Philip. *Capitol Men: The Epic Story of Reconstruction Through the Lives of the First Black Congressmen.* New York: Houghton Mifflin, 2008.

Edwards, Alba M. *Sixteenth Census of the United States: 1940, Population, Comparative Occupation Statistics for the United States, 1870 to 1940.* Washington, DC: United States Government Printing Office, 1943.

Garvey, Marcus (speech). Liberty Hall, New York, March 6, 1920, March 13, 1920, reprinted in *The Marcus Garvey and the Universal Negro Improvement Association Papers*, vol. 1, Berkeley: University of California Press, 1983.

Handbook of the America Republics. Washington, DC: Bureau of the American Republics, 1893.

Martin, Tony. *Amy Ashwood Garvey: Pan-Africanist, Feminist and Mrs. Marcus Garvey No. 1 or A Tale of Two Amies.* Dover: The Majority Press, 2007.

McKay, Claude. *Home to Harlem.* New York: Harper & Brothers, 1926.

National Association for the Advancement of Colored People. *Thirty Years of Lynching in the United States.* New York: Negro University Press, 1919.

Prince, Mary. *The History of Mary Prince, a West Indian Slave.* London: F. Westley and A.H. Davis, 1831.

Reid, Ira De A. *The Negro Immigrant: His Background, Characteristics and Social Adjustments, 1899–1937.* New York: AMS Press, 1939.

Thome, James A. and J. Horace Kimball. *Emancipation in the West Indies: A Six Months' Tour in Antigua, Barbados, and Jamaica in the Year 1837.* New York: American Anti-Slavery Society, 1838.

U.S. Census of Population, 1930 and 17th Census of the United States, 1950 Population Volume IV Special Reports.

U.S. Department of Justice, Immigration and Naturalization Service. Yearbook of Immigration Statistics.

Wells, Alan Frank and D. Wells. *Friendly Societies in the West Indies: A Report on a Survey.* Colonial Office, 1949.

Secondary Sources

Alleyne, Mervyn. *Roots of Jamaican Culture.* London: Pluto Press, 1988.

Anthony, TaKeia N. *The Universal Ethiopian Student's Association, 1927–1948: Mobilizing Diaspora.* Cham, Switzerland: Palgrave Macmillan, 2019.

Barrow, Christine. *Family Land and Development in St. Lucia.* Cave Hill: Institute of Social and Economic Research (Eastern Caribbean), University of the West Indies, 1992.

Bates, Beth Tompkins. *Pullman Porters and the Rise of Protest Politics in Black America, 1925–1945.* Chapel Hill: University of North Carolina Press, 2001.

Beito, David. *From Mutual Aid to the Welfare State: Fraternal Societies and Social Services, 1890–1967.* Chapel Hill: University of North Carolina Press, 2000.

Berg, Manfred. *The Ticket to Freedom: The NAACP and the Struggle for Black Political Integration.* Gainesville: University Press of Florida, 2005.

Blain, Keisha. *Set the World on Fire: Black Nationalist Women and the Global Struggle for Freedom.* Philadelphia: University of Pennsylvania Press, 2018.

—— and Tiffany Gill. *To Turn the Whole World Over: Black Women and Internationalism.* Chicago: University of Illinois Press, 2019.

Bolland, O. Nigel. *On the March: Labour Rebellions in the British Caribbean, 1934–39.* Kingston: Ian Randle Publishers, 1995.

Boyce Davies, Carole. *Left of Karl Marx: The Political Life of Black Communist Claudia Jones.* Durham: Duke University Press, 2008.

Brereton, Bridget. "The Development of an Identity: The Black Middle Class of Trinidad in the Later Nineteenth Century," in *Caribbean Freedom: Economy and Society from Emancipation to the Present*, ed. Hilary Beckles and Verene Shepherd. Kingston: Ian Randle Publishers, 1993.

Brown, Tammy L. *City of Islands: Caribbean Intellectuals in New York.* Jackson: University Press of Mississippi, 2015.

Brown, Vincent. *The Reaper's Garden: Death and Power in the World of Atlantic Slavery.* Cambridge: Harvard University Press, 2008.

Bryan, Patrick. *The Jamaican People 1880–1902: Race, Class and Social Control.* Jamaica: University of West Indies Press, 2000.

Bryce-Laporte, Roy S. and Delores M. Mortimer. *Caribbean Immigration to the United States.* Washington, DC: Research Institute on Immigration and Ethnic Studies, Smithsonian Institution, 1976.

Byrd, Brandon R. *The Black Republic: African Americans and the Fate of Haiti.* Philadelphia: University of Pennsylvania Press, 2019.

Cantres, James G. *Blackening Britain Caribbean Radicalism from Windrush to Decolonization.* London: Rowman & Littlefield, 2020.

Chambers, Glenn A. *Race, Nation, and West Indian Immigration to Honduras, 1890–1940.* Baton Rouge: Louisiana State University Press, 2010.

Chateauvert, Melinda. *Marching Together: Women of the Brotherhood of Sleeping Car Porters*. Chicago: University of Illinois Press, 1997.

Clarke, Velta and Bolarinde Obebe. *Adjustment of Caribbean Immigrants in New York: Educational Dimensions*. Brooklyn: Caribbean Research Center, Medgar Evers College, 1989.

Clarke, Velta. *Aliens in a New Frontier: Caribbean Immigration into the United States and the Interchange of Human Resources, Opportunities and Education*. Brooklyn: Caribbean Research Center, 1994.

Cobley, Alan Gregor and Alvin Thompson (eds.). *The African-Caribbean Connection: Historical and Cultural Perspectives*. Bridgetown: University of the West Indies, National Cultural Foundation, 1990.

Dray, Philip. *Capitol Men: The Epic Story of Reconstruction Through the Lives of the First Black Congressmen*. New York: Houghton Mifflin, 2008.

Erman, Sam. *Almost Citizens: Puerto Rico, the U.S. Constitution, and Empire*. Cambridge: Cambridge University Press, 2018.

Espin, Oliva. *Women Crossing Boundaries: A Psychology of Immigration and Transformations of Sexuality*. New York: Routledge, 1998.

Ferrer, Ada. *Freedom's Mirror: Cuba and Haiti in the Age of Revolution*. New York: Cambridge University Press, 2014.

Foner, Eric. *Reconstruction: America's Unfinished Revolution, 1863–1877*. New York: Harper Collins, 2002.

Foner, Nancy. *Islands in the City: West Indian Migration to New York*. Berkeley: University of California Press, 2001.

Gates, Henry Louis and Gene Andrew Jarrett. *New Negro: Essays on Race, Representation, and African American Culture, 1892–1938*. Princeton. Princeton University Press, 2007.

Gelderloos, Peter. *Anarchy Works: Examples of Anarchist Ideas in Practice*. San Francisco: Ardent Press, 2010.

Gitterman, Alex and Lawrence Schulman, *Mutual Aid Groups, Vulnerable and Resilient Populations, and the Life Cycle*. New York: Columbia University Press, 2005.

Giovannetti, Jorge L. "Black British Caribbean Migrants in Cuba: Resistance, Opposition, and Strategic Identity in the Early Twentieth Century," in *Regional Footprints: The Travels and Travails of Early Caribbean Migrants*, ed. Annete Insanally, Mark Clifford, and Sean Sheriff. Kingston: Latin American-Caribbean Centre, University of the West Indies, 2006.

Glaude Jr., Eddie. *Democracy in Black: How Race Still Enslaves the American Soul*. New York: Broadway Books, 2017.

Glaze, Anita J. *Art and Death in a Senufo Village*. Bloomington: University of Indiana Press, 1981.

Gomez, Michael. *Exchanging Our Country Marks: The Transformation of African Identities in the Colonial and Antebellum South*. Chapel Hill: University of North Carolina Press, 1998.

Gordon Nembhard, Jessica. *Collective Courage: A History of African American Cooperative Economic Thought and Practice*. State College: Pennsylvania State University Press, 2014.

Greer, Christina. *Black Ethnics: Race, Immigration, and the Pursuit of the American Dream*. Oxford: Oxford University Press, 2013.

Hammond Perry, Kennetta. *London Is the Place for Me: Black Britons, Citizenship and the Politics of Race*. Oxford: Oxford University Press, 2016.

Hamshere, Cyril. *The British in the Caribbean*. Cambridge: Harvard University Press, 1972.

Hastings, S.U. and B.L. MacLeavy. *Seedtime and Harvest: A Brief History of the Moravian Church in Jamaica, 1754–1979*. Barbados: Cedar Press, 1979.

Herskovits, Melville. *Dahomey: An Ancient West African Kingdom*. New York: J.J. Augustin, 1938.

———. *Myth of the Negro Past*. New York: Harper Brothers, 1941.

Hill, Robert A. (ed.), John Dixon, Mariela Haro Rodriguez, Anthony Yuen. *The Marcus Garvey and Universal Negro Improvement Association Papers, Volume 11: Marcus Garvey 1887–1940*. Berkeley: University of California Press, 1983.

Mark Lai, Him. *Becoming Chinese American: A History of Communities and Institutions*. New York: AltaMira Press, 2004.

Hoffnung-Garskof, Jesse. *Racial Migrations: New York City and the Revolutionary Politics of the Spanish Caribbean*. Princeton: Princeton University Press, 2019.

Holt, Thomas. *The Problem of Freedom: Race, Labor, and Politics in Jamaica and Britain, 1832–1938*. Baltimore: John Hopkins University Press, 1992.

Howell, Ron. *The Boss of Black Brooklyn: The Life and Times of Bertram L. Baker*. New York: Fordham University Press, 2019.

James, Winston. *Holding Aloft the Banner of Ethiopia: Caribbean Radicalism in the Early Twentieth Century America*. New York: Verso, 1998.

Johnson, Michele A. and Brian L. Moore. *Neither Led nor Driven: Contesting British Cultural Imperialism in Jamaica 1865–1920*. Kingston: University of the West Indies Press, 2004.

———. *"They Do as They Please": The Jamaican Struggle for Cultural Freedom After Morant Bay*. Kingston: University of the West Indies Press, 2011.

Johnson, Violet Showers. "Pan-Africanism in Print: The Boston Chronicle and the Struggle for Black Liberation and Advancement, 1930–1950," in *Print Culture in a Diverse America*, ed. James Danky and Wayne Wiegand. Chicago: University of Illinois Press, 1998.

———. "The Black Presence in U.S. Immigration History," in *A Nation of Immigrants Reconsidered: The U.S. in an Age of Restriction, 1924–1965*, ed. Maria Cristina Garcia, Madeline Hsu and Maddalena Marinari. Chicago: University of Illinois Press, 2019.

———. *The Other Black Bostonians: West Indians in Boston, 1900–1950*. Bloomington: Indiana University Press, 2006.

Kaba, Mariame and Alexandria Ocasio-Cortez. *Mutual Aid 101*, Tool Kit, 2020.

Kasinitz, Philip. *Caribbean New York: Black Immigrants and the Politics of Race.* Ithaca: Cornell University Press, 1992.

Kropotkin, Peter. *Mutual Aid: A Factor in Evolution.* New York: McClure Phillips, 1902.

LaBennett, Oneka. *She's Mad Real: Popular Culture and West Indian Girls in Brooklyn.* New York: New York University Press, 2011.

Laurence, K. O. *Immigration into the West Indies in the 19th Century.* Barbados: Caribbean Universities Press, 1971.

Lee, Erika. *At America's Gates: Chinese Immigration During the Exclusion Era, 1882–1943.* Chapel Hill: University of North Carolina Press, 2004.

Levine, Barry B. *The Caribbean Exodus.* New York: Praeger, 1987.

Lewis, Rupert and Patrick Bryan (eds.). *Garvey: His Work and Impact.* Trenton: Africa World Press, Inc, 1991.

Little, Kenneth. *The Mende of Sierra Leone: A West African People in Transition.* Oxford: Alden Press, 1969.

Litwack, Leon F. *Trouble in My Mind: Black Southerners in the Age of Jim Crow.* New York: Alfred A. Knopf, Inc., 1998.

Makalani, Minkah. *In the Cause of Freedom: Radical Black Internationalism from Harlem to London, 1917–1939.* Chapel Hill: University of North Carolina Press, 2011.

Marshall, Paule. *Brown Girl, Brownstones.* Old Westbury: Feminist Press, 1981.

Marshall, Woodville K. "'We Be Wise to Many More Things': Blacks' Hopes and Expectations of Emancipation," in *Caribbean Freedom: Economy and Society from Emancipation to the Present,* ed. Hilary Beckles and Verene Shepherd. Kingston: Ian Randle Publishers, 1993.

McDuffie, Erik. *Sojourning for Freedom: Black Women, American Communism, and the Making of Black Left Feminism.* Durham: Duke University Press, 2011.

McWhirter, Cameron. *Red Summer: The Summer of 1919 and the Awakening of Black America.* New York: Henry Holt and Company, 2011.

Mjagkij, Nina. *Organizing Black America: An Encyclopedia of African American Associations.* New York: Garland Publishing, Inc., 2001.

Model, Suzanne. *West Indian Immigrants: A Black Success Story?* New York: The Russell Sage Foundation, 2008.

Moore, Brian and Swithin Wilmont. *Before and After 1865: Education, Politics, and Regionalism in the Caribbean.* Kingston: Ian Randle Publishers, 1998.

Moore Turner, Joyce and W. Burghardt Turner. *Caribbean Crusaders and the Harlem Renaissance.* Urbana: University of Illinois Press, 2005.

Moyse Steinberg, Dominique. *A Mutual-Aid Model for Social Work with Groups.* London: Routledge Taylor & Francis, 2014.

Newton, Velma. *The Silver Men: West Indian Labour Migration to Panama 1850–1914.* Bridgetown: Institute of Social and Economic Research University of the West Indies, 1984.

Ngai, Mae M. *Impossible Subjects: Illegal Aliens and the Making of Modern America.* Princeton: Princeton University Press, 2014.

Opie, Fredrick Douglass. *Black Labor Migration in Caribbean Guatemala, 1882-1923*. Gainesville: University Press of Florida, 2009.

Palmer, Ransford W. *In Search of a Better Life: Perspectives on Migration from the Caribbean*. Westport: Praeger Publishers, 1990.

———. *Pilgrims from the Sun: West Indian Migration to America*. New York: Twayne Publishers, 1995.

Parascandola, Louis J. (ed.) *Look for Me All Around: Anglophone Caribbean Immigrants in the Harlem Renaissance*. Detroit: Wayne State University Press, 2005.

Paton, Diana and Pamela Scully (eds.). *No Bond but the Law: Punishment, Race, and Gender in Jamaican State Formation, 1780-1870*. Durham: Duke University Press, 2004.

Paton, Diana. *Gender and Slave Emancipation in the Atlantic World*. Edited with Pamela Scully. Durham: Duke University Press, 2005.

Perry, Jeffery B. *Hubert Harrison: The Voice of Harlem Radicalism, 1883-1918*. New York: Columbia University Press, 2009.

Putnam, Lara. *Radical Moves: Caribbean Migrants and the Politics of Race in the Jazz Age*. Chapel Hill: University of North Carolina Press, 2013.

———. *The Company They Kept: Migrants and the Politics of Gender in the Caribbean Costa Rica, 1870-1960*. Chapel Hill: University of North Carolina Press, 2002.

Rogers, Reul. *Afro-Caribbean Immigrants and the Politics of Incorporation: Ethnicity, Exception, or Exit*. Cambridge: Cambridge University Press, 2006.

Sanchez, George J. *Becoming Mexican American: Ethnicity, Culture, and Identity in Chicano Los Angeles, 1900-1945*. Oxford: Oxford University Press, 1996.

Schulman, Lawrence. *The Skills of Helping Individuals, Families, Groups, and Communities*. Chicago, Illinois: F. E. Peacock Publishers, 1979.

Simpson, George Eaton. "The Acculturative Process in Jamaican Revivalism," in *Men and Cultures: Selected Papers*, ed. Anthony F.C. Wallace. Philadelphia: University of Pennsylvania Press, 1960.

Soyer, Daniel. *Jewish Immigrant Associations and American Identity in New York, 1880-1939*. Cambridge: Harvard University Press, 1997.

Spade, Dean. *Mutual Aid: Building Solidarity During This Crisis (and the Next)*. New York: Verso Books, 2020.

Stephens, Michelle. *Black Empire: The Masculine Global Imaginary of Caribbean Intellectuals in the United States, 1914 to 1962*. Durham: Duke University Press, 2005.

Summers, Martin. *Manliness & Its Discontents: The Black Middle Class & the Transformation of Masculinity, 1900-1930*. Chapel Hill: University of North Carolina Press, 2004.

Sutton, Constance and Elsa M. Chaney. *Caribbean Life in New York City: Sociocultural Dimensions*. New York: Center for Migration Studies of New York Inc., 1987.

Taylor, Ula. *The Veiled Garvey: The Life and Times of Amy Jacques Garvey*. Chapel Hill: University of North Carolina Press, 2003.

Tye, Larry. *Rising from the Rails: Pullman Porters and the Making of the Black Middle Class*. New York: Henry Holt and Company, 2004.

Waldrep, Christopher (ed.). *Lynching in America: A History in Documents*. New York: New York University Press, 2006.

Warner-Lewis, Maureen. *Central Africa in the Caribbean: Transcending Time, Transforming Cultures*. Kingston: University of the West Indies Press, 2003.

Waters, Mary C. *Black Identities: West Indian Immigrant Dreams and American Realities*. Cambridge: Harvard University Press, 1999.

Watkins-Owens, Irma. *Blood Relations: Caribbean Immigrants and the Harlem Community, 1900–1930*. Bloomington & Indianapolis: Indiana Press, 1996.

Wilder, Craig Steven. *In the Company of Black Men: The African Influence of African American Culture in New York City*. New York: New York University Press, 2001.

Woodsworth, Michael. *Battle for Bed-Stuy: The Long War on Poverty in New York City*. Cambridge: Harvard University Press, 2016.

Vickerman, Milton. *Crosscurrents: West Indian Immigrants and Race*. Oxford: Oxford University Press, 1999.

Theses

Anderson, Beverley Joy. *The Decline of Friendly Societies of Jamaica: A Traditional Voluntary Association in a Developing Society*. PhD diss., Boston College, 1985.

Diggs, Charles. *Kin Meets Kin: An Analysis of Afro-American and Afro-Caribbean Relations in Harlem During the 1920's*. Master's thesis, Cornell University, 1988.

Moore, Garrie Ward. *A Study of a Group of West Indian Negroes in New York City*. Master's thesis, Columbia University, 1913.

Toney, Joyce Roberta. *The Development of a Culture of Migration Among a Caribbean People: St. Vincent and New York, 1838–1979*. PhD diss., Columbia University, 1986.

INDEX

ACKNOWLEDGMENTS

In essence, this book is about the networks of care that helped create and sustain communities of Caribbean immigrants making their way in an unfamiliar world. I am thankful for my own networks who have made the long journey to the completion of this book possible. To my very first mentor, Margaret Washington, who saw potential in a young budding historian from Brooklyn and took her under her wing—thank you! I want to thank my PhD advisor, Michael Gomez, for helping to shape not only my work, but me intellectually into the scholar that I am today and for modeling the scholar that I would like to become. I am eternally grateful to Irma Watkins-Owens, whose work is the foundation on which this book stands. I am thankful for the community of female scholars who have helped shape this book in its various stages, my dissertation and manuscript advisors: Ada Ferrer, Michele Mitchell, Lara Putnam, and Violet Showers Johnson.

I have been fortunate to have had several fellowships that supported the completion of this work. I want to thank the American Antiquarian Society, Boston College's African and African Diaspora Studies program, the Schomburg Center for Research in Black Culture's Scholars-in-Residence Program, Rutgers University's History Department and Institute for Research on Women, and Fordham University. My time at each of these institutions has expanded my network of scholars and friends who have been influential in the writing of this text. Thank you to Martin Summers, Rhonda Frederick, Régine Jean-Charles, Richard Paul, Brent Hayes Edwards, Imani Owens, Yuko Miki, Ayesha Hardison, Brian Jones, Anthony Rodriguez, Sister Aisha H. L. al-Adawiya, Naomi Lorrain, Deborah Gray White, Alexandria Russell, Sarah Tobias, Arlene Stein, Keisha N. Blain, and J. Marlena Edwards.

Research for this book has taken me to several archives around the world and I am thankful for the many archivists and staff members who opened their vaults to me. I am grateful to Edwina Ashie-Nikoi, one of the first archivists I met at the Schomburg Center. Thank you for giving me access to vital collections before they were even catalogued. Caribbean women are the center of this work, and I am especially grateful to the women of several mutual aid societies who shared their stories with me. I am eternally thankful for the kindness and generosity of the late Ivy S. Simons, who I open this story with, thank you for sharing your life story and ice cream with me. I am also grateful for Mona Wyre-Manigo, Danette O. Sampson, and Doreen Wilkinson. I am extremely grateful to my colleagues at Fordham University who have read several drafts of this work and provided invaluable feedback: Westenley Alcenat, Mark Naison, and Laurie Lambert. Laurie, I am especially appreciative for your mentorship and most importantly your friendship over the years. Many thanks to my colleagues in the Department of African & African American Studies, the History Department, and my wider Fordham community: Christina Greer, Dennis Tyler, Brandy Monk-Payton, Zein Murib, Claire Gherini, Christopher Dietrich, Meenasarani Murugan, Samantha Iyer, Nana Osei-Opare, Vivian Lu, Nelsy Rivera, and Rafael Zapata and the Office of the Chief Diversity Officer.

Academia can often be a lonely and isolating profession; however, I have been lucky enough to have experienced just the opposite throughout my career. I am indebted to my very first network of colleagues who continue to pour into me their wisdom and friendship, my NYU/African Diaspora cohort: Joan Flores-Villalobos, Ebony Jones, Beatrice Wayne, Alison Okuda, Jonathan Michael Square, Ademide Adelusi-Adeluyi, Shauna Sweeney, Max Mishler, Alaina Morgan, James Cantres, Amita Manghnani Cantres, Dominique Jean Louis, and Natasha Lightfoot. To my history cohort: Geoffrey Traugh, Alexander Manevitz, David Klassen, Marcio Siwi, Sarah Griswold, Eva Muschik, Gabriel Rocha, Samuel Dolbee, Arianne Urus, and Lana Povitz, I could not have asked for a better group of people to take the PhD journey with. Tanisha C. Ford, thank you for your mentorship and guidance. Michael J. Thate, I am grateful for your constant reassurance and support when impostor syndrome tried to take over. Thank you for always challenging me and pushing me to join you outside the box.

To my editor, Bob Lockhart at the University of Pennsylvania Press, thank you for your kindness, patience, and belief in the importance of this work. Without your invaluable feedback and masterful editing this book would not have been possible.

My most heartfelt thank you goes to my best friends: Jody Sadornas, who painstakingly read many versions of this work and provided support in innumerous ways that I cannot say thank you for enough—I love you, fili mou yia panda! Diamaris Welch, my Double Mint twin, and the entire McKenzie family—thank you for countless hours of encouragement, laughter, and sisterhood. Your friendship over the last twenty-plus years has been invaluable. Thank you to you and Harry P. Jones for always offering your support, food, and drinks when this process got extremely tough.

Finally, my deepest gratitude goes to my family, the Maddoxes and Henrys, who are the inspiration for this work. In the 1950s/1960s, both sets of my grandparents im/migrated to Brooklyn, New York, in search of a better life and greater economic opportunities, my dad's family from rural North and South Carolina and my mom and her family from the tiny island of Saint Lucia, BWI. My parents met one fateful day at Boys & Girls High School, where many young African American and Caribbean teens were first introduced. This meeting would serve as the genesis for my own interest in immigration history and the formation of Black identity. I want to thank my family for their love and unwavering support, even when they were not 100 percent clear on what I was doing. Your confidence and trust that I was working to make the family proud has meant the world to me. I love each of you greatly. Thank you to my father, Tyrone Maddox, whose stubbornness and "won't take NO for an answer" attitude has rubbed off on me in the best way possible. Finally, to my mother, Donna Henry, who has always been my biggest champion, thank you for teaching me to dream big even when I had no way of making those dreams a reality—Mommy, we did it! None of this would have been possible without your many sacrifices, unconditional love, and guidance.